GOA TRAVELS

Manohar Shetty has published seven books of poems including *Domestic Creatures* (Oxford University Press, New Delhi) and *Living Room* (HarperCollins, New Delhi). Several collections feature his work notably, *The Oxford India Anthology of Twelve Modern Indian Poets* (ed. Arvind Krishna Mehrotra, Oxford University Press, New Delhi), as well as anthologies edited by Eunice de Souza and Vilas Sarang. Shetty has been a Homi Bhabha Fellow and a Senior Sahitya Akademi Fellow. He has also edited *Ferry Crossing: Short Stories from Goa* (Penguin India). Manohar has lived in Goa since 1985.

GOA TRAVELS

Being the Accounts of Travellers from the 16th to the 21st Century

edited by

MANOHAR SHETTY

RUPA

Published by
Rupa Publications India Pvt. Ltd 2014
7/16, Ansari Road, Daryaganj
New Delhi 110002

Sales centres:
Allahabad Bengaluru Chennai
Hyderabad Jaipur Kathmandu
Kolkata Mumbai

ISBN: 978-81-291-2926-0

First impression 2014

10 9 8 7 6 5 4 3 2 1

Typeset by SÜRYA, New Delhi

Printed by Parksons Graphics Pvt. Ltd, Mumbai

CONTENTS

THE INQUISITION IN GOA

THE CONTEMPORARY TRAVELLER

Introduction

Manohar Shetty

Centuries before Goa became the tourist destination it is today, several European travellers set forth on hazardous sea journeys to explore the once-fabled metropolis of Old Goa and its surroundings. The galaxy of inveterate travellers and chroniclers, who saw Goa both in its prime and in its decline, included the Dutch merchant and spy John Huyghen Van Linschoten, the Italian nobleman Pietro Della Valle, the jewel merchant from France, Jean-Baptiste Tavernier, the pioneering English entrepreneur Ralph Fitch, the German diplomat John Albert de Mendelslo, the young Italian slave trader Francesco Carletti, the French sailor and soldier Pyrard de Laval, the Portuguese officials Duarte Barbosa and Tom Pires, the French priests Carre Barthelemy and Cottineau de Kloguen, the Italian writer and chronicler of the Moghul empire, Niccolao Manucci, the Englishmen Dr John Fryer and Dr Claudius Buchanan, the Scot Captain Alexander Hamilton, and Richard F. Burton, the Victorian Age author of *One Thousand and One Nights* and co-translator of *The Kama Sutra*, and his wife Lady Isabel Burton.

All these travellers and chroniclers have left behind an invaluable legacy on the social customs, economic activities, including the trading of slaves and horses, the sartorial styles and the culinary habits of the times. Among the pioneers was John Huyghen Van Linschoten, who spent almost six years in Goa from 1583 to 1588 during which time he also clandestinely copied confidential Portuguese nautical maps and charts. Despite his somewhat dubious reputation as a spy, he opened up the horizons for later adventurers and seafarers who relied on his storehouse of sea-routes to India, Malacca and beyond Malacca in the Malay

Archipelago, and up to the Chinese coasts. Linschoten was also an acute observer and meticulous recorder of the decadence in Portuguese Goa during its incipient decline from its giddy heights of glory. He died in 1611, aged forty-eight.

Even before Linschoten came the Portuguese factor Duarte Barbosa, who arrived before the Portuguese conquest of Goa in 1510 and lived in India for about sixteen years. In 1519, Barbosa joined his legendary brother-in-law Ferdinand Magellan who circumnavigated the globe and conclusively proved that the earth was round. Barbosa's book was one of the earliest examples of travel literature. Written in 1516, it found its way into print only 300 years later as *The Book of Duarte Barbosa*.

The most colourful of the intrepid travellers was the Italian Pietro Della Valle. Born in 1586, Della Valle was the scion of an illustrious family in Rome. After a voyage to Baghdad in 1616, he married an eighteen-year-old Assyrian Christian, Maani Giorida. Four years later the young bride died near the Gulf of Ormuz (Hormuz in Iran) from fever and an unhealthy climate. The grief-stricken nobleman had her body embalmed and preserved in a coffin. He kept the body on board when the ship arrived in Surat on 10 February 1623. From Surat he travelled to Calicut—the southernmost tip of his travels in India. He left Goa on 16 November 1624 for Muscat, and from there for Rome, still accompanied by his embalmed wife. Finally, he reached Rome in March 1626. It was only here, more than three years after her death, that Della Valle buried the remains of his beloved wife in the family vault.

A contemporary of Pietro Della Valle, Francois Pyrard has been described as a ' talkative and observant Frenchman of the seaman class'. He was arrested by the Portuguese after he lost his official papers in a shipwreck and was dumped into a dungeon in Calicut. His health deteriorating, he was sent in chains to Goa, where he was admitted in the Jesuit Hospital, then reputed to be the finest such institution in all of Europe and Asia. Pyrard recovered, and to save himself further long-term incarceration, volunteered to serve in the Portuguese army. During his ten years of service, he was a keen and insightful observer of the Portuguese and the surrounding environment.

Another Frenchman, Jean-Baptiste Tavernier, who arrived in Goa more than thirty years later, was a wealthy and famous jewel merchant, dealing mainly in diamonds with Indian royalty, high-ranked Portuguese officials and local businessmen. He spent a week in Goa in 1641 and a further few months seven years later when he noted the rapid decline in the prosperity of the Portuguese, some of who even secretly approached him for alms. Tavernier was also an accomplished raconteur as can be seen from his entertaining account of the adventures and misadventures of two of his fellow Frenchmen, du Belloy and des Merestes, one of whom met an ignominious end and the other a more heroic one.

The young Italian slave trader and merchant Francesco Carletti arrived in Goa exactly at the turn of the 16th century when he was just twenty-one years old. A few years later, in 1606, he would be known for introducing chocolate to Italy from Central America. During his twenty-month sojourn in Goa, he was much enamoured of the women, especially the Bengali women with Portuguese blood who were 'the most desirous creatures imaginable'. He appeared fixated by their 'members' (breasts) 'so rounded as to seem to have been formed on a lathe', and was also struck by the apparent possessiveness of their Portuguese husbands and their 'lubricity' shared in no small measure by their wives due to the 'continuous heat' of the region. The men apparently were so possessive of their wives that at any hint of infidelity they killed them 'every day, which they can do freely because it is permitted by the laws of the Portuguese'. Carletti, however, refrains from elucidating on his own conquests, if any.

Among the first Englishmen to arrive was the merchant Ralph Fitch who was brought to Goa in 1583 after being arrested in Ormuz by the Portuguese on an unspecified crime. The Jesuit priest from Oxford, Thomas Stephens, already in Goa at the time, offered surety to the Portuguese but Fitch escaped from Goa and travelled all round India, including spending a brief interlude in the court of Akbar. It was Fitch's pioneering account on India and Burma that first whetted the appetite of the East India Company on the riches to be had in the subcontinent.

There have been a few other travellers' accounts in the overcrowded

17th-century calendar, like that of another Englishman Peter Mundy, in Goa in 1635. Mundy describes in some detail the fruits and vegetation and 'many faire churches' and the fabled, prosperous estate of the Portuguese, once 'absolute Masters and Commaunders in these seas' who 'triumphed like petty Romans' but who are now 'much abated by the comming in of the English and Dutch'.

The Frenchman Francois Bernier, more famous for his accounts on the Moghul Empire, also visited Goa in the 17th century but left a very brief account as did Phillip Baldaeus, the minister with the Dutch forces who were forever squabbling with the Portuguese and were fierce trade competitors.

The heinous practice of Sati—not in Goa where it was banned by Afonso de Albuquerque but in the neighbouring kingdom of Vijaynagar—has also been well documented by some of these travellers, especially by the Portuguese official, Duarte Barbosa, in the first few years of the 16th century. Barbosa's visceral account is chilling and appears to be from a first-hand view. Della Valle's account is as nerve-wracking and his vain exhortations to a willing victim to desist from going through with the barbaric ritual appears authentic and heartfelt.

It would be a serious oversight to ignore the travels of the Jesuit priests. In their pursuit of proselytism, they were indefatigable. Their zeal took them across the vast expanse of the subcontinent up to Tibet, and beyond to Malacca and China. They were in fact the only Europeans in the 16th century—apart from the transitory visit by Ralph Fitch—to gain access into the courts of the Moghul Empire. Amongst these great travellers was Anthony Monserrate, who was part of the Jesuit mission to the court of King Akbar in 1580. He was also appointed tutor to Akbar's second son, Murad. But despite the long and learned debates in the Ibadat Khana (House of Worship), the mission failed in its zealous attempts to woo the eclectic and always attentive and respectful Moghul king into the folds of the Catholic faith.

The swift decline of the Portuguese from its halcyon days in the early 16th century came in for some harsh comment by most chroniclers. But none could match the vituperation of the French apothecary and collector of curiousities, Jean Mocquet, who visited Goa in 1609. In his *Voyages en Afrique, Asie, Indes Orientales & Ocidentales* (Paris, 1617; translated by J. G. Schochen) he puts it trenchantly: 'Nothing is to be found amongst them (the Portuguese) but lying, treachery, avarice, usury, hate, anger, strife, envy, jealousy, pride, arrogance, murder, homicide, gluttony, drunkenness, voluptuousness, sodomy, lechery, fornication, adultery, blasphemy, cursing, swearing, breaking of oaths and all other sins in full measure. Merely to witness this makes one's hair stand on end, and one cannot cease to wonder at God's patience with such wicked men.'

Mocquet apparently had little patience himself.

Adds the Dutch missionary Philip Baldaeus in the mid-seventeenth century: 'The men are also generally excessive proud, there being scarce any of them that thinks himself remov'd a little above the vulgar sort, but what has his Umbrella carried over his Head, another Servant to carry his Cloke after him, and another who holds his Sword: They use frequently Snuff, not excepting even the Maidens and Women: and as they walk along the Streets, they are continually stroking and setting up their Whiskers.' It must of course be remembered that the Dutch and French were bitter trade rivals of the Portuguese and, in missionary zeal and success, Portugal had far outstripped both nations, at least in India. Indeed, many of the travel accounts featured here were by written by men of the cloth from various European countries.

In comparatively more recent times, Richard F. Burton, translator of *A Thousand and One Nights* and author of several scholarly books, also expelled much bile on Goa in his racist and misanthropic *Goa and the Blue Mountains*. Readers may well wonder what affliction he suffered from during his 'six months of sick leave'. If it is any consolation, Burton was almost equally caustic with the White Sahibs stationed in Ooty. His wife, Lady Isabel Burton, who accompanied him on their second visit to Goa in 1876, was even more caustic. In her memoirs she writes: 'Goa was not healthy enough to sleep out *el fresco*...There was not a breath of air in Goa even at night and the thirst was agonizing; even the water was hot, and the more one drank the more one wanted: it was a sort of purgatory. I cannot think how the people manage to live there: the place was simply *dead*; there is no other word for it. Of all the places I have ever been to, in sandy deserts and primeval forests, Goa was the worst.' Times have indeed changed.

A more sympathetic account of the period comes from the French priest, Cottineau de Kloguen, who visited Goa twenty years before Burton. He found the clergy, though poor, 'most regular and exemplary in their manner' and of the general community he found that 'it would be difficult to find (one)…pursuing a more regular, tranquil and moral conduct, than that of the present inhabitants of Goa'.

The 18th century saw a drastic decline in the accounts of any new travellers. Goa by then was well and truly in a state of decline and perhaps not many travellers here at the time mixed business with the pleasures of observation. The English naval surgeon Edward Ives who visited Goa in 1754 wrote just one brief descriptive paragraph, commenting on the decline of the Portuguese: 'There are many churches and monasteries here, some of which were once superb; the decay of these and most of the other buildings, too plainly shews the present ruinous state of the Portuguese power and trade in this part of the world.'

But the chronicles of most of these travellers serve as significant signposts and channels of empirical evidence. More than the dry dates of history, they provide telling insights into Goa's colourful past.

The darkest chapter in the history of colonial Goa is the imposition of the Inquisition (1560–1812). Introduced into Goa at the behest of St. Francis Xavier, the Order of the Inquisition savaged the social fabric of the place. As the freedom fighter T. B. Cunha puts it in his essay, 'Denationalisation of Goans': 'The horrors of the Goa Inquisition, endured in its dungeons, the cruelty and sadistic ferocity of its penalties are even admitted by the impartial evidence of the Archbishop of Evora in a sermon proffered in Lisbon: "If everywhere the Inquisition was an infamous Court, the infamy, however base, however vile, however corrupt and determined by worldly interests, it was never more so than the Inquisition of Goa, by irony of fate called the Holy Office. The inquisitors even attained the infamy of sending to their prisons women who resisted them there, satisfying their beastly instincts and then burning them as heretics.'"

Fortunately Dr Gabriel Dellon, a French physician who was a victim of the Inquisition and incarcerated in its dungeons in present-day Old Goa in 1675, lived to tell the tale. His is possibly the only eyewitness account of the Inquisition in Goa, detailing all the diabolical rites of the Tribunal, the farcical trial, his harrowing incarceration on the flimsiest of charges, and his eventual liberation. The Inquisition in Goa claimed several European lives, especially during the peak of the anti-Jewish pogrom initiated by the Portuguese royalty and the Catholic Church in the 16th century. Among the more bizarre 'victims' was the famed botanist and physician, Garcia da Orta, a close friend of the poet Luis de Camoes and widely regarded as the pioneer of the autopsy in India. Garcia da Orta escaped detection as a Jew during his lifetime but, in 1580, twelve years after his death in 1568, he was *posthumously* convicted of Judaism, his bones disinterred and burned at the stake at an auto-da-fe. Such was the bloodcurdling zeal of Portuguese bigotry at the time. A year after da Orta's death, his sister Catarina too was burnt—alive—at the stake in Goa for the crime of practising Judaism.

In contemporary times, only a few Western writers in English have depicted Goa with some insight and accuracy. Graham Greene, after a visit in 1964, wrote a short essay; Somerset Maugham a brief portrait of a priest; Evelyn Waugh, a devout Catholic who visited Goa in 1952 during the Exposition of St Francis Xavier, wrote some detailed and dreary diary entries; and, in more recent times, there's been a cliché-ridden account by William Dalrymple. The fastidious V. S. Naipaul in *An Area of Darkness*, in his usual role as a glorified drain inspector, wrinkled his nose over squatters defecating by the River Mandovi. Others have fostered inaccuracies that could easily have been avoided with elementary research. Anita Desai in the novel *Baumgartner's Bombay*, for instance, believes that the 'poison called feni' is brewed from the cashew nut—not from the pulp of its discarded fruit. Did it occur to Ms Desai to compute the cost of country liquor actually made from expensive cashew nuts? John Irving in his otherwise admirable novel *A Son of the Circus* reckons that the smell of the 'heavy sickly fumes' of feni can drift all the way from Panjim to Baga—a distance of almost 20 kilometres.

More soberly intoxicated by Goa is David Tomory. His *Hello Goodnight: A Life of Goa* is a delightful travelogue on the changing face of Goa. He recalls with aplomb the glory days of the flower-power hippie generation of the 'sixties and early 'seventies and their decline into torpor, ennui, and failed nirvana.

Bromides and outright falsehoods on Goa are rife, and often go unchallenged or set right. Holiday destinations often meet this fate. Commercial Hindi cinema has reinforced these distortions, notably of the Catholic community—down now to less than a quarter of the population. But the history of Goa is unique and far removed from the rest of the subcontinent. The vivid accounts left behind by these travellers and chroniclers over the centuries provide a telling testimony on both the glory of Goa during its high-water mark in the early 16th century, its rapidly fading allure as a jewel in the Portuguese crown, and its recent resurgence as a star attraction for travellers from around the globe.

An omission I regret is the evocative essay 'Nirvana of a Maggot' by the painter F. N. Souza, but there were far too many obstacles in obtaining copyright clearances. I have also left out a rather dreary account by the English physician Dr John Fryer who made a stopover in Goa in 1675 and another account by the Portuguese apothecary, Tome Pires, who visited India in 1511, just a few months after Afonso de Albuquerque's conquest of Goa the previous year. Pires prophetically called Goa 'the coolest place in India', unwittingly echoing centuries ago a phrase more in keeping with advertising copy today. Curiously, not one of the old-time travellers mention even in passing Goa's now famed beaches.

The shelf on creative Portuguese literature on or from Goa is surprisingly bare, with only a few turgid, unwieldy novels and some quasi-mythological poetry. The epic poem 'The Lusiads' by Portugal's greatest poet Luis de Camoes is the only exception. There were, however, mitigating circumstances. Historically, the odds were against the flourishing of the arts. The unremitting focus on Commerce and Conversion meant that very few artistically inclined people made the rigorous journey from Lisbon to Goa. The decline of Portuguese influence in the East was also relatively swift, despite the long period of occupation. After its peak in the 'Golden Epoch' of the early 16th century, the Portuguese, meeting stiff competition from the aggressive Dutch and other colonial powers in the lucrative spice and slave trade, soon spiralled downwards. Even at the height of its powers, the mother country itself fell under the sway of the Spanish crown between 1580 to 1640. Goa, once the El Dorado, the prized possession of the Portuguese, was reduced to an outpost, as its rulers increasingly turned their attention to Brazil and their other smaller colonies. It was no longer a 'plum posting' and the soldiery and officials sent to Goa were invariably reluctant young draftees and conscripts, not much given to the literary arts.

But the travellers have a different story to tell. Adventurous, observant, loquacious, and not averse to spinning a yarn or two, they paint a picture of Goa that is at once entertaining and enlightening. They are the true storytellers on the rise and fall of the Portuguese empire in 'Golden Goa'.

The
Early
Traveller

'When the King dies four or five hundred women burn themselves'

Duarte Barbosa

Dio

After departing thus from these towns, Mangalor and Çuriate, along the coast there is a point where the land projects into the sea, on which is a great town named by the Malabares Devixa, and by the Moors of the land it is called Dio (Diu). It is on a small island, hard by the main, and has a right good harbour, a trading port used by many ships, with exceeding great traffic and commerce with Malabar, Baticala, Guoa, Chaul, and Dabul. Ships also sail hence to Meca, Adem, Zeila, Barbora, Magadoxo, Melinde, Brava, Mombaça and Ormus with the kingdom thereof. The articles of merchandize brought hither by the Malabares are as follows: cocoanuts (great store), areca, jagra, emery, wax, iron, Baticala sugar, pepper, ginger, cloves, cinnamon, mace, nutmegs, sandal-wood, brasil-wood, long peppers, and, besides these, many silks and other wares which come from China and Malaca. From Chaul and Dabul they bring thither great store of woven cottons and linens, and take them away again to Arabia, and Persia. The traders who bring these goods take in return much silk cloth and country cotton, many horses, wheat, gingelly (and the oil got from it), cotton, opium, both that brought from Aden and that which they make in Cambaya, which is not so fine as the former. They also take many of the common silk camlets made in Cambaya, which are good and cheap. From India also they bring many large carpets, taffety, cloth of scarlet-in-grain and other colours, spices and other things, and all these goods are carried by the folk of this country to Meca, Adem, Ormus and other parts of Arabia and Persia, to such a degree that this town now has the greatest trade of any found in these regions; and yields such a sum of money that it is an astonishing thing, by reason of the bulky and precious goods that are here laden and unladen.

Goa

Further along the coast there is a very fine river which sends out two branches to the sea. Between these two is an island on which stands the city of Goa. It belongs to the Daquem, and was a seignory over itself and over other lands around it further inland. There rules a great lord, a vassal of the said king, whom they call Sabayo, on whom this seignory of Goa was bestowed because he was a bold horseman and valiant in war, in order that he might wage war thence against the king of Narsyngua, as he did continually thenceforth until the day of his death; on which this city remained in the possession of his son the Çabaym Hydalcam.

The inhabitants thereof are Moors of distinction, many of whom are foreigners from divers lands. They were white men, among whom, as well as merchants of great wealth, there were also many husbandmen. The land, by reason that the harbour was exceeding good, had great trade, and many ships of the Moors came thither from Meca, the city of Adem, Ormus, Cambaya and Malabar. The Hydalcam had there a captain with many men at arms, who guarded it, and no man entered the island except under a strict regulation and a pass. He also kept there magistrates, scriveners and guards, who stopped every man who would enter, writing down who and whence he was, and what were his distinguishing marks; in this manner they allowed men to come in or to go forth. The city is very great, with good houses, well girt about with strong walls, with towers and bastions. Around it are many vegetable and fruit gardens, with fine trees and tanks of sweet water, with mosques and heathen temples. The surrounding country is exceedingly fertile. Here the Hydalcam had a great revenue as well from the land as from the sea.

Having heard the news of the overthrow of the Rumes before Dio by the Viceroy Dom Francisco Dalmeida [...], he sent to summon all those who had escaped thence, and they, leaving their Captain Mirocem in the kingdom of Guzarate, came to Goa. The Hydalcam received them well and determined to give them all the aid and succour of which they stood in need, and to set them up again by the help of other Moorish kings and of the merchants, to the end that they might wage war against our people; in such a way, that having gathered together a great sum of money they began to build in the Goa river fair galleys and brigantines after our fashion and style, as well as many pieces of ordnance of iron and copper and all other munitions of war needful for the sea, and made such good speed that in a short time a great part of the fleet was ready, as well as many great store-houses full of all necessaries in great perfection. Thus they were so confident that they put out to sea in atalayas and fustas to the zambucos, which were passing by with safe-conducts from the Captains of the King our Lord and from Afonso D'Alboquerque, who was then Captain-in-Chief of the Indian Sea, and took them. And as this continued to increase, the said Afonso D'Alboquerque, having information thereof, determined to pay them a visit and persuade all his ships, caravels and galleons; he entered the river, and attacking the said city, took it by force of arms. In this attack many noteworthy events took place, which I do not here relate, in order to cut my story short, 'for it is not my intention to write a chronicle, but only a short summary of that which can in truth be ascertained regarding the chief places in India'.

But, to return to the subject: In this fight perished much people of the city, and of the ships which they had made ready some were taken and more were burnt, and he brought the city forthwith under the rule and governance of the King our Lord, even as it now is, and built for its defence strong fortresses. It is, at this time present, inhabited by Portuguese, Moors and Heathen, in great numbers.

Duties on the fruits and produce of the land yield the King our Lord yearly twenty thousand cruzados, in addition to the port dues.

In this port of Goa there is great trade in many kinds of goods, from the whole of Malabar, Chaul, Dabul and the great kingdom of Cambaya, which are consumed on the mainlands, and from the kingdom of Ormus come every year many ships laden with horses, and great numbers of dealers from the great kingdom of Narsyngua and from Daquem come hither to buy them. They pay for them at the rate of two to three hundred cruzados a piece, as the case may be, and take them away to sell them to the kings and lords of their lands, and by this means one and all they make great gains, and the King our Lord as well, who receives a duty of forty cruzados on each horse.

[In this kingdom of Decam there are many great cities and many towns and villages in the inland country, inhabited by Moors and Heathen. The country is exceedingly fertile, yielding much food, and with great traffic.]

The Ormus merchants take hence in their ships cargoes of rice (great store) sugar, iron, pepper, ginger and other spices of divers kinds, and drugs, which they carry thither: and in all their dealings they are by the order of the King our Lord treated with greater mildness than by the Moorish kings.

The king of this land (Bahmani Kingdom of Mahmud Shah) and the whole Daquem kingdom is named Soltam Mahamude. He is a Moor, and resides always in one city which is called Bider, where there is great luxury, leading a very pleasant life. He does not govern himself, nor do anything concerning his government, but makes it all over to certain Moorish noblemen to govern, and each of these has charge of certain towns and cities, and governs those entrusted to him by the king. If any one of these rises against him the others all help obedience or destroy him. These Governors are often at war one with the other; they have many horsemen and are good archers, with Turkish bows. They are fair men and tall, and are attired in fine cotton garments, with turbans on their heads. They come from divers countries, and he pays them right well; they speak Arabic, Persian and Daquanim (Marathi) which is the native tongue of the land.

The Moorish noblemen in general take with them tents, with which they form encampments, on the halting-grounds, when they travel, or when they take the field to attack any town.

They ride on high-pommelled saddles, and make much use of zojares, and fight tied to their saddles, with long light lances which have heads a cubit long, square and very strong. They wear short coats padded with cotton, and many of them kilts of mail; their horses are well caparisoned with headpieces. They carry maces and battle-axes and two swords (each with its dagger), two or three Turkish bows hanging from the saddle, with very long arrows, so that every man carries arms enough for two. When they go forth to fight they take their wives with them, and they employ pack-bullocks on which they carry their baggage as they travel. Their king is often at war with the king of Narsyngua, from whom he has taken many towns, who in his turn endeavours to recover them. They are but seldom at peace, and were so even more seldom while the Sabayo yet lived. The Heathen of this Daquem kingdom are black and well-built, the more part of them fight on foot, but some on horseback, yet these are few. The foot-soldiers carry swords and daggers, bows and arrows. They are right good archers, and their bows are long like those of England. They go bare from the waist up, but are clad below; they wear small turbans on their heads. They eat flesh of all kinds, save beef, which is forbidden by their idolatrous religion, which they follow very strictly. When they die they order their bodies to be burnt, and their wives burn themselves alive.

Sati

In this kingdom of Narsyngua (Vijayanagar), there are three classes of Heathen, each one of which has a very distinct rule of its own, and also their customs differ much one from the other.

The principal of these is that of the King, the great Lords, the knights and fighting men, who may marry, as I have said, as many women as they wish, and are able to maintain: their sons inherit their estates: the women are bound by very ancient custom, when their husbands die, to burn themselves alive with their corpses which are also burnt.* This they do to

---

*The very full description here given of the rites of Sati as observed in the Vijayanagar kingdom is of great interest, and gives the impression of being drawn from personal observation. It may be compared with the similar description given by Fernao Nuniz (l.c. p. 391) which agrees with it in so many details as to

(Contd...)

honour the husband. If such a woman is poor and of low estate, when her husband dies she goes with him to the burning ground, 'where there is a great pit' in which a pile of wood burns. When the husband's body has been laid therein and begins to burn, she throws herself of her own free will into the midst of the said fire, where both their bodies are reduced to ashes. But if she is a woman of high rank, rich, and with distinguished kindred, whether she be a young maid or an old woman, when her husband dies she accompanies the aforesaid corpse of her husband to the aforesaid burning ground, bewailing him; and there they dig a round pit, very wide and deep, which the fill with wood (and a

---

(Contd...)

make it probable that Nuniz had seen a manuscript of Barbosa's work. The description given by Niccolo de Conti (*India in the Fifteenth Century*, II, 24) probably also refers to Vijayanagar, although it is not expressly mentioned. He had already mentioned (p. 6) the sati of all the king's wives. Other interesting descriptions of satis in other parts of India are given by Mandelslo, Peter Mundy and Thoman Bowrey. In the case of Mandelslo, the woman gave him one of her bracelets, no doubt in making a distribution of her jewels such as is described by Barbosa (*Travels*, English translation by John Davies, 1669, p.32). In the same way Thomas Bowrey was given by the widow some flowers from her hair (*Countries Round the Bay of Bengal*, H.S., p. 38). His description refers to Careda between Madras and Machhlipatan in the year 1672, while Mandelslo's refers to Kambayat. It is evident, therefore, that this custom was widely diffused.

Peter Mundy's account (*Travels*, 11, 32-36) refers to a sati at Surat of a Banya's widow in 1630, of which he has left his own sketch. In none of these cases is there anything to show that the cremation took place, as at Vijayanagar, in a deep pit into which the widow threw herself either while her husband's body was burning, or, in the case of persons of high rank, afterwards, with a procession on horseback, and great ceremonies. The custom of performing the cremation in a pit as described by Barbosa and Nuniz was evidently common in South India. Tavernier alludes to it in the seventeenth century as prevailing on the coast of Coromandel. His account, though short, shows that the ceremony was identical with that prescribed in the text (*Tavernier's Travels*, English, Ed. 1678, Pt. II, Bk. 111, P. 171) In general the cremation seems to have taken place on a pyre, and not in a pit, and such is the usage in cremations at the present day in Northern India. In Western India Mr. Crooke says (*Popular Religions of Northern India*, 1, 188) a grass hut was erected in which the widow sat, holding her husband's head in her lap, supporting it with her right hand and holding in her left a torch with which she kindled the hut. Such a sati is that described by Peter Mundy, and the hut or 'cottage', as he calls it, is shown in the background of his sketch.

great quantity of sandal wood therewith), and, when they have kindled it, they lay the man's body therein, and it is burnt while she weeps greatly.

Wishing to do all honour to her husband she then causes all his kindred and her own to be called together, that they may come to feast and honour her thereby, all of whom gather together at the said field for this ceremony, where she spends with them and with her kindred and friends all that she has in festivities with music and singing and dancing and banquets. Thereafter she attires herself very richly with all the jewels she possesses, and then distributes to her sons, relatives and friends all the property that remains. Thus arrayed she mounts on a horse, light grey or quite white if possible,* that she may be the better seen of all the people. Mounted on this horse they lead her through the whole city with great rejoicings, until they come back to the very spot where the husband has been burnt, where, they cast a great quantity of wood into the pit itself and on its edge they make a great fire. When it has burnt up somewhat they erect a wooden scaffold** with four or five steps where they take her up just as she is. When she is on the top she turns herself round thereon three times, worshipping towards the direction of sunrise, and, this done, she calls her sons, kindred and friends, and to each she gives a jewel, whereof she has many with her, and in the same way every piece of her clothing until nothing is left except a small piece of cloth with which she is clothed from the waist down. All this she does and says so firmly, and with such a cheerful countenance, that she seems not about to die. Then she tells the men who are with her on the scaffold to consider what

---

*The horse upon which the widow rode is described as 'ruco pombo se for posivel'. Probably there should be a comma after *ruco*. This word means ordinary light grey, with a dark skin beneath, while *pombo* is pure white, in which the pink skin shows beneath the hair. Horses of this colour are in great favour still for processions and ceremonies throughout India. In the north they are known as *Nukri* or 'silvery'. Nuniz (l.c. 391) describes the horse as worthless, and says nothing about the colour. Horses of this colour are not esteemed by Europeans.

**The scaffold or platform here described is *cadalfalso* in Portuguese, a word probably derived from *catafalco*, 'a catafalque'; in modern Spanish cadahalso. Akin to this is the Old French *escadafaut* from which our *scaffold* is derived.

they owe to their wives who, being free to act, yet burn themselves alive for the love of them, and the women she tells to see how much they owe to their husbands, to such a degree as to go with them even to death. Then she ceases speaking, and they place in her hands a pitcher full of oil, and she puts it on her head, and with it she again turns round thrice on the scaffold and again worships towards the rising sun. Then she casts the pitcher of oil into the fire and throws herself after it with as much goodwill as if she were throwing herself on a little cotton, from which she could receive no hurt. The kinsfolk all take part at once and cast into the fire many pitchers of oil and butter which they hold ready for this purpose, and much wood on this, and therewith, bursts out such aflame that no more can be seen. The ashes that remain after these ceremonies are thrown into running streams. All this they do in general without any hindrance, as it is the custom of all. Those who do not so, they hold in great dishonour, and their kindred shave their heads and turn them away as disgraced and a shame to their families. And as for some who have not done it, to whom they wish to show favour, if they are young they send them to a temple there to earn money for the said temple with their bodies. There are some temples which have a hundred or more women of good birth in them; and some unmarried women put themselves there of their own free will. They are forced to play and sing before the idols for certain hour every day, and continue to earn money for these for most of the time left them.

This abominable practice of burning is so customary , and is held in such honour among them, that when the King dies four or five hundred women burn themselves with him in this way*, for which they make the pit and the fire to such a size that they can hold any number who may

---

*As to the number of women who burnt themselves at the death of a king of Vijayanagar there is abundant testimony. Noccolo Canti mentions it in the first half of the fifteenth century (*India in Fifteenth Century*, II, 6). Nuniz also alludes to the practice (l.c. p. 293). The men who are said to have burnt themselves with the king belonged no doubt to the class of eunuchs who were the favourites alluded to by Nuniz, who says: 'Amongst these eunuchs the king has some who are great favourites and who sleep where he sleeps; they receive a large salary (l.c. p. 249).'

wish to throw themselves in; and for this too they keep ready great store of sanders-wood, eagle-wood, brazil-wood, and also of gingelly oil and butter to make the fire burn better. Some of these women throw themselves in suddenly while the king is burning, others with the ceremonies I have just described, and such is the rush as to who shall be burnt with him that it is a frightful thing.

'A magnificent Christian spectacle'

Fernao Mendes Pinto

Having departed from the bar of Ancola here, five leagues below Bhatkal, bound for Goa, the cutter arrived on Thursday, at eleven o'clock at night at our Lady of Rebandar, half a league from Goa, where the body (of St. Francis Xavier) was taken ashore, carried to the church, and placed next to the main altar, surrounded by many burning torches and tapers. Father Master Belchor who was now in charge of it, immediately sent someone to inform the viceroy, as he had asked him to do. He also sent word to the fathers of his college for them all to come and wait for him on the pier at daybreak, for he would be there by eight o'clock. After the father rector had taken care of everything he thought necessary at the time and rested a while, in the wee hours of dawn he said mass, which was attended by all the people who lived in the area, both native and Portuguese.

By this time as the day was breaking, six vessels arrived from the city with forty or fifty men on board who, during the lifetime of the deceased, had been very devoted followers of his, all of them carrying freshly lit candles in their hands with their slaves carrying tapers. Upon entering the church they all prostrated themselves face down on the dock as the cutter passed by them. Close behind them, in the same order, were ten or twelve vessels, so that by the time they reached the pier it must have been accompanied by twenty rowing vessels carrying about 150 Portuguese from China and Malacca, all very rich and respectable people. They were also carrying lighted torches and tapers while their servants, who probably numbered three hundred, were carrying candles as big as torches, creating altogether a magnificent Christian spectacle that inspired deep devotion in all those who beheld it.

When the cutter carrying this holy corpse arrived at the city pier where he was to dock, the viceroy was already there, waiting in full state, with footmen carrying silver maces accompanied by all the nobility of India, in addition to such an enormous crowd of people from the general population that four constables had all they could do to clear the way. Also there were the canons of the cathedral chapter, the supervisors and brothers of the House of Mercy, all in their vestments, with white tapers in their hands and a coffin with a brand-new cloth of brocade decorated with gold embroidery and fringes, which was not used because it seemed better to have him carried in the one in which he had come from Malacca. The fathers and brothers of the Society of Jesus—who were there in great numbers—boarded the cutter, which by this time had been made fast to the landing.

When they lifted the coffin on top of the deck house, a very devout crucifix appeared, which a large group of orphan children from the college had kept covered. One of them began to chant the psalm 'Benedictus Dominus Deus Israel', to which all the other responded together with a lamentation of very fine voices in perfect harmony that was so amazingly pious that it made everybody's hair stand on end just to hear them. Also, the tears and sobs were so widespread throughout the crowded Christian assembly that the mere sight of it was enough to make every sinner undergo genuine conversion.

The entire crowd set out from the pier in a very orderly procession and the holy corpse followed behind them in the coffin in which it had come from Malacca with a large brocade cloth on top and silver thuribles scenting it from both sides with the most delightful aromas, and the coffin belonging to the House of Mercy preceded it to the right. So that all in all the funeral was conducted that day with such great cost and splendour, for the honour of God and this servant of his that the native gentiles and Moors stuck their fingers in their mouths to show how deeply amazed they were as is their custom.

They passed through the city gate, proceeding in this manner along the main street, which at that time was very splendidly decorated from top to bottom with many carpets and silken hangings, and their windows were well fitted out and crowded with wives and daughters of all the noblemen, with many ingenious devices at the doorways below giving off perfumes and sweet-smelling aromas. And not only this street but all the others through which it passed as far as the college of St. Paul to which it was taken, were like this. Even though it was Friday of St. Lazarus, the college was festively bedecked with brocade frontals in all the altars, and lamps, candlesticks, silver crosses and everything else in sight were arranged in like manner.

After they reached the church in this way, it was placed next to the high altar on the Gospel side, where a solemn high mass was said with brocade pontifical and celebrated with beautiful chorus and many musical instruments befitting the solemnity of such an important festivity. But because the hour was very late and everyone was anxious to view the holy corpse, they dispensed with the sermon.

Once mass was over, the saintly body was exhibited to all the people who paid reverence to him with many tears. But since, as I said, there were so many people there and each was trying to get a closer view of it, the crush and press of the crowd was such that the grilles of the chapel, despite the fact that they were very sturdy, were broken into many pieces. Seeing that the tumult was steadily increasing and that they were unable to control it, the fathers covered the coffin again and told them that they would be able to view it more comfortably in the afternoon; and, with that, they all departed. Nevertheless, it was shown several times afterwards, and on some of these occasions, because of the enormous crowds that came, there was a great deal of shouting and disorder on the part of both women and children who were in danger of being suffocated.

'King Akbar most devoutly kissed the Bible'

Anthony Monserrate

Gift of a Bible

When the Fathers had refreshed themselves for a short time from the fatigue of their journey, they were again summoned before the King (Akbar). Whereupon they set their hands to the work on behalf of which they had undertaken so long and tedious a journey. For this purpose they made the following opening. On the 3rd of March they took to the audience chamber a copy of the Holy Bible, written in four languages and bound in seven volumes; this they showed to the King. In the presence of his great nobles and religious leaders Zelaludinus (Jalal-ud-din Akbar) thereupon most devoutly not only kissed the Bible but placed it on his head. He then asked in which volume the Gospel was to be found. When he was shown the right volume, he showed yet more marked reverence to it. Then he told the priests to come with their Bible into his own private room, where he opened the volumes once more with great reverence and joy. He shut them up again very carefully, and deposited them in a beautiful bookcase, worthy of such sacred volumes, which stood in the same private room, where he spent a great deal of his spare time.

Religious discussion

As a result of this an opportunity was given for a discussion, which was held at night, and in which the priests met the religious teachers and doctors and debated keenly with them the question of the accuracy and authority of the Holy Scriptures, on which the Christian religion is founded and that of the vanity and lies of the book in which the Musalmans put their faith treating it as though it had been given by God—although (to disregard other points) Muhammad stuffed it with countless fables full of futility and extreme frivolity. It was pointed out that the most ancient books of Moses and the Prophets bear testimony to the Gospel; and that Alcoranus (the Koran) itself, although it contends with the Gospel, and contains teachings so different from and indeed contrary to those of the Gospel, cannot avoid testifying, not only to the truth, but also to the sanctity of the Gospel. For Alcoranus says in more than one place that the Most High God gave the Gospel to Christ, although the author of Alcoranus most foolishly affirms that God gave the Gospel in a complete and finished state to Christ, just as He gave the Torah (that is the law) to Moses, the Zabur (that is the Psalms) to David, and to himself Alfurcanus (the Koran)—for I shall be excused if I mix up so many barbarian names. But indeed no one gave testimony to the truth of Alfurcanus; and so by the grace of God it came about that the opponents of the Fathers were reduced—their arguments against the Gospel having been refuted—to an inability to prove the very points by which they were attempting to defend their own book from attack. Thus, being thrown into confusion by observing the look on the King's face, they retired from the debate, and finally became entirely silent.

After the debate was finished the King retired, taking the priests with him, and said to them, 'You have proved your case entirely to my satisfaction, and I am well pleased with the religion contained in your law; but I should advise you to be cautious in speech and action, for your opponents are unscrupulous villains. Now I want more enlightenment on these points—how the Most High God can be both three and one, and how He can have a son, a man born of a virgin. For these ideas are entirely beyond my comprehension.' The Fathers replied, 'We will be cautious as regards the Musalman religious leaders, as you advise, not because we are afraid of them for ourselves, but because we wish to obey you. With regard to the other point, about which you ask for information, pray for enlightenment on it from God, who hath abundance and giveth generously to all men; then humbly wait to hear His answer to your prayer.'

The King was greatly impressed firstly with the fact that, although the Holy Bible is written in so many languages, yet no contradiction can be detected in it, but every language found in it expresses one and the same truth; and secondly with the fact that the Fathers were as well acquainted as their Musalman opponents with the Latin translation of Alfurcanus, which we owe to the great diligence and accuracy of Saint Bernard. The Musalman leaders were exceedingly mortified and chagrined by this fact. In addition to this the Fathers agreed together in their arguments but the Musalmans were by no means all of one mind in their defence of Alfurcanus. The King was greatly displeased by this.

This was what happened at the first discussion with the Musalman religious leaders. Three days later a second discussion was held, about heavenly bliss, which Muhammad most wickedly and lyingly asserted to consist in feasting and impure delights, and in other things absolutely the reverse of the teachings of the Holy Scriptures.

Akbar's kindness

Not to go into too many details, the Fathers frequently and freely admonished the King; but their conscientious readiness in doing this never lessened, still less put an end to, the kindly friendship of the King towards them. Nay more, when the King perceived that it was the sincerity of their hearts that led them to feel themselves free to correct him, he took it in such good part that he always seemed not only to favour them, but to heap honours upon them in his desire to show his affection towards them. For when they saluted him, which they did with uncovered heads, he answered with a nod and a bright smile. He did not allow them to keep their heads uncovered when they were in his presence. When a council was being held, or when he summoned them to his private audience-chamber for familiar conversation, he used to make them sit beside him. He shook hands with them cordially and familiarly.

He frequently left the public audience-chamber to converse with them in private. Several times he paced up and down with his arm round Rudolf's (Fr Rudolf Acquaviva) shoulders. Once, when he was in camp, he desired another of the priests, in the middle of a crowd of his nobles, to help him fasten on his sword, which service the Father performed, amidst the envy and wonder of all the courtiers. He wished the priests to be sharers of his inmost thoughts, both in good and ill fortune—no common mark of love and kindness. He ordered his door-keepers to grant them entrance, whenever they wished, even into the inner courtyard of the palace, where only the most distinguished nobles had the right of entrance. He sent them food from his own table—a mark of distinction which he is said never to have conferred upon anyone before. He visited one of the Fathers when he was ill, and greeted him in Portuguese as a sign of respect. There would have been no end to his gifts, had the Fathers not frequently told him that all they needed was food and clothing, and these of the most simple description. This reply pleased him so much that he repeated it publicly: and each month sent them as much money, under the guise of alms, as he thought would be sufficient for their daily expenses.

Monserrate has a discussion with the king

Two days after his son's departure Zelaldinus had the Priest conducted to him by night in order to ask him certain questions, both religious and secular. First of all he had an atlas brought and asked where Portugal was, and where his own kingdom. He wondered how we knew the names of the provinces and cities of India. Then he asked why the Priest was a celibate: for was it not a divine command, as it were, that all men should have wives: and he (the Priest) appeared either to condemn matrimony or to contradict himself when he said that celibacy was good and matrimony also good. The Priest replied, 'Does not your Highness know that, of two good things, one often happens to be better than the other? Thus silver is good, but gold is better: whilst wisdom is better than gold, and virtue than anything else. The moon is beautiful: but the sun is more beautiful, and superior to her.' The King agreed to this; whereupon the Priest added, 'Therefore priests remain celibate and unmarried, that they may follow better things: that they may imitate Christ: and that, free from the cares of a wife, children and family, they may spend their time apart from all desire. For by the sixth commandment of God all luxury is forbidden to Christians, and indeed to all mankind.' The King here interjected, 'You declare, do you not, that Christ is God. Do you not act rashly and insolently in wishing to be like him?' The Priest replied, 'We do indeed believe and asseverate that Christ is God, but we declare at the same time that he is man. And, being man, he practised chastity as an example to us, and also praised it highly very many times in the Gospel. As regards his being God, it would indeed be the mark of a proud and insolent mind to wish to be like Christ. It is indeed an impossible ambition; and hence to entertain it shows the height of folly and madness. But on the other hand it shows piety and devotion to follow his footsteps in practising the virtues which he himself practised. For one of the many causes which led him to wish to become man was his desire that (since we cannot imitate his work of creating and ruling the universe, and the other functions of his Deity) we might imitate him in the attributes and activities of his true manhood, such as his humility, self-sacrifice, chastity, poverty, obedience and other allied virtues. No painter or sculptor, however accurately and carefully he many paint his picture or carve his statue, endeavours actually to appropriate for himself the strength and virtue of nature. It has been found that, though we all struggle with our hearts to imitate Christ in those virtues which can be reproduced in a man, yet we are left far behind by him. Wherefore Christ greatly commends our endeavour to imitate himself, and is far from imputing it to pride or insolence or rashness.'

The King then added, 'The descent from Adam thus perishes in you.' The Priest replied, 'What if I had died when I was a boy eight years old, or (as frequently happens) just at the time of my marriage? What if my wife had been barren, or I myself, as many are? What if I had been born, or made, a eunuch, like the many that are in your palace? Let not your

Highness mistakenly imagine that marriage is enjoined. God indeed allowed much stress to be laid on the value of matrimony under the law of nature, in order that the human race might be increased: and also, amongst the Jews, under the law of Moses, in order that the religion and worship of the true God might be extended. But under the law of the Gospel, which excels all other laws as the substance excels the shadow, the human race having been sufficiently increased, Christ laid down the principle in regard to marriage that each man may freely follow that course he chooses, and stop where he wishes.' Here the King interrrupted (and not at all to the point), 'If God ordered anyone to cross a river, he would be a sinner if he disobeyed.' The Priest replied, 'That is true; but I declared a few moments since that marriage is not enjoined. Nor must you imagine that celibates, though they have no wives, lack offspring. For there is a spiritual begetting; and those whom a man instructs in the faith and virtues of Christianity are in a manner called his sons; for those whom he baptizes and whose confessions he hears are not less his spiritual sons than if he had begotten them by his body. Permit me to declare to you, O King, that if you listen to the advice of Rudolf and myself, you will be more truly and spiritually the son of Rudolf than the son of King Emaumus (Humayun). For those who are only parents by nature, merely beget a body: but he who baptizes you will beget a soul. It may of course happen that some are compelled and commanded to marry.' 'Who?' asked the King. The Priest replied, 'A king who must have an heir for the sake of peace and tranquility of the state. For this reason learned men urged Henry, King of Portugal, though he was a priest, to marry, and (in order that he might do so) to obtain a dispensation from the Pope, who has been constituted interpreter and high judge and moderator in such matters by Christ himself, whose representative he is. Yet King Henry was old and weak, and devoted to chastity, as he had ever been, and thus he died of old age still unmarried, as he desired.' This example was quoted because Zelaldinus was wont to respect and praise King Henry's sanctity, fortitude and constancy, as though he had been a second St. Sebastian.

When the question of celibacy and marriage had been so thoroughly dealt with that the King had no objections left to bring forward, he made detailed enquiries about the Last Judgment, whether Christ would be the Judge, and when it would occur. Having dealt with the other points the Priest said, 'God alone knows the time when the judgment will take place: and in his unsearchable wisdom he has desired this to be hidden from us. Christ himself refused to make it known to his disciples. He did not wish either that we should become negligent through knowing it to be far distant, or that we should be saddened by knowing that it is near at hand. But he wished us so prepare ourselves for that day that we may make good use of the gifts which he has given us, and abstain from sin and from all that he has forbidden, being in fear of the Judgment, though we know not when it will come. Yet signs shall precede that day which will enable men to conclude with confidence that it is at hand.' The King asked what these signs should be. The Priest replied, 'Christ mentioned especially wars and rebellions, the fall of kingdoms and nations, the invasion, devastation and conquest of nation by nation and kingdom by kingdom: and these things we see happening very frequently in our time.'

'Worshipfull and bountifull houses'

John Huyghen Van Linschoten

The 30 chapter

(Of the Portingalles and Mesticos, their houses, curtesies, mariages, and other customes and manners in India.)

The Portingals, Mesticos, and Christians, kéepe worshipfull and bountifull houses, having commonly (as it is said [before]) five, sixe, ten, twentie, some more, some lesse slaves, both men and women, in their houses every man according to his estate and qualitie, I meane married men. They are very cleanly and swéet in all things belonging to their houses, specially in their linnen, for that every day they change shirtes and smockes both men and women, and [their slaves and servants] likewise with other thinges that they weare, which they doe because of the great heat in that land. The Portingals are commonly served with great gravitie, without any difference betwéene the Gentleman and the common Citizen, [townesman] or soldier, and in their going, curtesies, and conversations, common in all thinges: when they go in the stréetes they steppe very [softly and] slowly forwards, with a great pride and vaineglorious majestie, with a slave that carrieth a great hat or vaile over their heads, to kéepe the sunne and raine from them.

Also when it raineth they commonly have a boy that beareth a cloke of Scarlet or of some other [cloth] after them, to cast over them: and if it bee before noone, hee carrieth a cushin [for his maister] to kneele on when he heareth Masse, and their Rapier is most commonly carried after them by a boy, that it may not trouble them as they walke, nor hinder their gravities. When they méete in the stréetes a good space before they come together, they beginne with a great Besolas manos, to stoope [with]

22

their bodies, and to thrust forth their foot to salute each other, with their hattes [in their hands], almost touching the ground: likewise when they come into the Church [where] they have their stooles ready, which their slaves have prepared for them: all that are by him that commeth in do stande [up], and with the same manner of bowing [of their bodies] doe him great reverence, and if it chaunceth that any doeth him reverence (as the manner is) and that he to whom it is done doth not greatly esteeme thereof, so that he doeth him not the like [curtesie], they do altogether for that cause go after him, and cut his hatte in peeces, saying that he had disgraced the partie, wherein it is not for them to aske wherfore they shold so do, for it would bee the greatest shame [and reproch] in the world unto them if they should not revenge [so great an iniury]: and when they séeke to bee revenged of any man that hath shewen them discurtesie, or for any other cause whatsoever it bee, they assemble ten to twelve of their friends, acquaintance or companions, and take him wheresoever they find him, and beat him so long [together], that they leave him for dead, or very neare dead, or els cause him to be stabbed by their slaves, which they hold for a great honor and point of honestie so to revenge themselves, whereof they dare boast [and bragge] openly [in the stréetes], but if they desire not to kil him, they baste him well about the ribs and all his body over with a thicke réede, as big as a mans legge, which is called Bambus, whereby for eyght dayes after and more he hath inough [to do to kéepe his bed], and sometime in that manner they leave him for deade.

This is their common custome, and is never looked unto or once corrected. Also they use long bagges full of sand, wherewith [they will give such blowes each upon other, that therewith] they will breake each others limmes, and [for ever after] make them lame. When any man goeth to visite an other in his house, although he which is visited be one of the principal Gentlemen [of the Citie], and the visitor but a simple soldier, or some other man it is the manner that hee which is visited commeth unto the doore of his house, with his hatte in his hand, and with great curtesie to receyve him that commeth to visite him, and so leadeth him up into his hall or chamber, wherein he will speake with him, where hee offereth him a chaire to sitte downe, and then hee himselfe sitteth [by him], then he asketh him what hee woulde have, which having understoode hee bringeth him downe againe to the dore in the like sort, and so with a Besolas manos biddeth him farewel, and if he should not doe so, or [when hee giveth him a stool], shold give him one unlined, or one yt is lesse or lower then that he taketh for himselfe, he that visiteth him woulde take it in evil parte, estéeming it a great scorne, and séeke to be revenged on him for the same.

When they have any weddinges and are married, whosoever they be if they have any wealth, all the friendes and neighbours come together, [every man] on horsebacke, and hee that hath not a horse wil borrow one, and are [every man] very costly apparelled, at the least some 50 to 100 [horses little] more or lesse, as the person is [of qualitie], and so they ride altogether in good order unto the Church with their seruantes, and [every man his] hatte for the Sunne, the parentes and friendes in the hinder part, and in ye last row the bridegroome betwéene two [of them], whom they call gossops: after them followeth the bryde between two Commeres, each in their Pallamkin, which is most costly made, and after them followe the slaves both men and women going in troupes, as if they ranne to hunt, and so comming to the Church, and being married according to the order used in the Church of Rome: they are in the same order brought home again, and passing [through the stréets], the neighbours leaning uppon Indian Carpets looke out of the windowes, and throwe Rose water upon the Bryde and Brydegroome, and other swéet smelling waters, with Roses and Sugar Comfets, or corne.

In the mean time their slaves play uppon Shalmes and Trumpets most pleasant [and melodious] to heare, and comming to the house where [the Bride and Bridegroome] dwel, with great reverence and curtesie bowing downe [their bodies], they take their leaves of all the company, which are all on horsebacke about the dore. And so the Bride, the Bridegroome, and the Commeres goe up and sit with great gravitie in a window, and then beginne the [horseman] that led them [to Church], in honor of the married couple, one after the other to runne a course, the gossops (godfathers) beginning first, and the rest following twice or thrice [one after the other], with continuall playing on Shalmes, which are very common in India, for that he which is of any wealth hath them of his own within his house. This being ended, they all passe before the window where the Bride and Bridegroome sit, with a [great] reverence, and so passe on all saving the Gossoppes, [for] they go up to the Bride and Bridegroome, and bid [God give] them joy, then is there some Comfets, and Marchpane brought forth, to drinke [a cuppe of] water withall, and after some [curteous] salutations [and congratulations] to the new married [couple, they take their leaves and] depart: so there remaineth with the Bride and Bridegroome but thrée or four of their nearest friends and kinsemen, for whome there is a dinner prepared, with little meate, yet [very] costly, which they passe over [very] lightly, and not many wordes, [which done] they presently bring the Bride to bed, without any other ceremonies or charges, wherewith the marriage is done and ended.

Oftentimes it chaunceth that they go to bed [at ye least] two houres before Sunne setting, not having the patience to stay so long as [we do] in these countries. When a childe is to be christened, it is likewise in the same sorte led to Church with horses, and last of all commeth the father alone, after whom followeth two men on foote, the one with a great silver or guilt vessell full of bread baked like cracklinges, which in Portingall are called Rosquilhos, and in the middle a great Waxe candle, well made and gilded, thrust through with some peeces of money of golde and silver, for an offering to the Priest that baptiseth the childe, and all over strowed and covered with Roses: the other carryeth a great silver or gilt saltseller in one of his handes, and a lampe of the same stuffe in [his] other hande, each with rich and costly Towels on their sholders: after that followeth two Pallamkins, on the one [side] ye Commere, on the other [side] the Midwife with the child, covered with a costly mantle, made for the purpose, and so the ceremonies of baptisme being ended in the Church, it is againe in the like sort brought home, and beeing there, they have the like manne of musicke [and] shalmes, running and leaping with their horses before the window where the Commere sitteth with the same ceremonies as at the wedding. This is the manner and costome of those that are married and kéepe house.

But concerning the souldier that is unmarried [thus it is]. They goe in the summer time into the Armado [lying] on the water, and being within the townes and on the land, they are very stately apparrelled, and goe verie gravely along the stréets with their slaves or [men] hired [for the purpose], that beare a hatte over them for the sunne and raine: for there are [many] Indians that are [daily] hired for the purpose, and have 12 Basarucos the day, which is as much as two stivers or a stoter, and they serve such as have no slaves, and that will not kéepe any to that end.

The souldiers dwell at least ten or twelve in a house, where they have among them a slave or hired Indian or two which serveth them, and washeth their shirts, and have foure or five stooles with a table, and every [man] a Bedde. Their meate is Rice sodden in water, with some salt fish, or some other thing of small value (without breade) and cleare fountaine water for their drinke, wherewith they are well pleased. They have amongst them all one or two good sutes of apparell, [all] of silke as the manner is there, and when one goeth abroad, the others stay at home, for in the house they have no néede of clothes (but sit whosoever they bee) in their shirts and a paire of linnen bréeches, and so [as it were] naked by [reason of] the great heate, for if some of them [have occassion to] goe out twenty times in one day, they must so often lend him their apparel, and hee must [likewise] put off his clothes, as often as he commeth home againe.

Some souldiers have a Gentleman or Captaine [to their friendes] which lendeth them monie to apparell themselves withall, to the end when summer time cometh, they may be ready to goe with them in Fléet to sea, as also to have their friendship, by night and [at] other times to beare them company, or to helpe them to bee revenged of any injury by them received as [I] said before: for that he which in India hath most souldiers to his friends, is most regarded and feared. So that to bee short, in this manner they doe maintaine themselves in common, [whereby they are able to come in presence] of the best of the countrie. Manie and most of them have their chiefe maintenance from the Portingales and Mesticos wives, as also the Indian Christians [wives], which doe alwaies bestow liberall rewardes and giftes [uppon them] to satisfie [and fulfill] their unchaste and filthy desires, which they know very well how to accomplish, and secretly bring to passe. There are some likewise that get their livings by their friends, travelling for them from place to place with some wares and merchandises, they are called Chattiins. These doe give over [and leave] the officer of a souldier in the Fléete, and the Kinges service: for as [it] is said there is no man compelled thereunto, although their names be registered in the office, yet doe they still kéepe the name of souldier, as long as they travaile abroad and are not married. The souldiers in these dayes give themselves more [to be] Chattiins (traders), and to deale [in Marchandise] then to serve the King in his Armado, because the Captaines and Gentlemen begin to be slacke in doing good unto them, as in times past they used to doe. Also they give themselves to rest and pleasure: wherefore if they can devise any meanes for it they had rather traveile and deale in trade of Marchandise, and to marie and be quiet, in respect that the common souldiers in these dayes are but slackely paide.

The 31 chapter

(Of the maner and customes of Portingale and Mesticos women in India)

The Portingales, Mesticos, and Indian Christian women in India, are little [séene abroad], but for the most part sit still within the house, and goe but seldome forth, unlesse it be to Church, or to visit their friends, which is likewise but verie little, and when they goe abroad, they are well provided not to be seene, for they are carried in a Pallamkin covered with a mat or [other] cloth, so that they cannot be seene.

When they goe to church, or to visit [any friend], they put on very costly apparrell, with bracelets of gold, and rings upon their armes, [all beset with] costly Jewels and pearles, and at their eares hang laces full of Jewels. [Their] clothes [are] of Damaske, Velvet and cloth of gold, for silke is the worst [thing] they doe weare. Within the house they goe bare headed with a wastecoate called Baju (short shirt), that from their shoulders covereth [their] navels, and is so fine that you may sée al their body through it, and downewardes they have nothing but a painted cloth wrapped thrée or foure times about [their] bodies. These clothes are very faire, some of them being very costly [wrought] with [loome worke, and] divers figures and flowers of all colours, all the rest of the body is naked without any hose, but onely bare footed in [a paire of] moyles (sandals) or pantofles, and the men in like sort.

This is their manner in the house both old, and young, rich, and poore, none excepted, for they goe forth but very little, and then they are [both] covered and carried, and what they néed abroad that the slaves both men and women doe fetch in. The women eat no bread or very little, nor yet the slaves, not that they refuse it for the dearnes [or want of bread, (for they have enough and great aboundance) but they are so used to eate rice, that they desire no other, which they séeth with water and eate it with some salt fish, or a [kinde of] salt fruit called Mangas (pickled mango), or with some other composition [both] of fish and flesh, with pottage (pepper water) which they powre upon it, and [so] eate it with their handes: for there they eate nothing with spoones, and if they should sée any man doe so, they would laugh at him. When they drinke they have certaine pots made of blacke earth very fine and thin, much like those that we use in Holland for flower pottes, having in the necke thereof a partition full of holes [with a spout], (and these cruses are called Gorgoleatta), to this end, that when they drinke, they may hold [the potte] on high, and touch it not with their mouthes, but the water running from the spout falleth into their mouthes, never spilling drop, which they doe for cleanliness, because no man should put it to [his] mouth, and when any man commeth newly out of Portingall, and then beginneth to drinke after their manner, because he is not used to that kinde of drinking, he spilleth it in his bosome, wherein they take great pleasure and laugh at him, calling him Reynol, which is a name given in iest to such as newlie come from Portingall, and with such ceremonies as the Portingales use there in India so that at the first they are much whooped and cried at in the stréets, untill by use [and practise] they have learned the Indian manner, which they quicklie doe.

The men are very jealous of their wives, for they will never bring any man into their houses, how speciall a friend [soever] hee bee, that shall sée their wives or [their] daughters, unlesse it bee some gossip or any other married man with his wife in companie. When they will goe together to some place to sport and solace themselves, they are alwaies well guarded by their slaves, both men and women both for their safety and service. If any man commeth to the doore to aske for the master [of the house], presently the wives and their daughters run to hide them (this is a Muhammedan habit), and so leave the man to answer him that standeth at the dore: likewise they suffer no man to dwell within their houses, where the women and daughters bee, howe néere kinsman [soever] he be unto them, being once 15 years of age, nor their owne sons, but have certaine chambers and places beneath, or besides [their] house where they lye, and may in no sort come among the women, and thether they send [them] their meate and [other] provisions, for it hath oftentimes béene séene [in those countries], that the uncles sonne hath laine by his aunt, and the brother by the brother's wife, and the brothe with his sister: whereof I have knowne some that have bin taken with the manner, and that [both] they and the woman have been slaine by the husbands. The women are very luxurious and unchaste, for there are verie few among them, although they bee married, but they have besides their husbands one or two of those that are called souldiers, with whome they take their pleasures: which to effect, they use al the slights and practises [they can devise, by] sending out their slaves and baudes by night, and at extraordinary times, over walles, hedges, and ditches, how narrowlie [soever] they are kept [and looked unto].

They have likewise an hearbe called Deutroa (Dhattura), which beareth a séed, whereof brusing out the sap, they [put into a cup or other vessel, and] give it to their husbands, eyther in meate or drinke, and presently therewith, the man is as though hee were halfe out of his wits, and without feeling, or els drunke, [doing nothing but] laugh, and sometime it taketh him sleeping, [whereby he lieth] like a dead man, so that in his presence with their friends, and the husband never know of it. In which sort he continueth foure and twentie houres long, but if they wash his féete with colde water hee presently reviveth, and knoweth nothing thereof, but thinketh he had slept.

Deutroa of some called Tacula, of others Datura, in Spanish Burla Dora, in Dutch Igell Kolben, in Malaba Vumata Caya, in Canara Datura, in Arabia Marana, in Persia and Turkie Datula. Of the descriptions of this bearbe and fruit you may read in the Herballes, if any man receaveth or eateth but halfe a dramme of this seed, hee is for a time bereaved of his wits, and taken with an unmesurable laughter.

There are many men poysoned by their wives, if they once be mooved: for they know howe to make a [certaine] poyson or venome, which shall kill the person that drinketh it, at what [time or] houre it pleaseth them: which poyson being prepared, they make it in such sort, that it will lye six years in [a man's] body, and never doe him hurt, and them kil him, without missing halfe an houres time. They make it also for one, two, or thrée yeares, monthes, or dayes, as it pleaseth them [best], as I have seene it in many, and there it is very common. There are likewise many women brought to their ends by [means of] their husbandes, and slaine when soever they take them in adulterie, or that they doe but once suspect them, [if they doe presently] they cut their throats, and bring three or foure witnesses to testifie that strange men entred into their houses by night, at unaccustomed times, or els by day, [and had their pleasures] of their wives, or in other sort as they will devise it, whereby they are presently discharged [of the crime] according to the lawes and ordinances [both] of Spaine and Portingall, and presently may marrie with another [wife]. This [notwithstanding] is no meanes to make the women feare, or once to leave their filthie pleasures, although there are everie yeare manie women without number so dispatched [and made away] by their husbands, and it is so common with them, that no man thinketh it strange, [or once wondereth thereat] because of the costume. The women also for their part say [and] flatly [affirme], that there can be no better death, than to die in that manner, saying that so they are sacrificed for love, which they thinke to be a great honour [unto them].

The women are by nature very cleanelie and neat, as well in their houses as in apparell, for that although all whatsoever she putteth on her bodie every day, is [both white, cleane and] fresh: yet they have a manner everie day to wash [themselves] all the body [over], from head to foote, and some times twyse [a day], in the morning and at evening: and as often as they ease themselves or make water, or [else] use the companie of their husbands, everie time they doe wash [themselves], were it a hundreth times a day and night: they are no great workers, but much delighted in swéet hearbs, and in perfumes and frankincense, and to rub their bodies and their foreheads with swéet sanders and such like woods, which with water they doe stéep or breake in peéces: also the whole day long they [doe nothing, but sit and] chawe leaves [or hearbes], called Bettele (betel), with chalke and a [certaine] fruit called Arrequa, whereof in an other place among fruites and hearbs I wil speake more.

This Arrequa, some of it is so strong, that it maketh men almost drunke, and wholly out of sense, although in shewe and in taste it is almost like wood or rootes: these things they sit all the whole day chawing [in their mouthes], like oxen or kyne chawing the cud: they let the sap goe down in [to their throats], and spit the rest out [of their mouthes], whereby they make their mouthes so red and blackish, that to such as know it not it is strange to sée—all which, with [their] washing, frankinscence, and rubing with sanders, they have [learned and] received of the Indian Heathens, which have had those costomes of long time, and yet till this day [use them]: they say it preserveth the téeth, and kéepeth them sound, good for the mawe, and against a stincking mouth and evill breath, insomuch as they are so used to chaw it, that wheresoever they goe or stand, they must alwaies have [of] those leaves carryed with them, and the women slaves do likewise goe alwaies chawing, and are so used thereunto, that they verily thinke, that without it they can not live, for their common worke is to sit all day, when their husbands are out [of doores], behind the mat, which hangeth at the winndow, alwaies chawing the [hearbe] Bettele, séeing those that passe by in the stréetes, and no man séeth them: but as any man passeth by which liketh them, and they will let them have a sight, they lift up the mat, whereby they doe the passinger a great favour, and with that manner of shewing themselves and casting lookes, they make their beginnings of love, which by their slavish women they bring to effect: to the which end they have all develish devises [that possible may be invented], for that both night and day they do practise nothing else, but make it their [onely] worke, and to make nature more lively [to abound and] move them thereunto, they do use to eate those Betteles, Arrequas, and chalk, and in the night it standeth by their bed [sides, this] they eate whole handfuls of Cloves, Pepper, Ginger, and a baked kind of meat calle Chachunde, which is mixed [and made] of all kindes of Spices and hearbs, and such like meates, all to increase their leachery.

And they are not content therewith, but give their husbandes a thousand hearbs for the same purpose, to eate, they not knowing thereof, thereby to fulfill their pleasures, and to statisfie their desires, which can not by any meanes be satisfied. They are likewise much used to take their pleasures in Bathes, by swimming therein, which they can very well doe, for there are very few of them, but they would easilie swimme over a river of halfe a myle broad.

This shall suffice for [their] women, now I will procéed to other matters. And the better to understand the shapes and formes of their women, together with their apparell, you may behold it here, when they goe to Church and elswhere, both wives, maids, and widdows, [everie one by themselves], as also how they goe in their houses, with their dish of Bettele in their hands, being their daylie chawing [worke]: also how they are carried in Pallamkins through the stréet, with their women slaves round about them: also with their husbands and slaves by night, going to anie sport, or els to Church, which they use after ye manner of pilgrims, for then they go on foot, whereby they thinke to deserve greater reward, which by day is not permitted them, for they are not so much trusted: these visitations or night pilgrimages they hold and estéem for a great recreation and fréedome, for that they hope, watch and looke for the same, as children doe for wake-dayes (fairs) and other playing times: likewise the women slaves doe make some account thereof, because they doe never go abroad, but only at such times, or to Church on festivall dayes behind their Pallamkins, upon the which dayes they advertise their lovers, and leave their mistresses in the Churches, or slip into some shoppe or corner, which they have redie at their fingers endes, where their lovers méet them, and [there] in hast they have a sport [which done] they leave each other: and if she chance to have a Portingal or a white man to her lover, she is so proud, that she thinketh no woman comparable unto her, and among themselves doe bragge [thereof], and will steale both from master and mistress to give them, with the which manie Soldiers doe better maintaine themselves, then with the kinges pay; and if [if chaunceth that] these slavish women be with child, they are their maisters [children], who are therwith very wel content, for [so] they are their captives, but if the father be a Portingale, or [some] other frée man, when the childe is borne, he may within 8 dayes challenge it for his, paying the maister a small péece of money [for it], [as much] as by law is thereunto ordeined, and so [the child shall ever after] be frée, but not the mother: but if he stay above 8 to 10 dayes, and within that time no man cometh to challenge it, although it be a free mans [child], and he after that shall come to aske it, then it is the mothers maisters slave, and he may hold it at as high a price as pleaseth him, without constraint to sell it, and it falleth out verie little, or [else] never that the mother destroyeth her child, or casteth it away, or sendeth it to the father, be she never so poore, frée or captive, for they delight more in [their] children, and take more pleasure in carrying them abroad, specially when it is a white mans [child], then in all the riches of the world, and by no means will give it to the father, unlesse it should be secretly stollen from her, and so conveyed away.

The nursing [and bringing up] of the Portingales 'Mesticos' children is, that from the time of their birth they are kept naked onely with a little short shyrt (like the womens Baju, [which they weare] about their bodies), and nothing else, till they be of yeares to weare breches, or other clothes. Some of them are nurssed by their slaves, and some by Indian women, which they hire, whose shape and forme you may sée, following the Palamkin wherein the wife is carried, even as they goe bearing their children.

The 36 chapter

(Of the Indians called Bramenes, which are the ministers of the Pagodes, and Indian Idoles, [and] of their manners of life.)

The Bramenes are the honestest and most estéemed nation amonge [all] the Indian heathens: for they doe alwaies serve in ye chiefest places about the King, as Receyvers, Stewards, Ambassadors, and such like offices. They are likewise [the priestes and] ministers of the Pagodes, or divelish Idoles. They are of great authoritie among the [Indian] people, for [that] the King doth nothing without their counsell and consent, and that they may be knowne from other men, they weare uppon their naked body, from the shoulder crosse under the arme over their body downe to the girdle, or the cloth [that is wrapped about their middle], 3 or 4 strings like sealing thréede, whereby they are knowne: which they never put off although it shoulde cost them their lives, for their profession and religion will not permit it. They go naked, saving [onely that they have] a cloth bounde about their middles to hide their privie members. They wear sometimes when they go abroad a thinne cotton linnen gowne called Cabaia, lightly cast over their sholders, and [hanging] downe [to the grounde] like some other Indians, as Benianes, Gusarates, and Decaniins. Upon their heads they weare a white cloth, wounde twice or thryce about, therewith to hide their haires, which they never cut off, but weare it long and turned up as the women do.

They have most commonly rounde rings of golde hanging at their ears, as most of ye Indians [have]. They eat not anything that hath life, but féed themselves with hearbes and Ryce, neyther yet when they are sicke will for any thing bee let blood, but heale themselves by hearbes and ointments, and by rubbing [their bodies] with Sanders, and such like swéet woods. In Goa and on the sea coasts there are many Bramenes, which commonly doe maintaine themselves with selling of spices and [other] Apothecarie ware, but [it is] not so cleane [as others, but] full of garbish [and dust]. They are very subtil in writing and casting accounts, wherby they make other simple Indians beleeve what they will.

Touching the pointes of their religion, wherein the common people beléeve them to be Prophetes: whatsoever they first meete withal in the stréets at their going forth, the doe they all the day [after] pray unto. The women when they goe forth have but one cloth about [their] bodies, which covereth their heads, and hangeth downe unto their knées: all the rest [of the body is] naked. They have ringes through their noses, about their legs, toes, neckes, and armes, and upon each hand seven or eight ringes or bracelettes, some of silver and gilt, if they be of wealth [and ability]: but the common people of glasse, which is the common wearing of all the Indian women. When the woman is seven years olde, and the man nine years, they do marrie, but they come not together before the woman bee strong enough to beare children.

When the Bramenes die, all their friends assemble together, and make a hole in the ground, wherein they throw much wood and other things: and if the man be of any accompt, [they cast in] swéet Sanders, and other Spices, with Rice, Corne and such like, and much oyle, because the fire should burne the stronger. Which done they lay the dead Bramenes in it: then cometh his wife with Musike and [many of] her néerest frends, all singing certain prayses in commendation of her husbands life, putting her in comfort, and encouraging her to follow her husband, and goe with him into the other world. Then she taketh [al] her Jewels, and parteth them among her frends, and so with a chéerfull countenance, she leapeth into the fire, and is presently covered with wood and oyle: so she is quickly dead, and with her husbands bodie burned to ashes: and if it chance, as not very often it doth, that any [woman] refuseth to be burnt with her husband, then they cut the haire cleane off [from her head]: and while she liveth she must never after wear any Jewels more, and from that time she is despised, and accounted for a dishonest woman.

This manner and custome of burning is used also by the Nobles and principallest of the Countrey, and also by some Marchantes: notwithstanding all their dead bodies in generall are burnt to ashes, and the women, after their husbands deathes, doe cut their haire short, and weare no Jewels, whereby they are knowne for widowes. The [first] cause [and occasion] why the women are burnt with their husbandes, was (as the Indians themselves do say), that in time past, the women (as they are very leacherous and inconstant both by nature, and complexion), did poyson many of their husbands, when they thought good (as they are likewise very expert therein:) thereby to have the better means to fulfill their lusts. Which the King perceiving, and that thereby his principal Lords, Captains, and Souldiers, which uphelde his estate and kingdome, were so consumed and brought unto their endes, by the wicked practises of women, sought as much as hee might to hinder the same: and thereupon he made a law, and ordayned, that when the dead bodies of men were buried, they shold also burne their wives with them, thereby to put them in feare, and so make them abstaine from poysoning of their husbands: which at the first was very sharply executed, onely upon the nobles, [gentlemen, and] souldiers [wives, as also the Bramenes (for that the common people must beare no armes, but are in a manner like slaves.)

So that in the ende it became a custome among them, and so continueth: [whereby] at this day they observe it for a part of their law and ceremonies of their divelish Idoles, and now they do it willingly, being hartened and strengthened thereunto by their friendes. These Bramenes observe certain fasting daies in a year, and that with so great abstinence, that they eat nothing all that day, and sometimes in 3 or 4 daies together. They have their Pagodes and Idoles, whose ministers they are, whereof they tell and shew [many] miracles, and say that those Pagodes have been men [living upon earth], and because of their holy lives, and good workes done [here] in this world, are [for a reward thereof], become holy men in the other world, as by their miracles, by the Divel performed, hath béene manifested [unto them], and by their commandementes their formes [and shapes] are made in the most ugly and deformed manner that possible may bee devised. Such they pray and offer unto, with many divilish superstitions, and stedfastly beléeve yt they are their advocates and intercessors unto God. They beléeve also that their is a supreme God above, which ruleth all things, and that [mens] soules are immortall, and that they goe out of this worlde into the other, both beastes and men, and receyve reward according to their workes, as Pythagoras teacheth, whose disciples they are.

'A great trade in spices, drugs, silk...'

Ralph Fitch

Ormus is an island about 25 or 30 miles in circuit, which is perhaps the most arid and barren island in the world, as it produces nothing but salt; all its water, wood, provisions, and every other necessity, coming from Persia, which is about 12 miles distant; but all the other islands thereabout are very fertile, and from them provisions are sent to Ormus. The Portuguese have here a castle near the sea, with a captain and a competent garrison, part of which dwell in the castle and part in the town; in which likewise dwell merchants from all nations, together with many Moors and Gentiles. This place has a great trade in spices, drugs, silk, cloth of silk, fine tapestry of Persia, great store of pearls from Bahrain, which are the best of all pearls, and many horses from Persia which supply all India. Their king is a Moor, or Mahomedan, who is chosen by the Portuguese, and is entirely under subjection to them. Their women are very strangely attired, wearing many rings set with jewels on their ears, noses, necks, arms, and legs, and locks of gold and silver in their ears, and a long bar of gold upon the sides of their noses. The holes in their ears are worn so wide with the weight of their jewels, that one may thrust three fingers into them.

Very shortly after our arrival at Ormus we were put into prison by order of Don Mathias de Albuquerque, the governor of the castle, and had part of our goods taken from us; and on the 11th October he shipped us from thence, sending us to the viceroy at Goa, who at that time was Don Francisco de Mascarenhas. The ship in which we were embarked belonged to the captain, who carried in it 124 horses for sale.

All goods carried to Goa in a ship wherein there are horses pay no duties; but if there are no horses, you then pay eight in the hundred for your goods. The first city of India at which we arrived on the 5th November, after passing the coast of Zindi [Sindi], was named Diu, which stands in an island on the coast of the kingdom of Cambaia, or Gujrat, and is the strongest town belonging to the Portuguese in those parts. It is but small, yet abounds in merchandise, as they here load many ships with different kinds of goods for the straits of Mecca or the Red Sea, Ormus, and other places; these ships belong both to Christians and Moors, but the latter are not permitted to pass unless they have a Portuguese licence. Cambaietta, or Cambay, is the chief city of that province, being great and populous and well built for a city of the gentiles. When there happens a famine the natives sell their children for a low price. The last king of Cambaia was sultan Badur, who was slain at the siege of Diu, and shortly after the capital city was reduced by the great Mogor, who is king of Agra and Delhi, forty days journey from thence. Here the women wear upon their arms a vast number of ivory rings, in which they take so much pride that they would rather go without their meat than want their bracelets.

Going from Diu, we came to Damaun, the second town of the Portuguese in the country of Cambaia, forty leagues from Diu. This place, which has no trade but in corn and rice, has many villages under its jurisdiction, which the Portuguese possess quietly during peace, but in time of war they are all occupied by the enemy. From Damaun we passed to Basaim [Baseen], and from thence to Tanna in the island of Salsette, at both which places the only trade is in rice and corn. The 10th November we arrived at Chaul on the firm land, at which place there are two towns, one belonging to the Portuguese and the other to the Moors. That of the Portuguese is nearest the sea, commanding the bay, and is walled round; and a little above it is the Moors town, subject to a king called Xa-Maluco. At this place is a great trade for all kinds of spices, drugs, silk raw and manufactured, sandal-wood, elephants' teeth, much China work, and a great deal of sugar made from the nut called gagara [coco]. The tree on which it grows is called the palmer, and is the most profitable tree in the world. It always bears fruit, and yields wine, oil, sugar, vinegar, cordage, coals, or fuel; of the leaves are made thatch for houses, sails for ships, and mats to sit or lie on; of the branches are made houses, and brooms wherewith they sweep them; of the wood ships. The wine issues from the top of the tree, and is procured thus: They cut a branch, binding it hard, and hang an earthen pot under the cut end, which they empty every evening and morning; and still the juice, putting raisins into it, by which it becometh strong wine in a short time. Many ships come here from all parts of India, and from Ormus and Mecca, so that there are many Moors and Gentiles at this place. The natives have a strange superstition, worshipping a cow, and having cow's dung in great veneration, insomuch that they paint or daub the walls of their houses with it. They kill no animal whatever, not so much as a louse, holding it a crime to take away life. They eat no flesh, living entirely on roots, rice, and milk. When a man dies, his living wife is burnt along with his body, if she be alive; and if she will not, her head is shaven, and she is ever after held in low esteem. They consider it a great sin to bury dead bodies, as they would engender many worms and other vermin, and when the bodies were consumed these worms would lack sustenance; wherefore they burn their dead. In all Guzerat they kill nothing; and in the town of Cambay they have hospitals for lame dogs and cats, and for birds, and they even provide food for the ants.

Goa is the chief city of the Portuguese in India, in which their viceroy resides and holds his court. It stands in an island about 25 or 30 miles in circumference, being a fine city and very handsome for an Indian town. The island is fertile and full of gardens and orchards, with many palmer trees, and several villages. Here are many merchants of all nations. The fleet which sails every year from Portugal, consisting of four, five, or six great ships, comes first here, arriving mostly in September, and remaining there forty or fifty days. It then goes to Cochin, where the ships take in pepper for Portugal. Often one ship loads entirely at Goa, and the rest go to Cochin, which is 100 leagues to the south. Goa stands in the country of Adel Khan, which is six or seven days journey inland, the chief city being Bisapor [Bejapoor].

On our arrival in Goa we were thrown into prison, and examined before the justice, who demanded us to produce letters [of licence?], and charged us with being spies; but they could prove nothing against us. We continued in prison till the 22nd December, when we were set at liberty, putting in surety for 2000 ducats not to depart from the town. Our surety was one Andreas Taborer, who was procured for us by father Stevens, an English Jesuit whom we found there, and another religious man, a friend of his. We paid 2150 ducats into the hands of Andreas Taborer, our surety, who still demanded more; on which we petitioned the viceroy and justice to order us our money again, seeing they had it near five months, and could prove nothing against us. But the viceroy gave us a sharp answer, saying, we should be better sifted ere long, and that they had other matter against us. Upon this we determined to attempt recovering our liberty, rather than run the risk of remaining as slaves for ever in the country, and besides it was said we were to have the *strapado*. Wherefore, on the 5th of April 1585 in the morning, we removed secretly from Goa; and getting across the river, we travelled two days on foot in great fear, not knowing the way, as having no guide, and not daring to trust any one.

One of the first towns we came to is called Bellergan, where there is a great market of diamonds, rubies, sapphires, and many other precious stones. From thence we went to Bejapoor, a very large city where the king keeps his court, in which there are many Gentiles, who are gross idolaters, having their idols standing in the woods, which they call pagodas. Some of these are like a cow, some like a monkey, some like a buffalo, others resemble a peacock, and others like the devil. In this country are many elephants, which they employ in their wars. They have great abundance of gold and silver, and their houses are lofty and well built. From thence we went to Galconda, the king of which is called Cutub de Lashach. In this country, in the kingdom of Adel Khan, and in the Decan, those diamonds are found which are called of the *old water*. Golconda is a pleasant fair town, having good and handsome houses of brick and timber, and it abounds with excellent fruits and good water. It is here very hot, and both men and women go about with only a cloth bound about their middles, without any other clothing. The winter begins here about the last of May.

'They eat everything from porcelain plates'

Francesco Carletti

In the city of Goa, which is located on an islet not more than fifteen miles in circumference and at sixteen degrees of latitude toward the north, I took a house. The houses there are very comfortable and good to look at, as also are the churches, particularly those of the Jesuits, of which there are three. These are that of the Novitiate, which they also call Our Lady of the Rosary, a monastery called The Jesus, and a college called Saint Paul's. In my time, at least, they kept the blessed corpse of their Father Francis Xavier, one of the first religious of the Society of Jesus to go to preach the Holy Evangel in that Orient of China and Japan.

It was necessary for me to remain in this city longer than I had thought when leaving China, and the reason was that other ship, which, as I told Your Highness, was unable to pass Malacca because of the unfavorable weather, so that in those twenty months during which I remained there awaiting the rest of my merchandise, which I had loaded on that ship and left behind, I resolved to sell all the silk that I had brought from China with me. And I sent it to Cambay, where it was sold and earned me seventy per cent and more of what it had cost me in China. From Cambay I had them send me, by way of a merchant of the Gujarati nation with whom I had correspondence, an equal quantity of linen cloths of the sorts that they call *canichini, boffettani, semiane,* and other sorts good for Portugal, and various other manufactures of cotton, such as bedcovers embroidered with curious, very beautiful designs in workmanship of a fineness rarely seen, which they also work on silk fabric. And I also had them send me a goodly quantity of things made of mountain crystal and other varieties of stones, such as blood agate, milk agate, and the like.

All this came from Cambay, a city located on the bank of the Indus River, in a latitude of twenty-three degrees north, it being about 450 miles distant from Goa. It is a land and region subject to the Great Mogul, monarch of the best and largest part of all that India, his dominion stretching even to Bengal, where the Ganges River is, and inland to the regions of Russia. And that is the king who buys all the balas rubies that are taken from all parts of the world to India, where they are sold to the great gain of those who sent or brought them there. He is so great a king that when he moves from one city to another, as happened in 1608—when he went from that of Lahore to that of Agra—it requires more than 200,000 men, 200,000 horses, and 6,000 elephants (which they also use for riding through the city, remaining seated on top with their feet folded under in the Moorish style, on rugs), and more than 40,000 camels, as well as oxen, which they use for carrying burdens, and almost innumerable other animals. And throughout the entire trip he always is housed in pavilions that are erected each evening and which, taken all together, make up an enormous city. I learned all this from a letter sent by a Jesuit who went on that voyage.

From Cambay the merchants of that country come to Goa each year with their merchandise in their own ships, and they all are gentle men, mostly Gujarati and Brahmins of that group that live according to the rules of Pythagoras and do not eat anything that lives or has the appearance of blood. They also carry a large quantity of diamonds, among which, Most Serene Lord, I saw one that was brought to Goa by an ambassador of the abovementioned Mogul king. It was in the shape of a pyramid, and it weighed 160 *mangelini*, which is equal to two hundred carats, as the *mangelino* is the same as five of our grains, or one carat and a quarter. And from that diamond he wanted to have removed certain of their letters which were carved into it, so that it then could serve on the headguard of the king's horse. All the above-mentioned merchandise is bought by the Portuguese, to be sent to Lisbon on the ships that go out from Goa and Cochin each year loaded, for the most part, with spices and drysaltery of all sorts. Pepper, on the other hand, is the King's or belongs to him who has a contract with His Catholic Majesty. And that pepper is taken from that coast of Calicut, Cananor, Mangalor, Onor, Barzalor, *(translator's note: Calicut, Cannanore, and Mangalore are easy to identify, but 'Onor' and 'Barzalor' defy identification)* and Cochin, cities to which the merchants from Cambay also go with the same goods for sale.

In Goa they have their houses and shops in a section of the city apart from the rest, and they live very civilly, and above all with much religion, feeling the greatest scruple about killing even a flea or any other viler little animal that there may be. And it is said that in Cambay they have a hospital made for this, where they take in and care for all sorts of sick animals, and that the old cattle and oxen wander through the streets, and that they are given things to eat out of charity, and that among the great lords of that region a festival is held upon the marriage of a cow with a bull, animals that those people hold in the greatest veneration, and that upon such feasts they spend thousands of scudos in order to regale their guests. But I know with certainty that in Goa I have seen them ransom from the hands of Portuguese boys birds, dogs, and cats that the boys, so as to extract money from them, had pretended to want to kill. And they gave such money gladly, and with a certain charity and unbelievable compassion they placed those beasts in safe freedom.

I also know, from long practice in dealing with this sort of men, that in carrying on business with them it is a marvelous thing to see how they cling to reality and are faithful in all their actions. And in buying and selling they are most truthful, and in every way they keep their word and supply what they promise. Finally, they are renowned for extreme moral virtue in everything that they do, so that it would take a long time to tell about it, I shall tell only of the strange way in which their merchants behave when buying and selling goods. They do not speak aloud. But a middleman, who must work out the price of the things desired, takes one hand of the selling merchant and covers it up with his garment (they wear it long, of white cotton cloth, almost in the Turkish style), and without saying a word or giving any other sign, he presses the fingers of this hand, and this in a way to refer to hundreds or thousands, it being agreed that each finger means one hundred or one thousand, and similarly, by the same arrangement, tens or even units. So that if the merchant wants to ask for 155 ducats for his goods from this middleman, he squeezes first a single finger of the hand, and by that action will say 'hundred,' Then he will take all the five fingers and, pressing them all at once, will say 'five tens/' Then, giving another squeeze to the five fingers, he will wish to say 'five,' and thus will have asked 155 ducats for his stuff without having spoken to the middleman. And then this latter, turning toward the buyer, takes his hand, and in the same manner and form tells him how much the seller is asking for his merchandise. If the buyer then wishes him to make an offer of 130 ducats, he takes one finger of the middleman's hand and, squeezing it, means: 'I will give one hundred ducats,' and then he squeezes three others together, and thus says 'and three tens more,' the sum of which makes up the 130. And thus—now with the buyer and now with the seller doing as I have described—the deal is consummated without a word being spoken. Then what has been agreed to by this dumb show is spoken aloud. And what the middleman says is inviolably observed. And he, if not in accord with the sale, is not required to say anything about either the asking price or the offer made for the merchandise, so that under such circumstances nothing at all is known, and thus the negotiations are disclosed only to the three of them—seller, middleman, and buyer—and in that manner the goods keeps its reputation better and is easier to sell to another merchant.

In addition to the observance of their religion, they also are very moral, and do not permit the taking of more than one wife. And they keep their wives delightfully, highly adorned with jewels of all kinds and with gold, with which some of them are so weighed down as to be immobilized. And they are very careful not to have anything to do with other women, and never eat outside their own houses—that is, with strangers or with any people not of their religion, which they esteem to be the best of all. But they do not for that reason damn that of the Christians. Also, one of them, my great friend and a very rich and talented person, often said to me: 'The Christians too, if they would live morally and civilly, would save their souls,' it being his idea that to be a good man and to do to others what you would wish to have done to yourself is sufficient, under whatever religion, to earn a place of repose after death. But I, as much as was possible, tried to show him the contrary—that there was no other way but baptism for anyone wishing to enjoy the glory of God in the other life.

But let us go back to the Portuguese, who live very lavishly and comfortably in Goa, going about constantly on horseback [the horses being brought from Persia with the ships from Ormuz, *(translator's note: Hormuz or Ormuz, the ancient Harmosia, is on the Iranian coast near Bandar Abbas)* and from Arabia, and they give them as feed a certain variety of small beans, but cooked]. And when they ride out they have before and behind them goodly troupes of slaves, including one slave carrying a club in his hand in the manner of a mace, opening up the way; one with an umbrella, without which they never leave the house, one who drives off the flies with a red-and-white horse's tail; and one who acts as a footman and one as a page. And in that style they go all over the city as if in triumph. And the city is made up of good houses and is well decorated.

From China comes everything good and beautiful which could be desired in the way of very rich adornments of gold and silk, beds, chests, tables, cabinets, and chairs, all gilded and with a black varnish that is made from a substance taken from the bark of a tree that grows in China and which at first flows like pitch, but then becomes so hard that it repels water and so shiny that one can use it as a mirror. And all this is very beautifully decorated. With these things, and with others from various parts of this India, they adorn their houses, in which they spend most of their time, the great heat allowing them to go out only during a few hours of each day—in the morning and in the late afternoon.

They eat everything from Chinese porcelain and, what is better, their foods are entirely made of exquisitely flavored birds. The country abounds in fowl, of which one sort has flesh—that is, skin and sinews—all black, and this is much more savory than the others. Of all the sorts they make an endless number of varied and excellent dishes, even to preserving them in sugar and to cooking them whole, boiled and roasted, without the bones, a thing no less marvelous than flavorful. My servant knew how to prepare them in this way and other ways never used in Europe, but native to that region. It also abounds in all kinds of domesticated and wild birds, all of them very cheap. From Ormuz come certain rock partridges that resemble hens, being very large, but having the same plumage and shape as ours.

And they eat everything with rice cooked simply in water, though they do not lack wheat for making bread, which can always be found for sale by anyone who wants to buy it. But in hot countries rice pleases more and is more easily eaten than bread. They also have an abundance of various sugar conserves of local fruit, very delicate and good—and what is best about them is that they cost practically nothing, as for one *giulio* one can get sixteen ounces of whatever fruit confection he may desire. These are the fruits already mentioned in these descriptions of the Orient, and they are sold in the streets by the slaves, who are no less beautiful than they are fervent and loving with themselves as merchandise, so that they rarely sell one without selling the other.

Furthermore, they are very devoted to their wives. And when they get married, they have the most sumptuous weddings, with large cavalcades and corteges of women to accompany the couple to the church when the ring is given and matrimony is contracted by the priest's words. And they make similar festivities of cavalcades and corteges at the baptisms of their children, who in this are more like princes than like private men. But these ostentations cost very little, as each one helps out the other as a mark of courtesy.

Today the wives are mostly those born there of Portuguese fathers and Chinese, Japanese, Javanese, Moluccan, and Bengali mothers, and even mothers from Pegu and various other nations of that region. These matches produce a somewhat brunette strain, but most of the women turn out to be very beautiful, and in particular well-formed as to person, and especially those who are born of the Bengali nation. These women are the best shaped and largest in body of all Indian women, and their members are so rounded as to seem to have been formed on a lathe. The face is rather round than long and is fully fleshed, and the complexion tends rather to the brunette than to the white. But when it is mixed with the Portuguese, it acquires some whiteness and perfection of style, so that those born of these Bengali women turn out to be beautiful women, and they commonly are called *mesticas* which means mixed-breeds.

They are the most desirous creatures imaginable. And further, because of this intensity of their love, they are very jealous of their husbands, as the Portuguese men are of their wives. But the women are that much more jealous of their lovers, of whom, whether married or unmarried, each of them professes to have one—but only one. And to him they give themselves as slaves for and in everything. And they pretend that this lover is as faithful to them as they profess to be to those upon whom they have settled their love. And for that reason it is necessary to be extremely careful that they not discover even a suspicion on which to become jealous. For when they feel themselves disdained, their vengeance is nothing less than poisoning their lover, using the cooked foods or sugar conserves that in that region they constantly give one another while eating their own table foods, sending them to friends and relatives.

And one often hears it said: 'So and so is dead from having eaten such and such a thing given to him by his woman,' who often is not found out or even identified, being a married woman. Women also do this to their husbands, it being a custom of that region. And it is said that it was to remedy that corruption that the law was made among the Indians that wives should be burned alive with the bodies of their dead husbands, so that then the women would not cause their husbands, death for the reason already mentioned or out of a capricious desire to marry some other man, a thing that is not allowed. And in many parts of India, women losing their husbands must observe that law unless they wish to be held to be infamous and shameless. And later this custom itself fell into such abuse that when some great personage or a king died—such as the King of Narsinga—all his wives and concubines and male and female servants, together making up a very large number of people, were burned with his body so that they might make a handsome entrance into the Inferno with their master.

But to speak further of the desirousness of the *mestiças* of Goa, they say that all of them want to have a lover because, it seems, that sky thus inclines each of the women, the lubricity of whom is owing not a little to the continuous heat, rather excessive than moderate, of the region that gave birth to their Indian mothers, who by nature are the most lascivious throughout that Orient or, to say it better, all that part of eastern Asia. And the Portuguese nation is not much behind nor much less desirous of Venus than she is of Love, both of whom seem to have their home particularly in Goa. And there, truly, are the elements essential to maintaining and increasing that kingdom: the lubricity and idleness of those soldiers, most of whom are unmarried gentlemen with no belongings but cloak and sword, and those along with youth, which they use up in that pastime, especially as during four months of the year they cannot sally forth in their ships because of the rains that, as I have said elsewhere, come during the months of May, June, July, and August.

During that period it is not possible to leave or enter any port of that entire coast of India with any vessel, no matter how small. This is because of the outside wind, which blows furiously in the south and southwest, and which lifts and moves so much sand with the heavy sea that it closes the mouths of those harbors. Later, in the month of September, the ships emerge from there, one going toward Cape Comorin, the other toward Cambay. And by patrolling those two coasts in oared ships in the style of galiots that they call galleys, they keep that sea free of the corsairs of the Indies. These, called Malabari, cruise about everywhere, seeking to harm anyone whatever, and especially the Portuguese merchants. And these latter also exist in that same idleness, and almost never have anything to do except when loading the ships for Lisbon. During the rest of the year, they devote themselves to their pastimes and to enjoying the love, the kindness, the cleanliness, and the prettiness of their wives or mistresses, of whom it never would be possible to say enough to explain how amorous, kind, attractive, and clean they really are—except by saying that in every way they lead all the women who have been or are endowed with similar graces, if not everywhere in the world, at least among those women whom I have seen and experienced in circumnavigating the world completely.

And to begin with, the disposition of their living and their lascivious, not to say shameless, costume, in the style of the Indian women of the Malabar region, which accompanies the very graceful motions that they make as they walk around in their houses, will give you good testimony, or rather, to say it better, knowledge of the charms of these women. The dress is only a very fine cotton cloth six arms long and two wide, entirely painted with various designs and embroidered with great artistry in gold thread. In it they wrap the body from the waist down to the insteps of the feet, which they always show naked in a low, heelless black velvet slipper. And that cloth does no more than just cover up their members which can be seen sculptured and in relief, in such a way that the eye can judge exactly how they are made, for it clings to and becomes one with the aforesaid members as if it were wet—this because of its fineness and because of the tightness with which they wrap themselves in it.

The rest of the body is covered, from the waistline up, in a bodice with very tight, long sleeves. This also serves them as a chemise, being of very fine and transparent cotton fabric woven thinner than any sort of veiling. And it is closed as far as the breasts, which are covered by the translucent bodice. At the neck this gives the effect of being a man's shirt with a collar, but is pleated—as also is the rest of the shirt—in the manner in which surplices and other garments of the religious are pleated, without starch, as the water and burning sun of that region are enough to hold those pleats and keep them stiff.

This is the costume that they wear in their houses, so that one could say that they are naked from the waist up, as one sees all of the shoulders, the breasts, and the arms through the transparent bodice—and from the waist down one sees but little less, as they display the outlines of the entire body which is made up of very well-proportioned members. And one rarely sees women with sagging breasts or with any of the other imperfections that fall upon our women after they have given birth. And I think—and even hold it to be certain—that few European women would be discovered to have such members that they would look well in this costume. One sees this in those women who come out from Portugal. Wanting to dress themselves in that manner, they are not successful, but lose a great deal because of the defects of their bodies.

As for ornamentation with jewels, the women wear on their arms bracelets with many thick, heavy golden bells. Each one of these weighs enough to be worth fifteen or twenty scudos, and they put ten or twelve of them on each arm. They wear many rings on their fingers, and pendants of two sorts in their ears. One sort they wear by piercing the ear, but much farther down than usual, and there placing a diamond or ruby jewel; the other sort, worn as among us, is a similar one or a pearl pendant. And they wear pearl ornaments, golden chains, and other similar things at the neck. They arrange their hair simply, pulling all the strands back equally and then forming many little curls without any other shaping. This is the way in which they get themselves up in their houses.

But when they are outside, they go about dressed in the Portuguese style, always carried in certain litters called palanquins, each borne by two or four male slaves. They sit in these with the thighs and legs extended, as if on a bed, and with cushions at the back and rugs beneath them. And they are covered with a mat that protects them from sun and rain, and also so that they may not be seen. And it also is customary for the men to go about in these litters, but they may not go covered up. The women never are to be seen going about in the streets on foot except for that short space which, having alighted from the palanquin, they must cross to enter the church. And it provides a good means of going wherever they wish without being either seen or recognized.

In those regions it is a very common thing for a woman to go in search of a man by that means, either because women are not held in as much honor as among us or, perhaps, because shame does not blot out desire, as it does in our women. I know that a certain married woman went one evening to seek a friend of mine at his house, making use of one of those palanquins. But my friend did not welcome her very well, this because of the danger in which that woman was placing herself and his interests. For if they had been discovered and then judged according to the laws observed among the Portuguese, they would have lost nothing less than their lives and property. And when he had told her that, she answered that man without fear that if she was risking her life and honor out of love for him, he well could do the same for her, that she had come there to stay with him for as much time as was granted her. And that action serves to testify to the second quality of the love that rules those women, it being at times so strong that it partakes more of the bestial than of the human, and they seem rather to wish to lose their lives than to take pleasure in that act.

Husbands kill their wives every day, which they can do freely because it is permitted by the laws of the Portuguese, which in this respect are most severe against the poor women, who very frequently die unjustly. This happened in my time to a young wife of only a few months, killed by her husband because of jealousy that he felt of a man who had fallen in love with her when she had been a girl, but who continued to pass through the street in which she lived with her husband. But in this matter the Portuguese nation is rather rash than jealous. Nor does even that fact succeed in placing any rein on the unrestrained desires of their women. And as for the kindness of these women, in that respect they also go to excesses, never stopping the giving of very noble gifts to the rich while at the same time giving to the poor everything necessary. And they vie with one another to see who can be the best in these matters.

In their gifts of things to eat, furthermore, they study night and day to make exquisite new dishes, which should be restorative above all. Nor do their slaves behave otherwise (they have large numbers of them in their service, and many of them have forty or fifty slaves of various nations, and most of them beautiful) as they precede and follow them with these dishes. From among these I shall tell you of only one, which is called 'royal food,' and which they prepare from the flesh of capons that have first been boiled or roasted. This they shred very fine and then mix and crush with almonds, sugar, amber, musk, ground-up pearls, rose water, and egg yolks, a mixture that restores and, while doing that, incites the lovers to indulge once more in the delights of venery. These gifts, besides being accompanied by beautiful and amorous ambassadors, also are sent with letters composed of amorous and graceful conceits never made use of among us, so that it is amusing to hear them because of what is in those rigmaroles. The slaves are so faithful that very often they have borne or bear insults and injuries to cover up for their mistresses when the latter are discovered in an error or are suspected by their spouses.

And this happened to a friend of mine who was surprised by the husband of a woman who had him come to her there so that she could delight herself with him while she was in the bath, which in that region they are accustomed to enter each evening before going to bed. And the door of the house was opened to him so that he could flee, this by a female slave who had been waiting to do exactly that. Then the slave, kneeling before the master—who was chasing my friend—begged forgiveness for a fault that she had not committed. For she pretended that the man had come on her account. And by the many blows that she accepted for this, she freed her mistress from the suspicion that the husband otherwise would have had of her. The mistress likewise went on scolding her, the better to make herself look innocent of this matter, which was entirely her fault and scheming, and not that of the slave girl. And the slave later was well repaid by both the mistress and her lover when they found themselves together again on a better occasion.

If I were to retell all the occurrences and cases that came to my notice during the twenty-one months when I was in Goa and to describe the ardor that those women have for putting them into effect, 1 never would reach the end of this chronicle, and would wrong the tales of Boccaccio. But, to return to the other quality of those women—that is, their cleanliness, in this they truly shame and outdistance all other women of the world of whatsoever nation, and this even though their habits come to them from the Indian women of Malabar. Both groups of women always wash themselves immediately with water after taking care of their natural needs, and most often with scented water. And they do this with the left hand only, because the right hand is used when eating and they therefore have the custom of never touching with it anything that can be considered dirty. And when they disport themselves with their husbands or lovers, they wash immediately afterwards, doing this as many times as they are made use of. And each evening before going to bed, as I have said, they enter the bath and wash the entire body. Then, all perfumed, they wrap themselves up in certain very fine cloths, also of cotton. These they suddenly let fall to the ground, thus remaining entirely naked.

Then they dally for a while to chew the leaf of the *betre*, which they also do in the daytime, and which they almost always have in their mouths. And this is the very same as that which in the Philippine Islands they call *buyo*, and which they mix with that fruit which they call *bonga* and those here in India call *arecca*, and which is a fruit as large as a walnut and is produced by a tree the shape of a palm as regards its trunk and leaves, but much smaller. It is of an astringent and rough flavor, which they mitigate with a lime made of marine shells. And the fruit having first been slaked with that, they rub it when they want to put it in their mouth. And it has the effects that I wrote about in my chronicle of the Philippine Islands. Further, I say that the smell of this leaf when it is being chewed resembles that of our tarragon and brings on a breath that greatly incites sexual desire and has that effect even more strongly on those who chew it, whom it also restores and strengthens and again invites to the pleasures of venery.

And also because of the great heat the Portuguese remain most of the time indoors, in shirt and white trousers, which they wear long enough to reach the insteps of their feet, and without stockings, but very abundant and wide, putting into each pair of them more than twelve arms of cloth as wide as a bolt of silk. They wear trousers in the same design to go out into the city. And as for the rest, they use a jacket and coat and overcoat in the Spanish style, but without lining. Likewise, they enjoy everything good and beautiful that is found throughout all those Indies, importing them from Bengal, whither each year they send their ships to take on rice, which is the best in the entire Orient, where there are more varieties and qualities of it than there are of grain among us.

From that region also they import an infinite variety of cotton cloths, some of them so fine that one can conceal many arms' lengths of them in the fist of a single hand. And I have had, and still have, shirts—as I have demonstrated to Your Serene Highness—that fit into the fist of my hand. Additionally, from that region come many other manufactures, such as the truly superb bedcovers and canopies, also of cotton, embroidered on cloth with the greatest lightness and beauty of workmanship, showing animals and other figures and adornments, in a certain grass the color of straw. This they spin out to a fineness more exquisite than that of silk, as well as being of greater strength and more lustrous and of much finer appearance. Further, from the coast of São Tomé, called Manipore and Coromandel, they get those beautiful fabrics in which, as I have said, their women dress or, to say it better, wrap up their members from the waist down, as do all the other women native to that region. And then from the kingdom of Pegú, which borders upon Bengal, they have huge quantities of gold and rubies and many other sorts of jewels. But now that kingdom has been destroyed, and all its mines are lost, having been destroyed and ruined by the King of Siam, as I pointed out to Your Serene Highness in the second chronicle.

The King of Siam, they say, undertook war against this King of Pegú in contention over a white elephant that the King of Pegú had. And he, knowing that this King of Siam had entered his country with an innumerable army, resolved that he did not wish to fight or to stand in the Siamese King's way. He decided to remain firm in his principal city with his great treasure, spending his time in various pleasures with his wives and uncounted concubines. And he ordered that no one ever should speak to him of the war or of what the enemy was doing, who thus came upon him without his knowing it. And he thought that he had remedied everything by having issued an edict throughout the country that his people should not sow the rice that they had been accustomed to sow.

And thereafter his people all perished of famine, a disaster that he either had not considered or that he did not mind so long as it also brought death to the enemy army. But the enemy, having heard of this barbarous decision, came with provisions and overran the whole country in a flash. He was able to do that easily because of the abundance of elephants and because those people require nothing more for life than a little rice and water. And rice is easy to carry, whereas water and other things could be found in the fields. But the people of Pegú were reduced to eating human flesh and, most of them, to dying of hunger. And they would have bought, and did buy, rice at the cost of gold when they could get it from the Portuguese who went there in some ships laden with the said rice. But they could not supply it to so large a number of people, who wholly died out, so that today it is very difficult to know where their great cities were which were destroyed with sword and fire by the King of Siam.

And in addition to the deaths that he had brought about, that King carried off a very great treasure in gold, rubies, and other jewels. It is said that the viceroy who then was governing India and who left for Lisbon in the year 1600 had wanted to license four or five hundred Portuguese to go to the kingdom of Pegu, because if they had sought it, it would have fallen into their hands for the same reason—that the King of Pegú, not wishing that anyone speak to him of war, would not have known of their coming, just as he did not wish to know about or to resist that King of Siam except in the manner mentioned above.

But, to return to the matter of the Portuguese, I say in a single word that one can describe as very happy the island, called Fizzuarin, on which the city of Goa is, and which is not longer than nine miles or wider than three. And though there is nothing more on that island than many of those palms which produce the nuts called cocos (cultivated by the natives living there, who are called Kanarese, lowly folk who go about almost naked and are rather black in color than merely brunette), nonetheless it overflows with every delight and every kind of goods, which are brought there from all sections of those Indies and Oriental regions of which (that is, of whose harbors and traffic) the Portuguese are in control, though many years ago the Dutch and the English and the French took away from them, one could say, the traffic of the Moluccas, wh'ence come cloves, nutmeg, mace, pepper, and other sorts of merchandise of those regions.

Also ruined is the traffic with China, to which they go constantly, meaning to enter with their ships and have commerce there, as they have had in the Moluccas, from which nonetheless almost exactly the same things continue to reach Goa each year by way of Malacca, but not at such favorable prices as formerly, this because of the abovementioned

Hollanders and others. These, having gone there with their multitudes of ships, have reduced everything to lower prices, buying with money of account those things which the Portuguese bought at a profit in exchange for cotton cloths from Negopatan, *(translator's note: the modern Negapatam)* Manipore, and Coromandel. From those places they brought each year huge quantities by their ships to Malacca and the Moluccas. Also, they have suffered in their trade with Portugal because the aforesaid Hollanders and others interfere with it by preying upon the carracks that ply to and from Lisbon in that trade, which is the splendor of all that Orient and which caused and still causes the whole world to marvel and is the greatest thing of usefulness accomplished by the Portuguese. For on the *reales* that come solely from Lisbon they earn more than fifty per cent, it happening that the *real* of eight *reales*, *(translator's note: the renowned 'pieces of eight.')* which is worth 320 *reis* in Portugal, is worth 480 and 484 *reis* in India. And thus similarly with other things brought from there to India, such as wines, oil, coral, glass, cats'-eyes, balas rubies, emeralds, large pearls, and various other goods. And on those items incredible profits were and still are made by means of the merchandise that they send from Goa to Portugal on the aforementioned carracks, which ordinarily leave in the month of December, as also in that of January.

[The Hollanders] infest those seas and keep them in continuous fear. And they are the reason why it now is with such small safety that they carry on, as they formerly carried on, the trade with Zoflala *(translator's note: the modern Sofala, a seaport in southeastern Mozambique)* and Mozambique, of great value for the captain who goes there to govern that region. For in three years he takes out more than 100,000 scudos, having from His Catholic Majesty the sole privilege of selling to the Negroes of that region the stuffs that are taken there, which are cotton fabrics—which are exchanged for gold, in which those areas abound, and also for amber and ivory and other strange goods and things, such as the tooth of the sea horse and that of the marvelous woman-fish, thus called because these animals resemble women so closely that it is said that the Negroes of the region, fishing in those seas, use them carnally as if they were in truth women. It is said that there is only one tooth that has the marvelous power to stanch the flow of blood, though they make crowns and rosaries and rings of them all, indifferently, as they do of the tooth of the hippopotamus, or sea horse, to which they attribute the same property, though it is not held in as great esteem.

Similarly, they have frightened those who trade through Ormuz, an island located at the entrance of the Persian Gulf, to which each year several ships from Goa go to bring back Persian and Arabian horses, merchandise in which much is earned because they are bought by the King of Mogor and the King of Narsinga, and by others throughout all of India, and at high prices, often reaching and surpassing a thousand scudos each. They also transport sugar and pearls, which are the largest and most beautiful fished anywhere in India, though the better and larger part of them are brought there by Persian, Turkish, and Hebrew merchants, who take them, together with other merchandise, in caravans leaving from Basra by the Euphrates River and going to Baghdad and then with the aforesaid caravans of camels overland to Aleppo and thence to Constantinople.

The Portuguese likewise go, with no less risk and fear, to China, whence they return with the abovementioned goods at a great profit. They leave Goa in the month of April, China in the month of December. And at the same time there goes thither the ship that passes from China to Japan with the same goods, this to the profit of the Portuguese inhabitants of Macao and of the captain to whom this voyage is conceded, along with the government of Macao for a year, by His Majesty, who thus remunerates him for services connected with war materiels in India. From this voyage, only from the freight, he takes out forty or fifty thousand scudos, he himself being paid by the merchants at the rate of ten per cent of the total amount of the loading and transporting of the merchandise that the ship carries to Japan.

To go back to questions concerning India, I say that they live, for all these reasons, in great trouble and fear for the causes already mentioned in this chronicle, but that otherwise there is no other region in the world in which it is possible to live better and more lavishly, and particularly in the city of Goa, in which there are many businesses that, without any loss on exchange in going and returning, earn from twenty-five to thirty per cent at the beginning of each year or, to say it better, at the end of each of the voyages I have named—to Zoffala, Mozambique, Ormuz, China, and the Moluccas, and also to Bengal—they giving to the captain of the ship or to other merchants their funds, this at the risk of the vessel and the goods both on the outward journey there and on the return voyage.

All of these voyages are made in less than one year, while the merchant is at his ease in the city, always engaged in festivities, songs, music, games,, and balls in the houses in which many have their music privately performed with the greatest attention to the rules by both men and women. And in the plazas and streets nothing is mentioned but pleasant things, loves and lovers, and there are female musicians and actresses and female dancers who go about to give pleasure to whoever wishes it, almost all of them being women so gracious and well-favored in their persons and appearance that no gentleman can be ashamed to welcome them to his home and to enjoy, in addition to the games that they play with great skill, their love-games. In these latter they are so lascivious and potent in promoting the effects that it is said that the King of Narsinga has employed more than six thousand of these dancers, sending them out with his army when it goes to war. And he does that so as to keep his soldiers in continuous happiness and pleasure. And it is a certain thing that they greatly enamor men by their curious, shameless movements, made with their bodies and accompanied with song and music that are no less gracious. But, not to become bogged down in these lubricities (of which it would be possible to tell many others, as it would also be possible to tell more of the customs of those people and others in that India; but I did not penetrate inland—nor is it the custom among the Portuguese to penetrate inland—and so did not experience them in a way to understand and see them, so that even if I desired to deal with them, it would all be by hearsay; and as much as I have been able, in these my chronicles I have claimed to tell Your Serene Highness only those things which I simply have seen and done), I shall tell you some other things that remain to be said of the fruit and tree of that palm which produces the nuts that the Portuguese call *cocos*.

As I have said, there are many of these on Goa's island, and they make it cool and delightful there. But there are, beyond any comparison, more of them on the uncounted islets of the Maldives, all of which are located to the south of Goa, beginning at one degree and stretching to eight degrees on the southern hand. And the nearest of them are 240 miles from Cape Comorin and 480 from Goa. On those islets, the Indian natives live by means of, dress from, and take all their needs from those trees, from which they make their houses and their boats. And each year they come to Goa with loads of merchandise made entirely from those palms—that is, wines, which they make in the manner I have described in my discourse on the Philippine Islands; oil, which they extract from the pit inside the nuts; vinegar, from the substance from which the wine also is made; cording, which they make from the husk that covers the said nut, it being a stupose thing and being prepared as hemp is made ready. And they make cables and ropes and rigging for servicing their ships, they being stronger and more resistant to rot the longer they remain in the water. And they also make mats, and from the leaves of the palms the sails for their vessels as well as covering for their houses. They also bring many of the fruits—that is, *cocos* or nuts—still green, with their pith inside, which is white.

And these nuts have their own milk, which is removed by breaking open the nuts, crushing them, and squeezing them, and which is good for cooking rice, and is excellent and of great substance and nourishment. They also eat the aforesaid pith, from which they also make bread and various other things, as has been mentioned elsewhere. From this plant, finally, not having any other, they extract all that they need for living in the way to which those people are used to live in this world, having no thought for any other delicacies.

From the abovementioned islands they bring another sort of nut, called Maldive coconuts, which are not found elsewhere. They grow in the depths of the sea off those islands, and from there are thrown up on the shore, where they are found. In shape, they are two nuts joined together, and they are longer by two times than the black *cocos*, but more solid. Inside, they have a pith that, though it looks the same, is very different in flavor and not at all good to eat, though it is excelling against poison and malignant fevers. It is held in great esteem among those Maldive people, and much more by their king, who does not permit it to be taken from his country. And for that reason very few of these come out, and they never are seen whole, though pieces of the pith are brought stealthily. I bought six ounces of these so-called Maldives in Goa, and I still have a little of them left. I have experimented with it, and have found it of good effect. I removed fragments of it by rubbing it on a stone with a little water—as 1 have said that they do with everything similar, instead of crushing it—in the Indian way.

There too, in addition to the many other marvelous things, grows a tree not very robust or large, but delicate and much resembling the elderberry in the color of its trunk, but having very different flowers with an odor and a shape much like the jessamine except that the little stem on which the flower emerges from the plant is of a yellow color and serves in place of saffron to give color to foods. This flower always remains closed, shut in upon itself, during the day, so that one scarcely notices it. But as evening comes on, it opens. And before the next morning sun comes, one finds the flowers all fallen to the ground. And for that reason they have been given the name of 'sad flowers'—that is, melancholy—and everyone goes out to collect them, making use of them for their odor and, like saffron, for their color. Many of these plants grow in the cemetery of the Goa cathedral, a very appropriate place for that flower, which produces the effect that here goes with the cypress.

But to bring this chronicle to an end, I say that, having spent twenty-one enjoyable months in that city, and the ship that had remained behind in Malacca having arrived, and I having received the rest of my goods, which I had loaded upon it, I gave thought to embarking with it and with the investment that I had made, after liquidating the silks I had sold, in diamonds and various sorts of cotton cloths, on the flagship galleon called the *Saint James*, which then was preparing to depart for Lisbon, as it did on the day of Christmas, 1601. Of that embarkation and of what followed thereafter during the entire voyage until arrival in Zeeland, I reserve the telling until tomorrow, for the next chronicle, if it thus please Your Serene Highness.

'Lady Mary is worthy of great veneration'

Pierre du Jarric

Chapter X | An embassy to Goa

About this time, Father Emmanuel Pigneiro, who had remained at Lahor, came to the camp, partly for the comfort of seeing Father Hierosme Xauier, for it was nearly three years since they had met, and partly to visit the King (Akbar). The latter had been apprised of his departure from Lahor, and was the first to inform Father Xauier of his coming. On his arrival, the two Fathers went to pay their respects to His Majesty; and as it was not customary to appear before him empty handed, they took with them as their present a picture of Our Lady very beautifully executed on paper. The King was seated at a window, listening, as was his custom, to those who sought speech with him. As soon as he saw Father Pigneiro, he invited him to approach, receiving him with much kindness, and bidding him uncover his head, and show him the present he had brought. On seeing the picture of Our Lady, he bowed his head and raised his hands to his face, which, amongst these peope, is a sign of great reverence. He then ordered the picture to be taken away and placed in his lodging; for he was seated upon his throne, and he deemed it unseemly that the picture of the Lady Mary should be below him. As he had ordered it to be removed so soon, the Fathers feared that it had not greatly pleased him, for the picture was on paper only, and, being drawn in ink, was uncoloured. Accordingly, they went on the following evening to his lodging, where he sat in less seat, and where those who spoke to him could come nearer to his person. Here none but

61

the most favoured persons were received. The Fathers, nevertheless, obtained entrance, and presented to him, besides some smaller gifts, another picture, this time of our Lady of Lorete, painted on gilded calaim. Calaim is a metal which comes from China. Though it resembles tin, it is a different metal, and contains a large proportion of copper. Nevertheless, it is white, and in India they make it into money. It can also be gilded, like silver. But to resume. Father Xauier addressing the King said that Father Pigneiro had come from Lahor to kiss his Majesty's feet, and begged that he might be permitted to approach. 'By all means let him do so,' replied the King; whereon the Father advanced and, bending down, embraced his feet. The King looked kindly on him, and in token of his good will laid his hands upon his shoulders, a mark of favour which he bestowed only on his chief captains and favourites. On seeing the picture of Our Lady, he bowed low, and taking it into his hands, placed it on his head. Then boldly, in the presence of the assembled captains and lords, he did reverence to it with clasped hands, paying it outwardly as much honour as though he had been a Christian, except that he did not go down on his knees, for this is not their custom even in their mosques and places of prayer. When the Father said that this Lady ought to be the guardian of his realm, he replied that he knew well that the Lady Mary was worthy of great veneration, and that it was for this reason that he had ordered the removal of the picture they had brought to him the previous day, for it did not seem fitting that he should be on a high seat, and the picture of Our Lady below him. He then placed the cover on the picture with his own hands, and gave it in charge to one of his personal attendants. After this, he asked various questions about the Pope, desiring to know, amongst other things, what ceremonial was observed when he was visited by the Emperor; and on being told that the Emperor kissed the Pope's foot, he exclaimed, 'Yes! That is because the Christians regard the Pope as the Vicar of the Lord Jesus.' The Father then explained that the Pope, to show that he does not regard such homage as due to himself, except in so far as he is our Lord's Vicar, wears a small cross on his foot, and that it is this cross that is kissed. On hearing this, the King and those with him marvelled greatly.

While they were still discussing the cross, and the reverence in which we hold it, a young noble who had been a disciple of Father Pigneiro, and who happened to be present, made the sign of the cross. The King asked if he had done it correctly; and the Father replied that he had. He then asked why it was made on the forehead, the mouth, and the breast, all of which was explained to him.

So greatly did this powerful monarch desire to make himself master of Goa and the Portuguese possessions in India, with the regions adjacent thereto, that he constantly referred to the subject when conversing with his friends. On one occasion, while speaking of these things to the nobles assembled in his palace, he told them with bold assurance that, having conquered the kingdom of Deccan, he would have little difficulty in overcoming Idalcan, after which he would soon have Goa, and all the Portuguese possessions in those parts. Now a certain Portuguese soldier, who on account of some misconduct had been obliged to quit India, happened to be present at this conversation, and hearing the King's remark, begged permission to speak. When this was granted, he said in the Persian language, 'Your Majesty appears to be very confident of accomplishing these designs; but, as we say in my country, there is such a thing as reckoning without one's host. If your Majesty's opinion of the valour of the Portuguese is as high as some people say, how can you expect to get the better of them so easily? Even though you regard them as so many chicken, yet chicken will peck before they allow themselves to be caught.' 'I have no intention,' said the King, 'of engaging them hand to hand. I shall overcome them by hunger.' 'Excellent! Sire,' said the soldier. 'You are of much the same mind as they are; for they intend to overcome your Majesty by thirst.' (This was, I conclude, an allusion to the dryness of the Mogor's territories.) The King was delighted with this repartee, and made much of the Portuguese soldier. Nevertheless, the conquests of the Portuguese was at the root of all his designs. With this end in view, he frequently sent his agents to Goa, ostensibly as ambassadors, but whose real business was to keep an eye on what the Portuguese were doing, and to ascertain their military strength. He always sent his agents at times when ships were said to be due from

Portugal, so that they might take note of what came in them, whether in the way of merchandise, or men.

It was in pursuance of this object that he despatched an ambassador who reached Goa at the end of the month of May, of the year 1601. The ambassador (Sultan Hamid) sent on this occasion was from the kingdom of Cambaya, a person of great wealth and influence, a Guzarate by birth, and of the sect of the Saracens. The alleged object of the mission was to establish a permanent peace by land and by sea with the Portuguese. The ambassador was also to make inquiry as to the most suitable present that his Majesty could make to the King of Portugal, to whom he contemplated sending an ambassador in order to confirm and strengthen their alliance.

The mission was received at Goa with great magnificence. It was met and escorted through the town by an imposing company of Portuguese nobles, and the ambassador was accorded all the honours usually paid to the representative of a great monarch. But the chief feature of his reception was a terrific salute of artillery which was continued throughout the day, both from the guns in the city and from those in other parts of the island; for the Portuguese had a great store of artillery of high quality. The ambassador fully appreciated the significance of this music. The gifts which he presented to the Viceroy on behalf of the Prince were some rich carpets, a panther which had been trained to the chase, another small panther, and a very valuable horse.

But far more valuable were the gift which Benoist de Goes, the companion of Father Xauier (who accompanied the ambassador by the King's command), presented to our Saviour and the Church; for he brought with him to Goa many half-casts of both sexes, the children of Portuguese, born amongst the thorny paths of Paganism and Mahometanism, who, upon the reduction of the fortress, became the slaves of the Great Mogor (Moghul), who handed them over to the said Benoist de Goes. These, after receiving some instruction in the Christian faith, were all baptised. The Viceroy showed them much kindness, and signified his desire to stand godfather to them. Amongst them was a Portuguese Jew who was ninety years of age. For more than forty years he had publicly professed Judaism; but God at last shed the light of heaven upon him, and he was converted to Christianity, and baptised. The letter which the ambassador carried to the Viceroy, setting forth the object of his mission, was to the following effect:

The message of the great Lord of the law of Mahomet, high and mighty King, slayer of hostile Kings, to whom the Great pay homage, whose dignity is unsurpassed, who is exalted above other kings, and whose government is renowned throughout the world, to Ayres de Saldagna Viceroy:

Meeting with favour and grace at the hands of the King of Kings, honoured and privileged by him, know that, by the grace of God, all the ports of Indostan, from Cinde to Chatigan and Pegu, are under our high prosperity; and it is always in our royal heart, and before our eyes, that the rich merchants and those who traffic may be able to go and come with all assurance and safety, so that they may continually pray to God for the increase of our prosperity, and especially the inhabitants of the kingdoms of the Portuguese, who, outside this kingdom, cannot go and come freely, and who are accustomed to navigate the sea of Indostan. (For this reason our royal honour has willed and arranged that one of our servants and courtiers has been sent as ambassador to confim once again the basis of the alliance, so that there may henceforth be no occasion to doubt it. On this occasion the Father Benoist de Goes has been sent together with our trusted servant Cogetqui Soldan Hama to your parts, where, after informing themselves with all diligence of things as they pass, they may accurately advise us, so that conformably to the status of each one, our good fortune may make provision for the going and the sending.) And if there are any skilled craftsmen who desire to visit our royal court, which is like the mansions of the blest, he shall give them all that they need in food and apparel, and bring them with him to this our court, the fulcrum of the world, on the understanding that, having been in our service, they shall have to leave to return to their country whenever it shall be their will to do so. It is fitting that they should be given good expectations, so that they may desire, of their own accord, to kiss the buttress of our throne. And as to whatsoever our ambassador may wish to purchase in the way of precious stones, fabrics, and other things of a like valuable nature, our desire is that he may be given all assistance therein, so that he may do his business and return speedily, since he is in our royal service. As to other matters, he will make them known to you by word of mouth. The 9th day of Fauardi of God, of the forth-sixth year of the era.

Such was the style in which this Prince wrote.

Chapter XVII | Events of the year 1602

Although in the conversion of souls there was not so much progress in this land of the Saracens, who are as hard as diamonds to work upon, as in other lands where this sect has not taken root, yet God did not withhold his mercies from his sheep scattered in this vast forest of unbelief.

In the year 1602, there were at Rantambur some forty persons, for the most part children or grandchildren of Portuguese, with their wives and relatives, who had been taken by the Great Mogor (Akbar) at the capture of the fortress of Syr, and had been enslaved. For though the King had led some of his prisoners to Agra, where he afterwards set them at liberty, trusting that they would not run away, he left the majority of them in the fortress of Rantambur, where they would have been completely forgotten, if the Fathers had not borne them in mind. Deeming the season of Lent, which was then approaching, a suitable time for visiting them, the Fathers went to the King and begged that, in as much as Christians are bound at this season to fulfil the principal obligations of their law, namely to confess and to communicate, his Majesty would be pleased to permit one of them to visit these Portuguese prisoners in order to instruct them, and enable them to do their duty as good Christians. The visit, they said, would not occupy more than twenty days. In reply, the King told them that the prisoners might be brought to Agra, which was what the Fathers most desired. They were straightaway sent for; and with them came five Turcs, that is to say, Turcs of Europe; for two kinds of Turkish soldiers are found in India, those of Asia, to whom the name Turc is given, and those of Europe, who are mostly from Constantinople, which has been called the New Rome, on which account they are called Rumes both by Indians and Portuguese.

These five Turcs, then, being also prisoners, were, through the interposition of the Fathers, brought to Agra, for which they showed themselves very grateful; for if they had not found this means of liberation, they could have hoped for no other. The prisoners were all brought in chains; but these were taken off at the solicitation of the Fathers, who also obtained the King's consent to their being employed in his service, and receiving food and clothing. In granting this petition, the King told the prisoners publicly that though they deserved death, because they had killed many of his people in the war, yet because of his love for the Fathers, he gave them not only life but liberty. It was the wish of one of the King's maistres d'hostel to place them in the service of an Armenian, who was the lord of certain villages; but the Fathers begged the King that they might remain near them, so that they might instruct them in the faith; since, if they were separated from them, they would soon become more uncivilised than they had been before. The King granted their request, and the prisoners were lodged close to them; and after they had instructed them in their faith, of which they knew little or nothing, they baptised all who had not been baptised before, which included the greater portion of them.

Now since these, and certain others who had come before, had been captured in Breampur and taken to places further south, their wives, daughters, and other relations had been left behind, and were in great need and peril. Accordingly, the Fathers, being unable as yet to withdraw these, despatched letters of credit to them, to provide them with a means of livelihood until they could be sent for. This could not be done for some time, owing to the debts which they and their husbands had incurred; for it was necessary to wait until these had all been paid. Subsequently, by the will of God, a young Armenian, of a very honourable disposition, whom the Fathers had commissioned to assist these poor people, brought them all back with him, trusting to the Fathers to repay him what he had spent, which they did very willingly, thanking him for having done so good a work. After they had arrived, and baptism had been administered to those who had not received it, they were re-married, according to the laws of the Church, to those who had also been baptised. Finally, and at their expense, which was a great blessing to these poor people; and they regarded it as a sign of God's special providence that in their captivity and misery He raised up the Fathers to succour them, who not only taught them the way of salvation, but ministered to their temporal needs with true paternal charity. Who can help marvelling at God's wisdom in using these means to make Himself known to these poor men and women, sprung from the Portuguese race, who, but yesterday, were dwelling amongst infidels, known only as Franks (for so they call Christians in these parts), without baptism, and without any knowledge of God; and who, to-day, are living like honest men, keeping the commandments of God and the Church, and recognising very clearly the truth of the Christian faith, and the grace which God has shown them in receiving them into His fold?

In the same year 1602, two ships of the Portuguese navy, while sailing northwards in the gulf of Cambaya, were wrecked on a portion of the coast which was under the sway of the King of Mogor. Some fifty Portuguese and fifteen servants contrived to reach land, but were instantly made prisoners by the captain who governed that country in the name of the King. The latter, to whom the circumstance was at once reported, ordered the prisoners to be sent to him. In the course of their journey, the poor fellows endured so many hardships that when they reached Lahor their plight was pitiful to behold. The King gave orders that they were to be imprisoned; but Father Xauier, who happened to be there, begged that they might be placed in his charge, promising to deliver them up to his Majesty's officers whenever so ordered. His request was granted, and the Fathers accordingly took the prisoners to their house where they sheltered them, and later transferred them to another house which the King placed at their disposal. They were supported throughout at the expense of the Fathers, but for whom, they would have perished miserably from hunger and other afflictions. That they found such a refuge was a manifestation of the providence of God. Their captains were Louys d'Antas Lobo and George de Castillo. The Fathers strove to secure their freedom, but for a long time their efforts were fruitless, since they lacked the wherewithal to make rich presents; for where avarice and disloyalty reign, nothing can be obtained except by money. The King, however, sent them four hundred xerafins for the purchase of clothing, and consented, at the instance of the Fathers, to grant the two captains an audience. A substantial donation was also received from the Prince (Jehangir), the eldest son of the King, who, so soon as he heard of the misery of these poor people, sent the Fathers a thousand crowns to relieve their necessities. Eventually, having been detained for more than a year, they were set at liberty. This they owned to the intercession of the Fathers in their behalf, as was stated in the letter which the King gave them when they were released, in which he wrote that he sent them back free men to please the Fathers. In consequence, these good Portuguese and the two captains in particular, knew not how to praise God sufficiently for His mercies, or how to thank the Fathers for their charity, without which they would one and all have died in captivity.

'Singing, laughing, and performing a thousand antics'

Francois Pyrard de Laval

The Jesuit hospital

So many visitors have left records that it is possible to construct Goanese society in some detail. To get the feel of the place, we can hardly do better than listen to Francois Pyrard while he describes his experiences there in 1608. He was a talkative and observant Frenchman of the seaman class, a brave homme, as will be seen, honest and careful. Leaving France in 1601 on board a ship fitted out by the merchants of St. Malo, he was cast away on the Maldives, then an island monarchy, and did not reach Calicut till 1607. Moving south to Cochin, like Calicut a Portuguese fortress, he was arrested because he had no papers and was thrown into prison. From thence, his health much impaired by the dreadful dungeon in which he was confined, they sent him in chains by ship to Goa.

Landing on the wharf near the Viceroy's palace, he expected to be lodged in the main gaol, the Sala das Bragas, and was surprised when out of pity the police took him to the Royal Hospital, a palatial institution controlled by the Jesuits. The Society was the most cultivated and modern element in Goa, and the hospital was administered by them in so admirable a fashion, that many declared it superior even to the Hospital of the Holy Ghost in Rome or the Infirmary of the Knights at Malta, the two leading hospitals of Europe at that time. Poor Pyrard, after his rough experiences, thought it a paradise. He was carried up 'a lofty and magnificent staircase' to a bed 'beautifully shaped and lacquered with red varnish', upon which was a mattress and silk coverlet, sheets of fine cotton, pillows of white calico, luxuries unknown in Europe among his class. A barber immediately shaved him, he was given pyjamas, a cap, and slippers, and provided with a bedside table on which was a fan, drinking water, a clean towel, and a handkerchief. Under the bed he noted a chamber-pot, an article which appeared to him the most satisfactory piece of furniture in the place after his experiences in Cochin gaol, where he had been herded with two hundred others in one room without any sanitary arrangements whatever. Supper brought further pleasant surprises. Each patient was served with a complete fowl, and the plates, bowls, and dishes were of Chinese porcelain, that is, of Ming porcelain, then such a rarity in Europe that Lord Treasurer Burghley thought 'a porringer of white purselyn garnished with gold' a very choice new-year present to give Queen Elizabeth.

When Pyrard felt better, he asked the head Jesuit physician for leave to go, saying that he longed to explore the great city of which he had heard so much. He seemed to think that the charge against him had been withdrawn, but the Jesuit knew better and out of kindness advised him to be in no hurry. Not taking his meaning, Pyrard agreed reluctantly to stay on, and when quite recovered pressed for his discharge. This time it was granted and he descended the grand staircase in the highest spirits. The Father had given him a new suit of clothes, a piece of silver, and his benediction. He had had a good breakfast, though, as he says, he 'little required it for the haste he was in to be off'. So it was a cruel shock when he was accosted by a sergeant at the bottom of the stairs and a warrant was flourished in his face. 'His partisans'—they were giant negro slaves imported from Africa—'seized me and bore me off in rough sort', he writes.

However, things did not go too badly. In his new clean suit and with the silver piece he won the heart of the gaoler's wife at the Sala das Bragas, for it was there that they took him. Instead of flinging him into the common dungeon where galley-slaves were confined, they put him, thanks to the lady, into a fairly decent room, a wonderful piece of luck, for the dungeon was 'le liue le plus ord et sale qui soit au monde comme ie croy', as he notes in his old-fashioned French.

There existed in Goa a prisoners' welfare society, at the head of which was a Jesuit. This Father came to see him, heard his story, considered that he had been unjustly arrested, since a ship-wrecked mariner can have no papers, and approached Dom Fr Aleixo de Menezes, the Archbishop and Primate, who was acting as Governor of the Indies, pending the arrival of a new Viceroy. This Augustinian friar, known in ecclesiastical history as the zealot who handed over many Nestorian Christians to the Inquisition, had lately, in his capacity as Governor, successfully beaten off a Dutch attack on Goa and was in no mood to have any truck with suspicious foreigners. To the Jesuit's solicitations he replied with heat that his protege deserved to hang. Had it not been that the Father persevered, such might have been the fate of the Frenchman. It seems that what turned the scale was his offer to enlist in the army of India.

Life of a soldier

For two years Pyrard served the Portuguese as a private soldier and has left an account of the way his companions lived. Most of the soldiers were recruited in Portugal. The prospects were good and, as a rule, volunteers came forward, but if they did not, they were pressed, even boys of ten years old being taken, for there was a great shortage of man-power in Portugal which had too small a population to meet the vast demands of its empire. Many of the soldiers were ex-convicts, released for the purpose, and all belonged to the lowest class, but as soon as they landed in India they became gentlemen. 'Des qu'ils sont la,' writes Mocquet, a traveller who arrived in Goa the same year as did Pyrard, 'pour vils et abjets qu'ils soient, ils s'estiment tous fidalques et nobles, changeant leurs noms obscurs a des noms plus illustres.' The real nobility winked at this practice. If Indians could be induced to believe that all Portuguese were aristocrats, or, at least, that all Portuguese in India were gentlemen of quality, so much the better. In this connection Mocquet cites the story of the swineherd, Fernando. On arrival at Goa this rustic followed the current practice and called himself Dom Fernando. One day, riding through the streets, well mounted and magnificently dressed, he met the son of his old master in Portugal. 'Good heavens! Fernando, is that you?' exclaimed the young gentleman. Fernando was put out, he tried to ride past, though it was an effort to pretend not to know his master's son. When the other rallied him: 'Come, come, Fernando, no need to pretend with me!' he could keep it up no longer and sheepishly dismounted. 'But don't tell anyone here,' he begged, as he knelt and paid the customary respects.

The common soldier was able to make this fine appearance for several reasons. His principal occupation was that of marine on board the warships which protected the convoys from the Dutch and the pirates, but during the monsoon from May to October, he lived in Goa as a private person. As there were no barracks, he rented a house along with a dozen comrades. Clubbing together they bought three or four good suits and engaged a few slaves to wait and cook. At home they would sit about in loose shirts and pyjama trousers, playing the guitar or gossiping with those who passed, but when they went out, which they did in rotation, the grand suits were put on. 'You would say there were lords,' says Pyrard, 'with an income of 10,000 livres, such is their bravery, with their slaves behind them and a man carrying over them a big parasol. There are places where these slaves are to be hired and one can be got for half a day for a copper.'

As they masqueraded in this fashion, they copied to the best of their ability the elaborate manners of their betters. Linschoten, who was at Goa in 1583, has some phrases which show the flourish they aimed at. 'They step very softly and slowly forwards, with a great pride and vain-glorieus majestie,' writes the bluff Dutchman of the way real fidalgos promenaded. When two met, while they were still some paces apart they began 'to stoope with their Hats in their hands, almost touching the ground'. Yet, behind this screen of manners they were watching each other narrowly, ready to take offence at the most trifling lapse in punctilio, such as a less number of bows returned, or the giving of a sober for an extravagant compliment. When such an insult was observed, the wronged man would allow no sign of resentment to escape him, but retiring with a smile would assemble his friends and presently lie in wait for the offender, set on him, and beat him with sandbags and bamboos. There were some even more fatal, who would order their slaves to deal a stab in the back.

Such behaviour having passed into the tradition of our melodrama, it is hard to believe that real people ever conducted themselves so.

Cheap though living was in Goa, the common soldier could hardly have managed on his pay alone to turn himself out so well. But he had another source of income. By 1600 the city was full of half-caste women. For a century the Government had been encouraging mixed marriages and there had also been the freest intercourse with female slaves. It is in the nature of Eurasian women to desire a man of pure European blood. The Portuguese soldiers were, therefore, in great demand. To get a soldier such a woman was prepared to house him, feed him, pay for his clothes, see to his washing, and provide him with pocket-money. No marriage usually took place, though the Government recognized the relationship to the extent of giving the children the right to inherit from both parents.

But Pyrard notes that, if a soldier left the house which he shared with his comrades and went to live with a Eurasian mistress, it was not as delightful as it sounded. The girls were temperamental and uncontrolled. They were more jealous and less amenable than either Portuguese or Indian women. Their whole life was to keep the man they had got. But he was surrounded by temptations to infidelity, as there were far more girls than white soldiers. If he yielded to the solicitations of another, or if, tired of his mistress, he sought to terminate the connection, he was in imminent peril. Unless he used the greatest cunning and dissimulation in quitting her, says Pyrard, she would infallibly poison him. What poison they used, Pyrard never precisely discovered. But he describes its effects, which were so curious that, had we not also Linschoten's testimony in addition, it would be hard to believe him. The action of the poison could be delayed by varying the dose. After taking it the victim might go a month, even six months, and be none the worse. Then one day he suddenly fell dead.

A soldier, were he good-looking or had he made a name for himself in fights with the Dutch, might also find women of the upper class eager for his aquaintance. In this class there were more women of mixed blood than of pure European descent. Dressed in a guaze blouse, a flowered skirt, and loose slippers, they idled indoors through the day, listening to the gossip brought in by their slaves, chewing betel or sucking sweetmeats. Even those of pure Portuguese extraction preferred rice to bread and ate curry without a spoon. It was to enliven this existence that they sought the attentions of handsome soldiers. 'They use all the slights and practices they can devise,' says Linschoten, 'by sending out their slaves and baudes by night, and at extraordinary times, over Walls, Hedges, and Ditches, how narrowly soever they were kept and looked unto.' For they were very narrowly kept in a seclusion hardly different from Indian purdah.

To introduce a gallant into the house would have been risky or impossible, had they not known how to use datura, a narcotic weed of the nightshade family, called in Europe stramonium. Administered in quantity it is a poison, but in small doses its narcotic properties merely weaken the will and confuse the intelligence. The husbands of these women, if a soldier-lover were coming to the house, used to be given sufficient of it to render them insensible, not wholly stupefied and sleeping, but rather tranced, and, so, ignorant of what happened even before their eyes, and when its effects had worn off, of the fact that they had been drugged. Pyrard had a passage describing such a scene. After stating that the datura is put in drink or soup, he says: 'An hour afterwards the husbands became giddy and insensible, singing, laughing, and performing a thousand antics (singeries), for they have lost all consciousness and judgement. Then do the wives make use of their time, admitting whom they will, and taking their pleasures in the presence of their husbands, who are aware of nothing.'

Anyone acquainted with the less reputable corners of the East will know that Pyrard was accurately describing what he had seen. Datura is still used by certain oriental women in ways not dissimilar. There are many cases of modern Englishmen who have been reduced to poor tame creatures on being dosed with this drug by their native mistresses.

A great lady goes to mass

In one of his most evocative passages Pyrard describes a woman of this upper class as she appeared at the Mass, practically her only distraction away from home. The scene is a medley of the Occident and the Orient, of the Latin and the Indian, of the Catholic and the Orient, of the Latin and the Indian, of the Catholic and the Pagan. It is a feast-day, a special occasion, and the lady is 'superbly attired in the Portuguese mode'. Her gown is gold brocade, which glows under a mantle of black silk gauze. She comes riding in a palanquin, seated on a Persian carpet and propped on velvet cushions. On foot behind are a score of maid-servants, slave girls from middle or upper India or negroes from Mozambique, bought for their looks and dressed to set them off in coloured smocks falling to the navel and wide silk pleated scarlet petticoats, some carrying a mat, a carpet, a prayer book, others a handkerchief or a fan. Escorting the palanquin are two Eurasian footmen, handsome and sleek, who at the church door help the lady to alight or, if she prefers to be carried into the nave, are ready there to hand her down.

When such a lady was on her feet, she seemed very tall, for she would be wearing chopines, a patten with a cork sole six inches thick, an extravagant fashion which was carried to fantastical extremes in Venice, and had even reached England, as is evident from Hamlet's exclamation to the actress: 'By'r Lady, your ladyship is nearer Heaven than when I saw you last by the altitude of a chopine.'

The progress down the aisle then began. Owing to the height of the chopines, and because it was undignified for a person of rank to walk otherwise than slowly, the passage to her seat took some time, as she paced along, leaning on the arms of the two footmen, her air languid, an assumed lassitude. Her maids were gone ahead to get ready her place, spreading her carpet, with a mat on top for coolness, arranging her cushions or sometimes setting a chair. There she would sit in the semi-darkness, for the churches in Goa had mother-of-pearl in place of glass window-panes, which suffused a soft yellowish under-sea light, sit there with her rosary of great gold beads, her pale olive face much painted, watching under her eyes, while her handsome maids fanned her nor dared smile back at their lovers who were signing to them in the shadow.

The life we were describing was the decadence into which the Portuguese fell when, no longer adequately reinforced and supported from home, they were losing the original energy which had driven them east. An oriental conquest, the wealth it brought, mixed marriages on a grand scale, and, perhaps, most deadly, the extensive use of slaves, had transformed the hard-bitten Portuguese of early days, the palandins of the Lusiads, the intrepid navigators, into a luxurious society, still able to hold what it had taken from ill-armed native kingdoms, but losing ground to the Dutch, who were coming upon the scene animated with the same pristine virtues that a century earlier had sustained da Gama and Albuquerque.

Slaves

Many of the slaves in Goa were household slaves. Their treatment was probably no worse than in Indian households. Rather, it was their influence upon their masters that was deplorable. If you walked up the Rua Direita, the great street which ran south from the main wharf at the Arch of the Viceroys, you came after a quarter of a mile to the principal square, the Terreiro da Sabaio, in whch were the Cathedral, the Senate House, and the Inquisition. On most days of the week a sale of slaves was here taking place. They stood so that you could examine them at your leisure, the dealers drawing attention to the points of their physique and detailing their skill in arts and crafts. 'You see there very pretty and elegant girls and women from all countries in India,' writes Pyrard. 'Most of them can play upon instruments, embroider, sew very finely, and do all kinds of work, such as making sweetmeats, preserves, etcetera.' In spite of their accomplishments they were very cheap, thirty shillings being the average price.

These slaves were docile. Not only did they do all the work of the house for their Portuguese owner, but they helped to support him, in some cases seem to have wholly supported him. They were trained to engage in retail trade on his behalf, selling in the bazaar the fruit and vegetables raised in his garden, or weaving, dyeing, and tailoring materials, from the sale of which a steady income was derived. The female slaves might become his concubines. Pyrard says negresses imported from Africa, 'wondrously black with curly hair', were the favourites in this respect. A grand lady might also make money by letting out her slaves as prostitutes. A certain class of Portuguese and Eurasians specialized in kidnapping for this market young people resident in the Indian states. The slave population in Goa was very great. For Latins the city was a paradise, a lotus-eating island of the blest, where you could sit on your veranda listening to music as the breeze blew in from the sea, with humble folk within call to minister to your every wish. No wonder it was called Golden Goa.

Pride, idleness, luxury and vice had so demoralized the Portuguese that Pyrard, though he tried hard to accommodate himself, found them intolerable. 'I cannot tell all the affronts, insults and ill-usage I suffered there,' he says. 'If they had believed that I so much as thought of recording anything about them, they would never have allowed me to return. I have but little of a high spirit, yet did I lead them to believe that I had much less for fear of giving them a bad opinion of me.'

'A Kingdom lying in the middle of Barbarians'

Pietro Della Valle

Portuguese vanity

The people is numerous (in 1640 AD, an estimated 190,000), but the greatest part are slaves, a black and lewd (ignorant) generation, going naked for the most part, or else very ill clad, seeming to me rather a disparagement than an ornament to the City. Portugals there are not many; they us d to be sufficiently rich, but of late, by reason of many losses by the incursions of the Dutch and English in these Seas, they have not much wealth, but are rather poor. Nevertheless they live in outward appearance with splendor enough, which they may easily do both in regard of the plentifulness of the Country, and because they make a shew of all they have; however, in secret they indure many hardships, and some there are who, to avoid submitting to such employments as they judge unbecoming to their gravity, being all desirous to be accounted Gentlemen here, lead very wretched lives, undergoing much distress, and being put to beg every Day in the Evening; a thing which in other Countries would be accounted unhappy and more indecent, not to say shameful, than to undertake any laudable profession of a Mechanick Art. They all profess Arms, and are Souldiers though marry'd, and few, except Priests and Doctors of Law and Physick, are seen without a Sword; even so the Artificers and meanest Plebians: as also silk clothes are the general wear of almost everybody; which I take notice of, because to see a Merchant and a Mechanick in a dress fit for an Amorato (dandy) is a very extravagant thing, yet amongst them, very ordinary, the sole dignity of being Portugals sufficing them (as they say) to value themselves as much as Kings and more.

Portuguese profligacy

April the ninth (1623). Early in the Morning F. Fra. Leandro sent a Palanchino, or litter, to fetch Mariam Tinatin, that she might go to Mass at his Church, and afterwards repair to the House of a Portugal Gentlewoman, called Sigra Lena da Cugna, living near the discalceated Carmelites and much devoted to them, whose House also stood right over against that which he intended to take for me. And this was done because the Portugals, who in the matter of Government took with great diligence upon the least motes, without making much reckoning afterwards of great beams, held it inconvenient for the said Mariam Tinatin to live with me in the same House, although she had been brought up always in our House from a very little Child and as our own Daughter. For being themselves in these matters very unrestrain'd (not sparing their nearest kindred, nor, as I have heard, their own Sisters, much less Foster-children in their Houses) they conceive that all other Nations are like themselves; wherefore, in conformity to the use of the Country and not to give offence, it was necessary for us to be separated; the rather too because strangers, who amongst the Portugals are not very well look'd upon and through their ignorance held worse than in our Countries Hereticks are, may easily expect that all evil is thought of them and that all evil may easily befall them in these parts; so that 'tis requisite to live with circumspection. And this may serve for advice to whoever shall travel to these Regions.

The rainy season

May the three and twentieth. The Sun entering into Gemini, I observ'd that the Rain began in Goa, and it happens not alike in all the Coast of India; for it begins first in the more Southerly parts of Cape Comorin, and follows afterwards by degrees, according as places extend more to the North; so that in Cambaia, and other more northern parts, it begins later than in Goa; and the further any place lyes North, the later it begins there. Whence it comes to pass that in the Persian Ephemerides, or Almanacks, they use to set down the beginning of Parsecal, or the time of Rain in India, at the fifteenth of their third Moneth, call'd Cordad, which falls upon the third of our June; because they have observ'd it to be so in the more Northern parts of India, as in Cambaia, Surat and the like, where the Persians have more commerce then in other more Southern places. In Goa likewise for the most part the beginning of the Rain is in the first days of June; yet sometimes it anticipates, and sometimes falls something later, with little difference. 'Tis observ'd by long experience that this Rain in India, after having lasted some days at first, ceases, and there return I know not how many days of fair weather; but, those being pass'd, it begins again more violent than ever, and continues for a long time together. By this Rain, as I observ'd, the heat diminisheth, and the Earth, which before was very dry and all naked, becomes cloth'd with new verdure and various colours of pleasant flowers, and especially the Air becomes more healthful, sweet and more benigne both to sound and infirm. The arm of the Sea, or River (Mandovi and Zuari), which encompasses the Island of, and is ordinarily salt, notwithstanding the falling of the other little fresh Rivers into it, with the inundation of great streams which through the great Rain flow from the circumjacent Land, is made likewise wholly fresh; whence the Country-people, who wait for this time, derive water out of it for their Fields of Rice in the Island of Goa and the neighbouring parts,which, being temper'd with the sweet moisture, on a sudden become all green.

A goodly prospect

In the evening I went with Sig. Ruy Gomez Baroccio, a Priest and Brother of Sig. Antonio Baroccio, to the Church of Saint James, which stands somewhat distant without the City, upon the edge of the Island towards the main Land of Adil-Sciah, which is on the other side of a little River, or Arm of the Sea. For which reason the Island is in this as well as may other dangerous places fortifi'd with strong walls; and here there is a Gate upon the pass, which is almost full of people going and coming from the main Land, and is call'd by the Indians Benastarim, by which name some of our Historians mention it in their writings concerning these parts, as Osorius Maffaeus, etc., which Gate, as likewise many others which are upon divers places of passage about the Island, is guarded continually with Souldiers, commanded by a Captain who hath the care thereof, and for whom there is built a fine House upon the walls of the Island, which in this place are very high, forming a kind of Bastion, or rather a Cavaliero, or mount for Ordnance; not very well design'd, but sufficiently strong, wherein are kept pieces of Artillery for the defence of the place.

We went to visit the said Captain, who was then Sig. Manoel Pereira de la Gerda, and from the high Balconies of his House and the Bastion we enjoy'd the goodly prospect, of the Fields round about, both of the Island and the Continent, it being discernible to a great distance. The Captain entertain'd us with the Musick of his three Daughters, who sung and play'd very well after the Portugal manner upon the Lute, after which we return'd home. About the Church of Saint James are some few habitations in form of a little Town, which is also call'd Santiago; and the way from thence to the City is a very fine walk, the Country being all green, and the way-sides beset with Indian Nut-trees (which the Portugals call Palms, and their fruit Cocco), the Gardens and the Houses of Pleasure on either side contributing to the delightfulness thereof, being full of sundry fruit-trees unknown to us; as also because in Winter-time the very walls of the Gardens are all green with moss and other herbs growing there, which indeed is one of the pleasantest sights that I have seen in my days, and the rather because 'tis natural and without artifice. The same happens, I believe, not in the Island only, but in all the Region round about.

In the field adjoining to the City, near the ruines of a deserted building, once intended for a Church, but never finish'd, is a work of the Gentiles, sometimes Lords of this Country, namely one of the greatest Wells that ever I beheld, round, and about twenty of my Paces in Diameter, and very deep; it hath Parapets, or Walls, breast-high, round about, with Gates, at one of which is a double pair of Stairs leading two ways to the bottom, to fetch water when it is very low.

A masquerade

On the twelfth of February, in the presence of the Vice-Roy and of all the Nobility and People of the City, (for whose conveniency scaffolds and seats were erected in the Piazza round about the Theatre, both for Men and Women) the first Act of the above-said Comedy, or Tragedy, (as they said) of the Life of Santo Sciavier was represented. Of which Tragedy, which was a composition represented by about thirty persons, all very richly clothed and decked with Jewels, no less extravagant than grand, whereunto they entered to act the rare Musick, gallant dances, and various contrivances of Charriots, Ships, Galleys, Pageants, Heavens, Hells, Mountains and Clouds, I forbear to speak, because I have the printed Relations by me.

On the eighteenth of Febraury, the Viceroy being indispos'd, the proceedings were suspended and nothing was done. But on the three following dayes, by two Acts a day, the whole Tragedy was rehearsed. It comprehended not onely the whole Life, but also the Death of San Francesco Sciavier (Francis Xavier), the transportation of his Body to, his ascension into Heaven, and, lastly, his Canonization.*

A Kanarese wedding

On May the nineteenth (1624), one Ventura da Costa, a Native of Canara, was married. He was a domestick servant to Sig. Alvaro da Costa, a Priest and our Friend, Lord of a Village near Goa; for whose Sake, who was willing to honour his servant's wedding in his own House, I and some other friends went thither to accompany the Bride and the Bridegroom to the Church of San Biagio, a little distant in another Village, which was in the Parish of the Bride, where the Ceremonies were perform'd in the Evening for coolness' sake. The Company was very numerous, consisting of many Portugal Gentlemen,

---

*Peter de Catelnau, one of the monks of Citeaux and of the monastery of Fortfroide, in Narbonnese Gaul, who was commissioned by Pope Innocent III to preach against the heresies of the Waldenses in 1203, and who was in this way the instrument for founding the Inquisition. He was assassinated in the dominions of the Count of Toulouse, and beatified in 1208.

such, perhaps, as few other Canarini have had at their marriages. The Bride and Bridegroom came under Umbrellas of Silk, garnish'd with silver, and in other particulars the Ceremonies were according to the custom of the Portugals; onely I observ'd that, according to the use of the Country, in the Company before the Married Persons there march'd a party of fourteen, or sixteen, men oddly cloth'd after the Indian fashion, to wit naked from the girdle upward, and their Bodies painted in a pattern with white Sanders, and adorn'd with bracelets and necklaces of God and Silver, and also with flowers and turbants upon their heads, in several galant fashions, and streamers of several colours hanging behind them. From the girdle downwards, over the hose which these Canarini use to wear short, like ours, they had variously colour'd clothes girt about them with streamers, flying about and hanging down a little below the knee; the rest of the leg was naked, saving that they had sandals on their feet. These danc'd all the way both going and returning, accompanying their dances with chaunting many Verses in their own Language, and beating the little sticks which they carry'd in their hands, afte the fashion of the Country, formerly taken notice of at Ikkeri. And indeed the dances of these Canarini are pleasant enough; so that in the Festivities made at Goa for the Canonization of the Saints Ignatio and Sciavier, though in other things they were most solemn and sumptuous, yet, in my opinion, there was nothing more worthy to be seen for delight than the many pretty and jovial dances which interven'd in this Tragedy. They marry'd Couple being return'd from Church to the Bride House, we were entertain'd with a handsome Collation of Sweet-meats in the yard, which was wholly cover'd over with a Tent, and adorn'd with Trees and green boughs, the Company sitting round, and the marry'd Couple, on one side at the upper end, upon a great Carpet under a Canopy. After which we all return'd home, and the Husband stay'd that night to sleep in his Wife's House.

A priest-ridden city

On February the nineteenth a very solemn Procession was made from San Paolo Vecchio to Giesu, through the principal streets of the City:

which Procession exceeded all the rest in number of Pageants, Chariots and Ships, and other Erections, filled with people who represnted several things, and good Musick, accompanyed with several Dances on Foot, and many other brave devices: of all which things I speak not, because I have a printed Relation thereof by me. In the rear of the Procession was carried by many of the Fathers, dressed in their Copes, the Body of San Francesco Sciavier, inclos'd in a fair and rich Silver Coffin, with a Silver Canopie over it, made very gallant, and the Effigy of the Saint behind. Then came, a great Standard with the pourtraytures of the Saints, carry'd likewise by some of the Fathers; and after that, all the Crosses of their Parishes of Salsette, and onely one Company of the Fryers of Saint Francis. Of the other Religious Orders in Goa none appeared here; because they said they would not go in the Processions of the Jesuits, since the Jesuits went not in those of others. With this Procession, which ended about noon, ended also the solemnities for the abovesaid Canonizations.

On February the twenty-fifth, this day being the first Sunday of Lent this year, the Augustine Fathers, according to custom, made a solemn Procession, which they call 'dei Passi', in reference to the steps which our Lord made in his Passion, conducted to several places. They carried in Procession a Christ, with the Cross on his shoulders, and many went along disciplining and whipping themselves, being cloth'd with white sack-cloth, gallant and handsome, very gravely according to the humor of the Nation. In several places of the City certain Altars were plac'd, where the Procession stood still; and, after some time spent in singing, the Christ turn'd backwards, representing that passage 'Conversus ad Filias Jerusalem, dixit illis, Nlite flere super me', etc. At which turning of the sacred Image the people, who were very numerous and fill'd the whole streets, lamented and utter'd very great cries of Devotion. At length the Procession, being come to the Church Della Gratia, where it ended, after the Augustine Nunns (whose Convent stands near that of the Fryers in the same Piazza) had sung a while, an Image, 'Del volto Santo' (of our Lord's Countenance), like that at Rome, was shown to the people, gathere'd together in the said Piazza, from a window of one of the Bell-turrets which are on either side of the front of the said Church; and so the Solemnity ended. But the above-mention'd Altars in the streets are every Fryday during Lent adorn'd in the same manner, and visited by the people every day and also at many hours of the night; just as the Church of Saint Peter at Rome is visited every Fryday of March; and they call this visiting, 'Correr os Passos', that is going about and visiting the steps of our Lord; which serves the people during this time of Lent no less for devotion than for pastime.

On March the first there was also another Procession in Goa of the Disciplinanti (Flagellantes), which I went not to see; the like is made every Fryday during all Lent, and therefore I shall not stay to describe it. I believe there is no City in the world where there are more Processions than in Goa all the year long; and the reason is because the Religious Orders are numerous, and much more than the City needs; they are also of great authority and very rich and the People, being naturally idle and addicted to Shews, neglecting other Cares of more weight and perhaps more profitable to the Publick, readily employ themselves in these matters; which, however good as sacred ceremonies and parts of divine worship, yet in such a City as this which borders upon Enemies and is the Metropolis of a Kingdom lying in the midst of Barbarians and so alwayes at War, and where nothing else should be minded but Arms and Fleets, seem according to worldly Policy unprofitable and too frequent, as also so great a number of Regious and Ecclessiastical persons is burdensome to the State and prejudicial to the Militia.

On the twenty-ninth of the same month (April) being the day of S. Pietro Martire 1, who, they say, was the Founder of the Inquisition*

---

*The Inquisition was founded by Pope Innocent III early in the 13th century, when he appointed a commission for the persecution of the Waldenses. It was established in the Portuguese dominions by King John III in 1536.

The Inquisition at Goa was abolished by Royal letter in 1774, re-established under Dona Maria 1 in 1779, and finally abolished in 1812 (see Eastwick's

(Contd...)

against Hereticks, the Inquisitors of Goa made a Festival before their House of the Inquisition which is in the Piazza of the Cathedral and was sometimes the Palace of Sabaio, Prince of Goa, when the Portugals took it, whence it is still call'd la Piazza di Sabaio. After solemn Mass had been sung in the Church of San Dominico, as Vespers had been the day before, in presence of the Inquisitors, who, coming to fetch the fryers in Procession, repair'd thereunto in Pontificalibus, in the evening, many careers were run on horse-back by the Portugal Gentry, invited purposely by the Inquisitors; and a day or two after (for this Evening was not sufficient for so many things) there was in the same Piazza a Hunting, or Baiting, of Bulls after the Spanish fashion; but the Beasts, being tame and spiritless, afforded little sport; so that I had not the curiosity to be present at it. This is a new Festival lately instituted by the present Inquisitors, who, I believe, will continue it yearly hereafter.

Widow-burning

I heard related at my first coming that a Rajia (Raja), that is, an Indian Prince (one of the many which are subject to the Moghol), being slain in a battle, seventeen of his wives were burnt alive together with his body; which in India was held for great Honour and Magnificence.* I have heard say (for I have not seen any woman burnt alive) that when this is to be done the Wife or Wives who are to be burnt inclose themselves in a pile of wood, which is lay'd hollow like the rafters of a house, and the entrance stop'd with great logs, that they may not get out in case they should repent them when the kindled fire begins to offend them: yea, divers men stand about the pile with staves in their hands to stir the fire,

---

(Contd...)

Handbook of Bombay, p.225), or in 1814, according to Mr. Sandberg (*Murray's Magazine*, Nov. 1890). See also Fonseca's *Hist. Sketch of Goa*, p.219, and Capt. Marryat's tale of *The Phantom Ship*.

*A remarkable and circumstantial account of a case of self-immolation of three wives of one husband is related in the *Journal of the Royal Asiatic Society* (vol. ix, part 1, 1876), given at length in the Introduction to the *Commentaries of Afonso Dalboquerque* (Hakluyt edition, vol. ii, p. lxx).

and to poure liquors upon it to make it burn faster; and avoid the flames, they would knock her on the head with their staves and kill her, or else beat her back into the fire; because 'twould be a great shame to the Woman and all her kindred, if she should go to be burnt, and then, through fear of the fire and death, repent and come out of it. I have likewise heard it said that some Women are burnt against their own will, their Relations resolving to have it so for Honour of the Husband; and that they have been brought to the fire in a manner by force, and made besides themselves with things given them to eat and drink for this purpose, that they might more easily suffer themselves to be cast into the fire; but this the Indians directly deny, saying that force is not us'd to any, and it may be true, at least in Countries where Mahometans command, for there no Woman is suffered to be burnt without leave of the Govenour of the place, to whom it belongs first to examine whether the woman be willingl; and for a Licence there is also paid a good sum of money.

Nevertheless 'tis possible too that many Widows, being in the height of their passion taken at their word by their kindred who desire it, go to it afterwards with an ill will, not daring to deny those that exhort them thereunto, especially if oblig'd by their word, nor to discover their own mind freely to the Governour; things which amongst Women, with their natural fearfulness and modesty, easily happen. And I would to God that in our countries in sundry cases, as of marrying or not, and the like matters, we had not frequent examples which Women not seldom give of great Resolutions, not forc'd in appearance, but indeed too much forc'd in reality, for avoiding displeasure and other inconveniences. In the Territories of Christians, where the Portugals are Masters, Women are not suffer'd to be burnt, nor is any other exercise of their Religion permitted them.*

A Market was kept this day in Sagher, as 'tis the custom every Sunday

---

*Widow-burning was prohibited by Afonso Dalboquerque when he took the city of Goa (see *Commentaries of Afonso Dalboquerque*, vol. ii, p. 94, Hakluyt edition). It is a reproach to the British Government that not until the year 1829 was the practice of widow-burning forbidden by law in British territories.

and at Ikkeri every Fryday. There was a great concourse of people, but nothing to sell besides necessaries for food and clothing after their manner. The way between Ikkeri and Sagher is very handsome, plain, broad, and almost always direct, here and there beset with great and thick trees which make a shadow and a delightful verdure. As we returned home at night we met a Woman in the City of Ikkeri, who, her husband being dead, was resolved to burn herself, as 'tis the custom with many Indian Women. She rode on Horse-back about the City with face uncovered, holding a Looking-glass in one hand and a Lemon in the other, I know not for what purpose; and beholding herself in the Glass, with a lamentable tone sufficiently pittiful to hear, went along I know not whither, speaking, or singing, certain words, which I understood not; but they told me they were a kind of Farewell to the World and herself; and indeed, being uttered with that passionateness which the Case requir'd and might produce they mov'd pity in all that heard them, even in us who understood not the Language. She was follow'd by many other Women and Men on foot, who, perhaps, were her Relations; they carry'd a great Umbrella over her, as all Persons of quality in India are wont to have, thereby to keep off the Sun, whose heat is hurtful and troublesome. Before her certain Drums were sounded, whose noise she never ceas'd to accompany with her sad Ditties, or Songs; yet with a calm and constant Countenance, without tears, evidencing more grief for her Husband's death than her own, and more desire to go to him in the other world than regret for her own departure out of this: a Custom, indeed, cruel and barbarous, but, withall, of great generosity and virtue in such Women and therefore worthy of no small praise. They said she was to pass in this manner about the City I know not how many dayes, at the end of which she was to go out of the City and be burnt, with more company and solemnity. If I can know when it will be I will not fail to go to see her and by my presence honor her funeral with that compassionate affection which so great Conjugal Fidelity and Love seem to me to deserve.

'Remember me in your prayers'

Nikola Ratkaj

Nikola Ratkaj was born in Veliki Tabor, Croatia, in 1601, into an aristocratic family at a time when Croatia was an integral part of the Habsburg Monarchy or Austrian Empire. At the age of fourteen Ratkaj began his schooling at the Zagreb* Jesuit Collegium, and finished his novitiate in Brno, before leaving first for Graz to study philosophy, and then for Rome to pursue his theological studies. It was from there that he was finally in 1623 sent to the East as a missionary.**

From Rome he travelled to Lisbon in 1623, where he boarded a ship for India. After a taxing and arduous journey during which he caught malaria, he arrived in Goa and was ordained the following year. Ratkaj arrived at the Portuguese Goa Dourada*** some two decades after its commercial peak of power.† Luís Vas de Camões, a 16th-century Portuguese poet who spent part of his life in the power- and money-driven Goa of the times, in a sonnet likens the city to Babylon:†† 'Here,

---

*The city of Vienna was then the opulent royal seat of power, while Croatia's capital, Zagreb, was a provincial town in a farflung corner of Europe.

**Bašiæ, Karmen. *Putnici u Indiju iz naših krajeva*. Zagreb: Section for Oriental Studies of the Croatian Philological Society, Faculty of Philosophy, 1999.

***Ratkaj's Indian surroundings were the same as those of the Croatian, Ragusan colony in Goa (Ragusa is the old name for the city of Dubrovnik), and Ragusan trade with Indian spices along the overland Levant or sea routes.

†Krizman, and Matišiæ.

††According to Borges, the Jesuits in Goa made large profits as well, through (royal) grants and gifts, but also illegal trade in silk, pearls, precious stones and spices, for which they continuously competed with the secular authorities (Borges, Charles J. *The Economics of the Goa Jesuits, 1542-1759: An Explanation of Their Rise and Fall*. New Delhi: Concept Publishing Company, 1994.

where fecundity of Babel frames/Stuff for all ills wherewith the world doth teem,/Where loyal Love is slurred with disesteem,/For Venus all controls, and all defames;/Where vice's vaunts are counted, virtue's shames...'* This setting, that was so antipodean and perhaps conducive to young Ratkaj's missionary zeal was slowly revealing cracks in its cosmetic façade—the Portuguese were already defending their endangered positions against other European powers (on which Ratkaj comments in his letters), and by 1635 the heyday of the Portuguese power in India was over.**

In 1624, the same year Ratkaj was ordained, a Portuguese missionary António de Andrade*** penetrated Tibet from India, crossing the Himalayas, and founded a Jesuit mission in the city of Tsaparang, for which Ratkaj was later designated and eagerly awaited to join. In his letters from Goa, Ratkaj describes the work of the pioneering missionaries in Tibet, along with the Plateau's religion and customs, but he personally most probably never made it there repla his descriptions were based on Andrade's detailed official reports. It was the Jesuit missionaries' duty to send reports on their work and circumstances to their superiors, and to do so with pre-defined regularity, in order to inform and network.† This custom initiated the intelligence system of the Jesuits, which, according to historian Donald F. Lach, surpassed anything Europe had at the time,

---

*Camões, Luís Vas, 'Babylon and Sion/Goa and Lisbon' Trans. Richard Garnett. *Hispanic Anthology*. Ed. Thomas Walsh. New York City: G. P. Putnam's Sons, 1920.

**Scammell, G. V. 'England, Portugal and the Estado da India c. 1500-1635.' *Modern Asian Studies*, Vol. 16, No. 2 (1982).

***Father António de Andrade (1580-1634) was a Jesuit priest in charge of the Jesuit mission in Agra (at that time Goa was the seat of a diocese and the Jesuit province to which Andrade belonged), as well as one of the first known Europeans who travelled to Tibet, and in 1625 established the first Catholic mission in the Western Tibetan kingdom of Guge, in the capital city of Tsaparang, aided by its king.

†Boswell, Grant. 'Letter Writing among the Jesuits: Antonio Possevino's Advice in the "Bibliotheca Selecta" (1593).' *Huntington Library Quarterly*, Vol. 66, No. 3/4 (2003): 255-260. Print.

except perhaps the one operating in the Republic of Venice.* Ratkaj's letters were no exception, and were, also following the Jesuit tradition, fine exercises in rhetoric, with Cicero's Latin letters serving as examples of grammar and style.** Ratkaj's ornate baroque letters, sometimes written in the style of sermons, were read out loud in the drawing rooms of Croatian castles, as well as among the novices and priests of the Zagreb Jesuit Collegium, and were instrumental in fuelling their imagination or faith with select glimpses of the Orient.

In the letters that have survived,*** Ratkaj never writes about Goa— its people, customs, landscape. However, we have to bear in mind that these few letters have been preserved due to their legal significance.† On the other hand, those other letters which might have contained such descriptive passages may simply be forever lost to us or lying undiscovered in some dusty archives.

—Lora Tomas

Goa, 5 February 1625

Letter to the Rector of the Zagreb Jesuit Collegium
(Translated from the Croatian by Lora Tomas. Original letters translated into Croatian from Latin and Italian by Mate Krizman.)

Reverend Father in Christ!
Grace and Peace of Our Lord be unto you!
I cannot begin to express in words how much the passing of my

---

*Lach, Donald F. *Asia in the Making of Europe, Vol. I, The Century of Discovery*. Chicago and London: University of Chicago Press, 1965. 315. Print.

**Boswell: 249-250.

***The six original Ratkaj letters, written in Latin, are now kept in the Croatian State Archives in Zagreb, while the Italian and Portuguese ones are in the Roman Jesuit Archives.

†Some of Ratkaj's letters have been partly written in legal code to serve as documents in court in the inheritance case he fought against his brothers. For those reasons the Zagreb Jesuit Collegium kept them safe, since its Rector was Ratkaj's fiduciary in the matter (Krizman, and Matišiæ: 47).

immensely pious mother has wounded my otherwise resilient heart. Even the time that covers the other pangs with a scar of healing could never remedy this wound of mine: it is, in the prolonged course of this too heavy a loss, rendering itself even deadlier. The only one that succeeds in quenching my anguish is the one that singes me with it–my own mother; I am soothing my yearning for my late parent by remembering her undying virtue. Indeed, I realize that, in such a profound grief, I do have a good reason to be joyful in having such a worthy relief for this terrible misery. She, namely, lives–for herself and, as we hope, for Heaven, and here for me—albeit her life has extinguished itself. I believe this about her so devoutly due to the remembrance of her extraordinary, fierce and persistent faith and devotion to God, the vast contempt towards human affairs, and not less towards her own self, as well as her ability to rise above the gravest of troubles. What else could await her as a deserved reward to a person endowed with such brilliant attributes of Christian virtue, if not life eternal?

Not letting the repeated praise of such a revered mother torment me further now that she is no more, I am turning my attention to other matters. I am at the moment, with the grace of God, already recovering from the two-year-long sickness that was eating me away throughout my journey to India, and even after, and which almost killed me. I am also, slowly but steadily, bringing to an end my theological studies, hopefully by the end of this year. In the meantime, I am preparing for a new mission–either the Ethiopian or the Mughal one,* though I believe it will be the latter, more so, its newly discovered and established outpost, Tibet. Its area and expanse will not to be described now—it would be more appropriate to do so once I get there. Some of it has been revealed in the annual reports of the Jesuit Society. It is a country which borders with China and the Mughal Empire, more accurately, it is situated right in the middle, and by its majesty comparable to both. Its people are half-

---

*From the 16th to the 18th century, North India was under Mughal rule, and the Mughal mission Ratkaj is referring to was the one with its central outpost in Agra, under whose jurisdiction was also the newly founded mission in Tsaparang in northwestern Tibet, for which Ratkaj was preparing himself.

Christians:* they profess, namely, the threefold nature of God, the message of the Son of God; they worship the virginal motherhood of the Mother of God; they celebrate a few sacraments, for example, confession, but only on certain occasions. Their lamas–which is what they call the priests who run their churches or places of prayer—take the vows of poverty and purity. Every day, in a kind of Liturgy of the Hours, two hours before sunrise and then another four or five times during the day, accompanied by music as we similarly do in our churches and cathedrals, they worship and honour, as they say, the Threefold God. However, among those signs of true faith they also entwine a whole host of falsehoods. This country, now discovered for the first time by one of our fathers** who withstood the greatest travails and dangers, promises an abundant harvest.

As far as the family affairs are concerned, especially the matter of the inheritance which needs to be demanded from my brothers, I have written to both of them about it. I have also written to the Emperor*** so that he can, if they would be causing any trouble, use his powers, although I do not assume that will be necessary. Still, since it is not possible for me to take care of this, I pray Your Excellency to do so in my name. In that regard, I grant you full authority over the matter or, as they say, the proxy which would entitle you to, according to the laws of the Kingdom of Croatia† and on account of my authorization, ask from my genteel brothers, Pavao and •igmund, my share of the inheritance,

---

*The Jesuits heard stories about the so-called Tibetan Christians from the Muslim traders at Akbar's Court, and concluded those must be the same pre-colonial Christians the Portuguese, upon arrival, encountered in India, tracing them back to the days of the first evangelist, the apostle Thomas. The Jesuit reports revealed the missionaries believed that the Tibetan form of Buddhism was either some form of corrupted Christianity or simply paganism. (Toscano, Giuseppe M. *Alla Scoperta del Tibet: Relazioni dei missionari del. sec. XVII.* Bologna: EMI, 1977.

**Father António de Andrade.

***Ferdinand II (1619-1637) was a member of the House of Habsburg, the Holy Roman Emperor, King of Bohemia, and King of Hungary and Croatia.

†The Kingdom of Croatia, with Zagreb as its capital, was an administrative unit within the Habsburg Monarchy between 1527 and 1868.

whether in assets or in an equal worth of money of good composition. Since I have never renounced this due right that belongs to me as one of the brothers, I want that the said share, in movable property and real estate, be returned to me and that Your Excellency safekeeps it in your Collegium as a deposit, until you inform me of its amount and I use it the way I see fit. At the moment I am not doing any of it, both because I don't know how much that share of inheritance might amount to, and because it will be better done once the money has been asked for and received. That is why I pray Your Excellency to inform me on the matter as soon as possible. Otherwise, if my brothers fail to pay the entire due share in its money's worth, but pay at least part of it, and the other part in real estate, Your Excellency will be entitled to administer these properties until I decide something about them, or you decide it is profitable to either exchange or sell them. Until you get its money's worth, you are free to have that real estate at your disposal for the needs of your Collegium, unless you decide differently. I pray Your Excellency to endeavour to arrange this matter, appealing to the Emperor if need requires, to whom I have already written about this, as well as to the other public authorities, above all to the Illustrious Lordship, the Viceroy of Croatia:* I want to entreat him to use his authority to help me in this matter, as well as the other persons to whom this matter may be of concern. I expect Your Excellency to inform me about all of this, and mostly about the amount of my share, in real estate and movable property, so that I can use them the way I see fit in Our Lord.

Last year the Ethiopian Patriarch** ordained me as a priest, and on St. Matthew's Day I delivered my first mass in our Collegium,*** in a

---

*The Viceroy or the Ban of Croatia was the title of the local rulers of Croatia. When Ratkaj wrote his letters, he was not aware of who held the office, since the letters sometimes took over a year to reach their destination. He thus addresses them to 'whoever he [Ban] may currently be'.

**Alfonso Medina.

***St. Paul's College in the city of Goa, once attached to the now dilapidated St. Paul's Church, was the leading Indian Jesuit establishment at the time and housed the first printing press in India.

festive way, accompanied by the music of Santa Fe seminary, on the behest of all the fathers and brothers of that seminary, although it was my desire to do so over the relics of St. Francis Xavier. On the occasion, I remembered as appropriate, Your Excellency and the whole of the Zagreb Collegium, which I continue to do even now, in the hope that Your Excellency, with all of the others, remembers me in your prayers far more often than I am worthy of.

I would have, withal, some news to send to you from here, the East, but I will avoid that in the hope that the Assistant Father, to whom everything is being sent, will do so instead. We still have not received any news from Japan or China. This is also the reason why I am not sending you any gifts: namely, the ships from China and Japan have not docked for two years now. In 1622, the fourteen of ours were, grievously, burned alive for the name of Christ, and as many of them from other orders, together with several laypeople, whose number soars up to almost three hundred: their lot was partly the same, and partly included a different kind of martyrdom. I hope that the Assistant Father informs you on the manner of their martyrdom. Next year, by God's grace, I will send you a letter with more news, along with the gifts.

Two months ago, eight mammoth ships set sail from here, of which I had already written to you last year, stating their size, shape, strength, etc. Each of them carries fifty or even sixty cannons whose brass balls weigh seventy to eighty pounds each, and are on their way to Ormuz*— a citadel at the gates of Persia, taken away from us three or four years ago, which we are now so ardently trying to occupy and make ours again.** God grant them success. I greet the Reverend Father Stjepan Ratkaj, whom I remember and bless now and always, both during his lifetime and in his death, as I do all of the other fathers and brothers in the said Collegium, praying the Father for at least two holy masses for my desired

---

*In 1507, the Portuguese captured Ormuz, an island off the coast of Persia (today Iran), which served them as the outpost from which to control the trade route between India and Europe. Aided by the British and the Dutch in a series of conflicts, it was regained by Persia in 1622.

**As a Catholic, Ratkaj strongly identifies with Portuguese rule.

purpose, and the brothers for two-three rosaries for an occasional good deed.

Otherwise I am extremely eager to hear about the state in your Austrian and Czech provinces, and above all about my old friends. May Almighty and Merciful God keep them healthy to the glory of His name. The letters Your Excellency or anyone else wishes to send me should be addressed in this manner and no other: to Father Nicolaus Georgii* of the Society of Jesus, etc. For some reasons I have, with the permission of the Reverend Father General, changed my surname.

Handed in Goa, 5 February 1625.

Your Excellency's worthless servant in Christ, Nicolaus Georgii, former Ratkaj, in my own hand.

Postscript

I haven't received any letters about the passing away of my Illustrious Mother, not even from Father Faro;** may be the letters have perished. I note to Your Excellency that, when you wish to write to me, it would be wise to choose two or three different mail routes, so that the copies of the letter could be carried by different ships. That way, even if one is lost, not all of them will perish together, but at least some of them would be saved on other vessels. From the letter of the Honorable Assistant Father for Germany I gathered that the Reverend Archbishop of Zagreb gave the memorial service speech for my Illustrious Mother. I would think it highly appropriate indeed if Your Excellency expressed my deepest gratitude to him; I have also reminded my two brothers to do the same. I expect to receive from Your Excellency the news about the circumstances of my Illustrious Mother's death.

---

*Ratkaj changed his name for political reasons, since the Portuguese secular authorities did not favour foreign missionaries in their colonies until the mid-seventeenth century. Italian missionaries were exempt from this rule because of the consideration Portuguese had towards Rome and the Papal States.

**Father Faro was the Rector of the Zagreb Jesuit Collegium from 1617 to 1624.

'Chastity is so strange a virtue in those parts'

J. Albert de Mendelslo

Chapter VII

The *Mary*, with the English President and Mandelslo on board, set sail from Surat bar on 5 January 1639, and got the same night in sight of the town of Daman. The reference which our traveller makes to the siege of Daman,* which was invested by the Mogul army at this period, is of great interest as a proof of the credibility of his narrative:

> The governor sent us a vessel of wine, about the bigness of a barrel, and some other refreshments, notwithstanding the siege which the King of Deccan, his neighbour, then maintained against the place, but with little good success, in regard the haven being not blocked up, the Indians could not prevent the sending in of relief into the city, even in the day-time.**

---

*This was the great siege of Daman in 1638-9 during the reign of Shah Jahan. The city was invested from the land side by a Mogul army of 5,000 foot and as many horse under the command of a general who was acting under the orders of Prince Aurangzeb, then viceroy of the Deccan provinces, with its headquarters at Daulatabad. The siege lasted for many months for the garrison kept up a spirited defence, the sea being open to them for receiving supplies. At last a settlement was effected through the efforts of Mir Musa, the Governor of Surat, who was helped in the matter by President Fremlin of the English factory, *The English Factories in India 1634-1636: A Calendar of Documents in the India Office, British Museum and Public Record Office*, William Foster (ed.), Clarendon Press, Oxford, 1911, pp. 123-4, 203, 214-6.

**Mandelslo, op. cit., p. 89. Here follows an interpolation by Olearius on the kingdom of the Deccan, etc., covering some eight pages of the text (pp. 89-97).

Two days later, the ship reached Bassein, then in the possession of the Portuguese, where it was welcomed with seven guns. Here, at the governor's desire, a frigate belonging to this nation was allowed to accompany the ship under the English colours in order to escape falling into the hands of the Dutch who were constantly moving up and down the coast. On 9 January the *Mary* passed by the islands of Bandra and Bombay, and on the 11th it entered the harbour of the great city of Goa.*

As Methwold had some important financial affairs to settle at Goa**, he and his German companion remained as guests in the capital of Portuguese India for ten days. A visit from the English President at Surat to the city of Goa was an event of special importance and he was accordingly received with the highest honours. The Portuguese admiral, described as the 'General of the Galleons', who was then in the port with his fleet to operate against the Dutch squadron, welcomed the President with a volley from his largest guns, and soon after came up in person on

---

*This was Old Goa, the famous city founded by Albuquerque in 1510, near the site of the town conquered by him from the Bijapur State. By the end of the sixteenth century it had grown into one of the finest capitals in India with a large population, stately buildings and extensive commerce, and it was a current proverb to say: 'If you have seen Goa, you needn't go to Lisbon.' After the middle of the seventeenth century its decline began, first owing to the attacks of the Dutch whose fleets blockaded the harbour, and also because its site became pestilential, the city began to be deserted. 'It is now literally a city of ruins, and is so hidden from view by the foliage of the jungle which has occupied it that the stranger approaches it unawares, and drives into the midst unconscious that he is traversing streets of ruined, empty dwellings, occupied by coconut and other tall trees instead of human beings. In the midst of all this ruin Goa remains a city of magnificent churches, four or five ranking as first class and in perfect preservation.'—John Murray, *A Handbook for Travellers in India, Burma and Ceylon*, Thacker, Spink, & Co., Calcutta, 1926, p. 492.

**President Methwold specially called at Goa on his homeward voyage to secure the payment of a large sum of money due to the Surat factory from the Portuguese authorities at Goa, a matter which had been long pending settlement. According to Mandelslo (p. 60) he was 'to receive fifty thousand rials, which the Portuguese were to pay in execution of the treaty of peace they had made with the English, to be employed in the Indies according as the President of Surat should dispose thereof'. See also *The English Factories in India*, pp. 111, 203.

board the *Mary* in a gilt gondola covered with scarlet cloth. After these formalities were over, the President left his ship and proceeded up the river to the city with his trumpets sounding before him. On arrival at Goa, his first visit was to the house of the Fiador da la Fazenda or the 'Overseer of the Exchequer',* it being with him chiefly that he was to negotiate the business which had occasioned his calling at Goa. This officer was sick in bed, but received his visitor with great civility, and as they had long been friends promised to give him all possible help. Methwold was then conducted in a palankeen to the residence arranged for him; and having asked for an audience with the viceroy** immediately proceeded to wait on the latter who lived in royal style at Goa.

The viceroy's palace lay on the river side, and Methwold and his companions proceeded thither by boat. They were met by several *fidalgos* or gentlemen of the viceroy's retinue who conducted them into the hall where the audience was to be given and which was richly furnished and full of pictures of several princes of Europe.*** The guards, who were clad in livery, presented arms and stood in two files in the antechamber through which the hall was to be entered. The viceroy, who was dressed in black, rose from his chair at the President's coming in and did not sit down again till the other was seated. All the rest of the company stood before the viceroy except some of the gentlemen who conducted Mandelslo and others into one of the side rooms to entertain them. The President

---

*The office of Fiador da Fazenda was the most important at Goa next to that of the viceroy. 'As there was no efficient audit of his accounts, and it was no crime for a Portuguese at this period to cheat the King of Spain, his embezzlements were on a vast scale.' See *The Voyage of Francois Pyrard de Laval to the East Indies, the Maldives, the Moluccas and Brazil* Volume II, Albert Gray and H. C. P. Bell (trans.), The Hakluyt Society, London, 1887, p. 2111.

**The viceroy's name was Dom Pedro da Silva de Menezes (1635–9). He died on 24 June 1639, some months after Mandelso's visit. See Frederick Charles Danvers, *The Portuguese in India: Being a History of the Rise and Decline of Their Eastern Empire* Volume II, W.H. Allen & Co. Limited, London, p. 267.

***These guards formed a company of 100 men, all clad in blue livery. They were Portuguese, carried halberts, and kept close to the viceroy's person in the palace or wherever he went. See *The Voyage of Francois Pyrard de Laval to the East Indies, the Maldives, the Moluccas and Brazil* Volume II, op. cit., p. 51.

having discussed his business took leave of the viceroy who brought him to the hall door and stood bare till the visitors were all gone. The gentlemen of his retinue accompanied the guests to their boat on the river, showing them on the way twelve fine horses, sumptuously covered and harnessed, which had been specially brought up there to give the visitor an impression of the viceroy's magnificence.*

The party had hardly dined after return to their lodgings, when visitors began to pour in. Most of the Portuguese lords came to 'salute' the President and there was not a monastery in Goa which did not send its deputies to 'compliment him'. The ten days of their stay in the city were thus spent in reciprocal visits and continual feasting. One of the noblest entertainments given to them was on 15 January, when they were invited by a Portuguese lord who had been Governor of Bassein and had been recently appointed to the government of Mozambique. Mandelslo's account of the feast may be quoted here:

> Every course consisted only of four dishes of meat, but they were so often changed. and the meat so excellently well dressed, that I may truly say I never was at the like. For with the meat there was brought such variety of excellent fruits that by the continual change and inter-mixture of both the appetite was sharpened and renewed. But what was most remarkable was that though the Portuguese ladies are as seldom seen as those of the Muscovites and Persians, yet this lord, knowing he could not in any way more oblige the English than by allowing them the sight of women, we were served at table by four handsome young maids of Malacca, while he himself was attended by two pages and an eunuch. These maids brought in the meat and filled our wine; and though he himself drunk not any, yet would he have the English treated after their own way, and drink to what height they pleased.**

The next day, being 16 January, the President as well as Mandelslo was invited by the Jesuits to a sumptuous feast at the New College of

---

*Mandelslo, op. cit., pp.98.
**Mandelslo, op. cit., pp. 98-9.

St. Paul,* though our traveller may be excused for mistaking it for the Professed House of the Jesuits. The account given by Mandelslo is by far the most interesting that has been written of this college, which was perhaps the greatest and most splendid building which the Society of Jesus had in the city of Goa. He testifies to the magnificence and order which prevailed in the institution under the management of the Jesuits:

> There were in this house a hundred and fifty fathers, and at least as many scholars or students, yet did not that great number fill that noble structure, which was four stories high, and had the pleasantest prospect in the world, as well towards the sea as on the land side. They first showed us all the conveniences of the house, their wealth, and the order they observed in their economy. Then they brought us into a fair arched hall, as big as an ordinary church, which was beset with tables placed all along the walls. The cloth was laid with the trenchers, the drinking cups, and earthen pots, and they had brought in bread and fruit. In the midst of the hall, there was another little square table, covered and furnished as the rest, for those who were to do penance for their having done anything contrary to the discipline of the order. In the midst of the entry to this hall, there was a pillar, out of which issued a spout of water for the washing of their hands. Then they carried us up to the third storey, to another hall, which was not as large as that below, but so richly furnished as might become the apartment of a very noble house, as well in point of tapestry as other things. The table prepared for us was very large, and placed in the midst of the hall, covered with a noble cloth, beset

---

*The New College of St. Paul, or the Convent of St. Roch, as it was generally called, was one of the finest edifices of Goa. To it was transferred, about 1610, the Old College of St. Paul which had played so conspicuous a part in the early history of the Catholic Church in the east, but which was abandoned on account of its unhealthy site. The new college was erected by the Jesuits in the face of great opposition. It suffered also from successive outbreaks of fire, but the Jesuits rebuilt what was destroyed. See Tavernier, op. cit., Volume 1, p. 197. Its professors were generally men of eminence from Europe. After the expulsion of the Jesuits from Goa in 1759 the college closed, and in course of time the building fell into decay and ruin. Its materials were used for constructing the new barracks at Pangim. See Jose Nicolau Da Fonseca, *An Historical and Archæological Sketch of the City of Goa, Preceded by a Short Statistical Account of the Territory of Goa*, Thacker & Co. Limited, Bombay, 1878, pp.315-20.

with fruit and bread and China dishes, which persons of quality in those parts do prefer before those of silver. The Father Provincial having given the President the precedence sat down by him, and afterwards ordered all our company to be so placed as that between every two there were two Jesuits to entertain and discourse with us; the rest standing behold to wait on us. The meat was brought in little dishes of porcelain, to every man his own dish; and this for several courses, both of flesh and fish, all excellently well dressed. The dessert was suitable to the rest of the entertainment and consisted in tarts, florentines, eggs dressed after the Portuguese way, admirably well perfumed, marchpains, and conserves both dry and liquid.*

On rising from this sumptuous repast, the guests were conducted into several chambers where they reposed during the great heat of the day. Later on they were taken into a hall where the 'divertisement' of a ball had been arranged to entertain them, and which danced by Indian children who had been baptised and instructed in the Roman Catholic faith. The Archbishop of Goa, who was Primate of all the Indies, was also present there, both to participate in the 'divertisement' and to entertain the President, by order of the viceroy. The ball, the details of which are given at length, being over, the guests stayed on to hear some music. On taking leave of their hosts, the latter informed them that they made use of such amusements not only to induce the Hindus and Muhammadans of those parts to embrace the Christian religion but also to amuse the children who had been baptised and to give them some diversion after their studies.**

On the 18th the visitors were invited to dinner by the Jesuits of the Professed House of Bom Jesus*** which Mandelslo confuses with the College of St. Paul described above. They were received at the entrance by some of the 'most ancient' Fathers, who showed them round the halls and chambers hung with pictures of distinguished persons who had been

---

*Mandelslo, op. cit., p. 99.

**Mandelslo, op. cit., pp. 99-100.

***A Professed House is a convent or the place of abode of a fraternity that has taken the vows of some religious order.

members of their order, and who related the history of those of their society who had suffered martyrdom for the Christian religion 'among whom the authors of the Gunpowder Plot in England were not the last. But they forebore giving us the explication thereof; only they entertained us with a long relation of the cruelties, exercised some years before, upon those of their society in Japan, where the emperor had made use of the most exquisite torments (that) could be invented, upon the Christians, as well the foreigners who had spent their endeavours in planting religion in those parts, as upon the Japonnesses who had made profession thereof.'*

The Fathers next conducted the President and Mandelslo to the famous Church of Bom Jesus** which was attached to the house which still remains in all its imposing splendour when so many other magnificent edifices which adorned Old Goa have long ago crumbled to pieces. Mandelslo's brief description deserves to be given:

'They brought us into the church which is no question one of the most sumptuous the Jesuits have in all Asia. The structure is vast and magnificent, and the ornaments are so suitable to the greatness thereof that it were not easy to imagine anything more noble. The first thing we were showed was the High Altar; but though it were one of the noblest I ever saw, yet came it not, in wealth, near another lesser one, which had been built in honour of St. Francis Xavier, whom they call the Apostle of the Indies. We were showed his image, which was upon wood, drawn

---

*Mandelslo, op. cit., p. 100.

**The stately Church of Bom Jesus at Goa was begun in 1594 and consecrated in 1605 and is still in excellent preservation, chiefly because it contains the tomb of St. Francis Xavier. The facade is an elaborate piece of workmanship and excites the admiration of the spectator. It is built of black granite and is 78 feet high and 75 feet broad. The pillars supporting the choir within bear two inscriptions, one in Latin and the other in Portuguese, recording the consecration of the church by Dom Aleixo de Menezes, Archbishop of Goa and Primate of the Indies, on 15 May, 1605. On the other side of the wall is the cenotaph of Dom H. Mascarenhas, Captain of Cochin and Hormaz (Ormuz), at whose cost the church was built. The main altar contains the statue of the Infant Jesus as also another very large image of St. Ignatius Loyola, the founder of the Society of Jesus. There are two chapels, one dedicated to St. Francis Borgia, the patron saint of Portugal, and the other in honour of the immortal St. Francis Xavier, whose splendid sarcophagus it contains. See Fonseca, op. cit., pp. 283-6.

according to the life, but we were told his body was still to be seen in that Church. In the same posture as it was at the time of his departure.'* Though not specifically mentioned, Mandelslo must without doubt have seen the coffin of the saint in the famous chapel dedicated to St. Francis Xavier in this church.**

Mandelslo gives here the following interesting account of St. Francis Xavier whose name has become immortal in history as the 'Apostle of the Indies':

> The Jesuits told us that the body of the said Saint Francis Xavier was found in the island of Ceylon, and that it was discovered only by a most delightful smell, which had brought those who had found it many leagues distance from the sea to the place where it was hidden. Which story does not agree very well with what others write of the same body. For besides that the scent which is carried from the island of Ceylon so far into the sea proceeds from the groves of cinnamon wherewith that island is in a manner covered, Maffaeus, one of the gravest authors that ever were of the Society, says in express terms that Francis Xavier, not satisfied with the progress he had made in the Indies by the means of his preaching the faith of Christ, would needs try whether it might have the like success in China, but that he died on the seaside as soon as he landed. 'Whereto he adds that the Master of the Ship, which had carried

---

*Mandelslo, op. cit., p. 100.

**In 1624, during the solemnities at Goa connected with his canonization, the body of St. Francis Xavier was removed by the Jesuits to the Church of Bom Jesus from St. Paul's where it had been deposited after it was brought from Malacca. The ceremonies have been fully described by Della Valle who was in the city at the time. The remains were first deposited in the Chapel of St. Francis Borgia, and later transferred to the beautiful chapel which is named after Francis Xavier. The interior of this is richly gilded and adorned with 27 choice pictures representing the life and miracles of the apostle. An altar under the arch of the chapel supports an image of the saint in solid silver four feet high gifted in 1670 by a pious Genoese lady who spent £300 on its execution. The image bears a staff in each band, one of silver and the other of Indian cane. The latter is taken by the governors of Goa previous to assuming charge of their office, in exchange for a new one which they offer to the saint, to secure his protection over the Portuguese territories. See Fonseca, op. cit., pp.286-9.

him thither, caused the corpse to be put into unslaked lime to the end he might carry away the bones after the flesh had been consumed; but that after certain days that consuming matter had not made any impression upon it, and that the body instead of being corrupted smelled very sweetly; and that thereupon they resolved to carry it to Goa where it was received with great ceremonies. They related to us a great many miracles wrought by that Saint; but I remember only two or three of the most considerable; to wit, that he had caused the sun to come back an hour after it was set: that he commanded the sea and the winds with the same power as Our Saviour had sometimes done; and that he had raised up two men, one whereof had been buried a whole day before.*

After Mandelslo and the President had been shown round the great church, they were brought to the refectory, which was a large hall capable of accommodating two hundred persons at the tables placed all along the walls. At dinner only four Fathers, 'the chiefest of the order', sat down with the guests, while all the rest stood and waited on the party. 'We were as well treated by these,' says our author, 'as we had been by the others; but I must confess these gave us the best canary that ever I drunk.'** After it ended they were taken right up to the steeple, 'whence we could take a view of all the city, the sea, the river, and all the adjacent champion, as far as the mountain, much better than we could have done from the fourth story of the Professed House (i.e. the New College of St. Paul)'.***

---

*Mandelslo, op. cit., pp. 100-101,

**Mandelslo, op. cit., p. 101

***St. Francis Xavier (1506-52), commonly known as the 'Apostle of the Indies', was born in Spain in the castle of Xavier at the foot of the Pyrenees. After completing his studies at the University of Paris, he joined Ignatius of Loyola and five others and established the Society of Jesus in 1534. In 1542, he arrived at Goa in charge of the mission sent by the King of Portugal to his Indian dominions. And laboured in the east for the next ten years. The work he accomplished was enormous, for he inaugurated new missionary enterprises from Ormuz to Japan. At Travancore he is said to have founded no less than forty-five Christian

(Contd...)

The next morning two of the Fathers came to the President's lodgings and took him and his companion out to see the great hospital at Goa, of which the Jesuits were then in charge. It is described by our author as a noble structure, capable of accommodating above a thousand sick persons and fully equipped with all necessary things. The noblest apartments in the hospital were the 'kitchen' and the 'apothecary's shop' belonging to it, both well furnished. There was at the time a large number of patients in the infirmary, most of them suffering from the 'pox' or 'bloody flux'. Those whose life was despaired of were carried to a private room where each was attended by a priest who remained there till the end came.*

(Contd...)

settlements, and he also visited Ceylon, Malacca, the Malay Archipelago and Japan. In 1552 he left Goa on a missionary enterprise to China but died of fever in the island of Chang-Chuen (St. John's) off the province of Kwang-Tung (December 2). He was buried close to the cabin in which he died. But his body was later transferred to Malacca and thence to Goa (1554) where it was deposited in St. Paul's in a crystal coffin enclosed in another of silver. In 1624 the body was removed to the Church of Bom Jesus where it still lies in a magnificent Shrine. St. Francis Xavier was canonized by the Pope in 1621. Many miracles have been ascribed to him, an official list of which is preserved in the Vatican library. Though an ascetic and a mystic, to whom things spiritual were more real than the visible world, he possessed strong common sense which made him supreme as an organizer. He seems also to have had a singularly attractive personality. Not without much justice has Xavier been regarded as the greatest of Christian missionaries since the first century A.D. For literature of the life of St. Francis Xavier see *Encyclopedia Britannica* 14th edition, Volume XXIII, p. 835; also Gray's note in *The Voyage of Francois Pyrard de Laval to the East Indies, the Maldives, the Moluccas and Brazil* Volume II, op. cit., p. 62.

*Mandelslo, op. cit., p. 101. The Royal Hospital at Goa was a splendid institution founded by the great Albuquerque after the conquest of Goa in 1510, and it was the pride and care of successive viceroys and kings of Portugal. In 1591 its administration was placed in the hands of the Jesuits who erected a splendid building for it, and under their fostering care the hospital acquired great celebrity. The most detailed account of the institution is that given by Pyrard de Laval who was treated here in 1608. Tavernier first visited it in 1641, only two years after Mandelslo and again in 1648. He says that it 'was formerly renowned throughout India' but that on his second visit he found that the inmates were not well treated (Tavernier, op. cit., vol. I, p. 198). Even in the days of its greatness, the mortality in the hospital appears to have been excessive (*Pyrard de Laval*, vol. II, p. 11). No doubt this was largely due to cholera, scurvy, enteric venereal diseases which the science of the time was not able to deal. The practice of

(Contd...)

The last institution among the religious edifices of Old Goa to be visited was the monastery of the Augustines which was also known under the name of the Convent of Our Lady of Grace. 'It is seated,' says our traveller, 'upon a little eminency, so that seeing it at a certain distance, a man would take it for one of the noblest palaces in the world.' The friars conducted them round the building and redoubled their civilities when Mandelslo delivered to them the letters of recommendation which the Augustines at Ispahan had given to him in Persia for the purpose.

Chapter VIII | Mandelslo's general account of the Portuguese in Goa

President Methwold at last completed his business with the viceroy who paid him nine thousand pounds sterling in ready money, and promised that the rest would be paid, either in money or in commodities, to those English merchants whom the President had for that purpose brought with him from Surat. Methwold now took leave of all those whose civilities he had received. The viceroy, the general of the galleons, and the principle lords about the court sent him very considerable presents. The viceroy presented him with several sticks of cinnamon, a biggel*, some butts of sack, sheep and baskets of fruit. The Jesuits sent him aquavitae**, a good store of all sorts of conserves, dry and liquid, and requested that he would take along with him to England certain Jesuits, one of whom had lived long enough in China to be thoroughly acquainted with that country.

(Contd...)

bleeding patients as often as thirty or forty times had also something to do with this heavy toll of life (Fryer, *East India and Persia*, Hakluyt Society (1909-12) vol.II. p. 14). The hospital was intended only for soldiers and for such as had no home in the city. See also Fonseca. op. cit. pp. 228-36.

*The biggel is apparently the *nilgau* or blue cow. Mandelslo says that with the horses in the viceroy's establishment at Goa he saw a biggel, 'which is a creature about the bigness and much the same colour as a *renne*, but is headed like a horse, maned like an ass, having black and cloven feet, and upon his head two black horns'.—Mandelslo, op. cit., p. 98.

**Aquavitae (*L.* water of life) any form of ardent spirits such as brandy, whiskey, etc.

Mandelslo's *Travels* refer to a very important topical episode at the time of his arrival at Goa, namely, the fact of the port being then under a formal blockade imposed by a dozen Dutch ships. This was the very period when Portuguese supremacy at sea and their possessions in the east were challenged by this energetic Protestant nation; and throughout the first half of the seventeenth century the power of the former was on the decline.* The blockade by the Hollanders, however, could only prevent the galleons and the carracks** from leaving the harbour, for Mandelslo saw one day about three hundred frigates and boats enter the port and proceed up the river to the city laden with all sorts of provisions and commodities such as pepper, ginger, cardamom, sugar, rice, fruits and conserves.***

On 20 January 1639, the President and his party left the city of Goa by the river, and as soon as they got out of it they made for the general's galleon which was called the *Bom Jesus* and which is described as 'one of the noblest vessels I ever saw', for it carried 60 brass guns, all cannon or culverings, with 600 men, mariners and soldiers, on board:

> The General received the President with much civility, and brought
> him into his chamber, and after a collation of conserves and sack,
> contrary to the custom of the Portuguese, who never proffer a man
> drink unless he ask for it, he showed us all the ship, which had the
> name of a galleon, but might very well be accounted a carrack by
> reason of the bigness of it. The other vessels of the fleet were also

---

*Before the Dutch had beaten down the power of the Portuguese in India, one saw at Goa nothing but magnificence and wealth, but since these late comers have deprived them of their trade in all directions, they have lost the sources of their gold and silver, and are altogether come down from their former splendour.—Tavernier, *Travels in India*, translated by Ball, London (1889) vol. I, p. 187.

**These carracks are ordinarily of 1,500 to 2,000 tons' burthen, sometimes more, so that they are the largest vessels in the world; they cannot float in less than ten fathoms of water.'—*Voyage of Pryrard de Laval*, translated by Gray and Bell, Hakluyt Society (1887) vol. II, p. 181.

***Mandelso, op. cit., pp. 98, 102.

very noble ones. there being not anyone among them that had not fifty guns at least.*

The President at last took leave and came on board the *Mary* to the booming of guns from the Portuguese fleet, and his ship took up a position in the roadstead between the two hostile fleets. After two days, on the 22nd, Methwold dismissed the two ships that had come with him from Surat and which were to carry thither the money that had been received at Goa.** The admiral in charge of the Dutch fleet, whose name is given as Van Keulen,*** was expected to pay him a visit in view of the fact that he had requested the President to convey some of his letters to his superiors in Europe. But finding at last that the Dutch fleet had sailed away in the direction of Ceylon. Methwold gave orders to proceed on the voyage.†

Mandelslo at this stage devotes several pages to a general account of the city of Goa,†† including its topography, its Portuguese inhabitants, the habits of their women, the life of Hindus and Muslims of this place, the court, the powers of the viceroys and other topics. We shall very briefly review this account, indicating some of the interesting features of the life of the people and the character of the government.

The name of the viceroy at Goa at the time of Mandelslo's visit was Dom Pedro da Silva, but we are told that his person was not in

---

*Mandelslo, op. cit., p. 102.

**Two ships, the *Blessing* and the *Michael* had accompanied the *Mary* from Surat to Goa. The former was old and worn out and it was intended to sell her to the Portuguese. The pinnace *Michael* was to bring back the crew of the *Blessing* and also Cogan and Wylde, members of the Surat council, who had accompanied the ex-President Methwold to Goa to receive the money promised by the viceroy and to assist in the disposal of the other ship.—*English Factories in India (1637-41)* edited by Foster pp. 88, 118-9.

***The name is Antonio Caen according to the *Hague Transcripts*, series I, vol. XI, nos. 350, 358, 360.

†Mandelslo, op. cit., p. 108.

††Dr. J. Fryer (1675) says: 'The city is a Rome in India, both for absoluteness and fabrics, the chiefest consisting of churches, and convents, or religious houses.'—*East India and Persia*, Hakluyt Society (1909-12) vol. no. II, p. 26.

conformity with his high position.* He had about him a court of more than fifty gentlemen who gave him the same respect that was due to the king in Europe. The viceroy was changed about every three years: partly because the king thought it unsafe to allow a subject to hold such a dignity for long, and also because the King of Spain desired to distribute his patronage among a large number of his nobles so as to enable them to amass a fortune in a short period.** This was possible because the court of the viceroy at Goa was maintained at the king's expense and also because the disposal of all the revenues was left in his hands. Every year the viceroy made an extensive tour over the territories under his control, and this brought him a large sum of money by way of presents from the neighbouring princes and from the governors and other subordinate officers.*** The viceroy was supreme civil and criminal judge and only in rare cases was an appeal allowed to the king. At his arrival in the Indies a

---

*One of the best accounts of the viceroys of Portuguese India, their court, their magnificence and their government is given by *Pyrard de Laval*, op. cit., vol II, p. 76-88. For example: 'The viceroy treats none with familiarity, nor ever goes to assemblies or banquets. He goes abroad but rarely, except on the great festivals. On the evening preceding the day when be intends to go forth, drums and trumpets are sounded throughout the whole town as a warning to the nobility, 'who assemble in the early morning before the palace, all on horseback and in grand array.'—pp. 78-9.

***'This frequent change of viceroys is displeasing to the Portuguese and to the Indians as is no less that of the governors of the various forts and other officers. To illustrate which they tell a parable: how that one day there lay a poor man at the door of a church, his legs full of ulcers and so covered with flies as was pitiful to behold; up came a neighbour who, thinking to do him a kindness drove away the flies: whereat the poor patient was much vexed, saying that the flies he drove away already had their bellies full, and would not bite him more. whereas those that would come would be hungry and would sting him worse. So it is, they say with the viceroys, for the gorged depart and the hungry arrive.'—*Pyrard de Laval*, op. cit., vol. II, p. 87.

***Tavernier says: 'It was formerly one of the most splendid posts in the world for a noble to be viceroy of Goa, and there are few monarchs who are able to bestow governments worth so much as are those which depend upon this viceroy.'—op. cit., vol. I. p. 190. These governors, who were appointed by the viceroy, also held office for three years. There were five of them in charge respectively of Mozambique, Malacca, Hormaz, Muscat and Ceylon. Besides these the viceroy had the patronage of a number of high offices in Goa and other places.

new viceroy used generally to land at the island of Bardes, to the north of the capital, from which place he sent his agents to Goa to take possession of the new charge and all its appurtenances. His predecessors made way for him on the first news of his arrival, unfurnished the palace, and left him only the guards and the bare walls.*

The Portuguese inhabitants of Goa are described as falling into two classes: the Castiços, born of Portuguese parents; and Mestiços, born of a Portuguese father and an Indian mother.** The latter were distinguished by their olive colour, and those of the third generation were as dark as the natives of the country. Persons of quality never went abroad on foot ; but were either carried about in a palankeen by their slaves, or rode on horseback or went in gilt and painted gondolas. They were always attended by a slave who carried a fan or an umbrella. The Portuguese, says Mandelslo, had the reputation of being highly conceited of themselves; but those of Goa were prouder in their gait and actions than any others of their nationality.*** They were also most punctilious and 'excessively civil one to another' in their social life.†

Mendelslo's account of the dress and habits of the Portuguese women at Goa is interesting. His reference to the decay of Portuguese morals, both among the men and women, and the general corruption of society, is amply confirmed by the French traveler Pyrard de Laval who resided in Goa for twenty months some thirty years before the visit of the German traveller. This social decline has generally been acknowledged by historians to form, along with the implacable hostility of the Dutch and the

---

*Mandelslo, op. cit., p. 108.

**The Portuguese, whether of Europe or Brazil, are at Goa called indifferently *Frangues* or *Fringuins*; those born in India of pure Portuguese blood, Castiços, corresponding to the *Creoles* of America; half castes are *Mestiços*.' *Pyrard de Laval*, op. cit., vol. I, p. 188.

***The Portuguese who go to India have no sooner passed the Cape of Good Hope than they all become *Fidalgos* or gentlemen and add *Dom* to the simple name of Pedro or Jeronimo which they carried when they embarked; this is the reason why they are commonly called in derision, 'Fidalgos of the Cape of Good Hope.'—Tavernier, op. cit., vol. I. p. 188.

†Mandelso, op. cit., p. 103.

devastating effects of successive epidemics, one of the causes of the decline and fall of Portuguese greatness in the east.*

'There are few Portuguese women or Mestiços,' says Mendelslo, 'seen going about the city; and when they go abroad, either to church or upon necessary visits, they are carried in close palinkeens or are attended and watched by so many slaves that it is impossible to speak to them. When they appear in public, they are all richly attired in velvet, flowered satin or brocado, and adorned with abundance of pearls and precious stones;** but at home they go in their hair, and have about them only a smock which reaches to the navel; and thence downwards they have petticoats of painted cloths falling down to the feet which are bare.*** They eat no bread, as liking the rice better. Now that they are accustomed to it; nor do they fare over-deliciously as to other things, their ordinary sustenance being salt fish, mangas,† or only rice soaked in a little flesh or fish-broth. They make use of certain bottles made of a kind of black earth, which they call gorgolettes,†† and have a pipe coming up to the brims so that

---

*For other causes see H. Heras, 'The Decay of the Portuguese in India', *Journal of the Bombay Historical Society*, 1928, vol. I, pp. 36-41.

***'The rich ladies of quality go but seldom to church, save on the great feast days, and then superbly attired in the Portuguese mode. Their gowns for the most part are of gold, silk and silver brocade, enriched with pearls, gems and jewels at the head, arms, hands and waist. Over all they wear a veil of the finest crape in the world, reaching from the head to the foot. They never wear stockings. Their patterns, or *chapins*, are open above, and cover only the soles of the feet; but they are all broidered with gold and silver, hammered in thin plates which reach over the lower surface of the chapin, the upper part being covered with pearls and gems and the soles half a foot thick with cork.'—*Pyrard de Laval*, op. cit., Vol. II, p. 102.

***The women take their ease in their smocks or *bajus*, which are more transparent and fine than the most delicate crape of these parts; so that their skin shows beneath as clearly as if they had nothing on; more than that, they expose the bosom to such an extent that one can see quite down to the waist.'—*Pyrard de Laval*, op. cit., vol. II, p. 112.

†*Mangas de velludo* (Port. = velvet sleeves) are a kind of sea mew, white all over the body and having black wings. Mandelso, op. cit., p. 248.

††*Gorgoleta* (Port.) are earthen and narrow-mouthed vessels for storing drinking water. They are so called from the gurgling sound that is made when water is poured out of them into the mouth from a distance, so as to avoid contact. The word is still current under the form of 'goglet'. The Indians call it *kunja*.—*Pyrard de Laval*, op. cit., vol. I, p. 329 *n*; vol. II, p. 74; Fryer, op. cit., vol. I, p. 125.

they may suck up the water without lifting up the bottles to their mouths.*

The corruption of morals was perhaps the most serious canker in Portuguese society at Goa during the first half of the seventeenth century, and the reference to it may be given here:

> The men there are so jealous of their wives that they permit not their nearest relations to see them:** for chastity is so strange a virtue in those parts, that there is no woman but contrives all the ways imaginable to pursue her enjoyments. never minding the breach of those laws which God and nature hath imposed upon them, though the frequent misfortunes which happen upon that occasion should engage them to be more cautious and reserved. The perpetual idle life they lead makes them so high in their desires for they do not anything of business in the world but spend the day in chewing of beetle which adds fuel to the flames, as do also the cloves and nutmegs which they eat out of an imagination that they prevent the corruptions of the teeth and stomach. which commonly make the breath stink.***

Slavery appears to have been an accepted institution in Portuguese India. though there is no evidence to show that the masters were inhuman in their treatment of this unfortunate class:

> 'Most of the Portuguese,' says our traveler, have many slaves of both sexes,† whom they employ not only about their persons, but also

---

*Mandelslo, op. cit., p. 105.

**Fryer says: 'They being jealous of their honour, pardon no affront; wherefore to ogle a lady in a balcony (if a person of quality) it is revenged with a bocca mortis' (Port. *bacamarte* = a blunderbuss).—op. cit., vol. II, p. 26. So also Tavernier: 'It may be said that the Portuguese dwelling in India are the most vindictive and the most jealous of their women of all the people in the world.'— op. cit., vol. I. p. 188.

***Mandelslo, op. cit., p. 105. cf. *Pyrard de Laval*, op. cit ., vol. II, pp. 113-14; Fonseca, *Sketch of the City of Goa.* pp. 161-2; *Voyage of J. Huyghen van Linschoten*, edited by Burnell and Tiele, Hakluyt Society, (1885) vol. 1, pp. 208-14.

†Pyrard de Laval gives a good account of the sale of slaves in the market-place at Goa. 'In this place are to be seen numbers of slaves whom they drive there as we do horses here; and you see that sellers come with great troops following.'—

(Contd...)

upon any other business they are capable of, for what they get comes in to the master. Whence it comes that handsome wenches are sought after, to be employed in the selling of fruits and such commodities as the Portuguese send to market, to the end their beauty might draw in customers. Their keeping, as to diet, stands them in very little. The children born between slaves belong to the master, unless the father will redeem them within eight or ten days after they are born.'*

The old city of Goa still maintained its position as the centre of a very flourishing trade which was carried on by the Portuguese with Bengal, Pegu, Malacca. China and Gujarat:

No person of quality at Goa but goes once a day to the market, whither the merchants, nay most gentlemen come, as well to hear what news there is, as to see what there is to be sold; for, from 7 in the morning to 9 (after which the heat is such as that a man is not able to stay there) the public criers, whom they call *laylon,* sell there by outcry all sorts of commodities, but especially slaves of both sexes and jewels…There are also to be sold there Persian and Arabian horses, spices, all sorts of aromatic gums, alcatifs, porcelain, vessels of agate, several things made of lacque, and whatever is thought precious or rare in any other part of the Indies. Merchants and tradesmen are distinguished by streets; so that silkmen are not shuffled in among linen drapers, nor the druggists among those who sell porcelain. The greatest profit they make is in the exchange of money.**

(Contd…)

op. cit., vol. II. pp. 65-6. Again, 'As for the slaves of Goa, their number is infinite; they are of all the Indian nations, and a very great traffic is done in them. They are exported to Portugal and to all places under the Portuguese dominion.—ibid., p. 39.

*Mandelslo, op. cit., pp. 105-6.

**The principle thoroughfare and business centre at Goa was the *Rua Direita* or the Straight Avenue, which was lined on both sides by fine buildings where lapidaries, goldsmiths, bakers and all the leading merchants and artisans at Goa

(Contd…)

In the account of the Hindu residents of Goa, one point deserving notice is that there were among them several able physicians who were so highly respected at Goa that they were permitted to have their umbrellas carried with them, a privilege which was extended only to persons of quality. We are told that the Portuguese, and even the viceroys and the archbishop requisitioned the service of these physicians in preference to those of their own nation.

(Contd...)

carried on their business. There were Portuguese, Germans, Italians, etc. The locality was densely thronged by people who attended auction sales held there from morning to noon.—Fonseca op. cit., p. 198. Mandelslo says that the public criers were called *laylon*, while Pyrard (op. cit., vol. II, p. 52) gives this name to the locality. The Portuguese word *leilao* = auction is oriental in origin, being derived from the Arabic *i'lam* = proclamation or advertisement.

'They all become Fidalgos or gentlemen'

Jean-Baptiste Tavernier

Chapter III | Remarks upon the present condition of the town of Goa

Goa is situated in latitude 15°N 73°E, on an island of six or seven leagues circuit, upon the river Mandavi, which two leagues farther down discharges itself into the sea. The island abounds in corn and rice, and produces numerous fruits, as mangues, ananas, figues d'Adam, and cocos (mangoes, pineapples, plantains and coconuts); but a good pippin is certainly worth more than all these fruits. All who have seen both Europe and Asia thoroughly agree with me that the port of Goa, that of Constantinople, and that of Toulon, are the three finest ports in both the continents. The town is very large, and its walls are built of fine stone. The houses, for the most part, are superbly built, this being particularly the case with the Viceroy's palace. It has numerous rooms, and in some of the halls and chambers, which are very large, there are many pictures representing each of the vessel which come from Lisbon to Goa, and those which leave Goa for Lisbon, with the names of each vessel and that of the Captain, and the number of guns with which it is armed. If the town were not so shut in by the mountains which surround it, it would without doubt be more numerously inhabited, and residence there would be more healthy than it is. But these mountains prevent the winds from refreshing it; this is the cause of great heat.

Beef and pork afford the ordinary food of the inhabitants of Goa. They have also fowls, but few pigeons, and although they live close to the sea fish is scarce. As for confectionery, they have many kinds, and eat a large quantity. Before the Dutch had overcome the power of the Portuguese in India, nothing but magnificence and wealth was to be seen at Goa, but since these late comers have deprived them of their trade in all directions, they have lost the sources of supply of their gold and silver, and have lost much of their former splendour. On my first visit to Goa I saw people who had property yielding up to 2,000 écus of income, who on my second visit came secretly in the evening to ask alms of me without abating anything of their pride, especially the women, who came in pallankeens, and remained at the door of the house, whilst a boy, who attended them, came to present their compliments. You sent them then what you wished, or you took it yourself when you were curious to see their faces; this happened rarely, because they cover all the head with a veil. Otherwise when one goes in person to give them charity at the door, the visitor generally offers a letter from some religious person who recommends them, and speaks of the wealth she formerly possessed, and the poverty into which she has now fallen. Thus you generally enter into conversation with the fair one, and in honour bound invite her in to partake of refreshment, which lasts sometimes till the following day.

If the Portuguese had not been occupied with guarding so many fortresses on land, and if, owing to the contempt they felt for the Dutch at first, they had not neglected their affairs, they would not be today reduced to so low a condition.

The Portuguese who go to India have no sooner passed the Cape of Good Hope than they all become Fidalgos or gentlemen, and add Don to the simple name of Pedro or Jeronimo by which they were known when they embarked; this is the reason why they are commonly called in derision 'Fidalgos of the Cape of Good Hope'. As they change their status so also they change their nature, and it may be said that the Portuguese dwelling in India are the most vindictive and the most jealous of their women of all people in the world. As soon as they entertain the least suspicion about their women they will, without scruple, make away with them by poison or the dagger. When they have an enemy they never forgive him. If they are of equal strength and dare not come to a struggle, they employ their black slaves, who blindly obey their master's order to kill any one; and this is generally accomplished with the stab of a dagger, or the shot of a blunderbuss, or by felling the man with a large stick of the length of a short pike which the slaves are accustomed to carry. If it should happen that too long a time is spent in tracing the man they wish to murder, and they cannot find him in the fields or in the town, then without the slightest regard for sacred things they slay him at the altar; I have myself seen two examples of this—one at Daman, and the other at Goa. Three or four of these black slaves having perceived some persons whose lives they wanted to take attending mass in a church, discharged blunderbusses at them through the windows; without reflecting whether they might not wound others who had no part in the quarrel. It happened so at Goa, and seven men were slain near the altar, while the priest who was saying mass was seriously wounded. The law takes no cognisance of such crimes, because their authors are generally the first in the land. As for trials, they never come to an end. They are in the hands of the Kanarins, natives of the country, who practise the professions of solicitors and procurators, and no people in the world are more cunning and subtle than they are.

I departed from Vengurla on the 20th of January 1648, and arrived at Goa on the 21st. As it was late, I postponed till the morrow going to pay my respects to the Viceroy Doffi Philippe de Mascarenhas, who had formerly been Governor of Ceylon. He received me well, and during the space of nearly two months which I spent at Goa, on five or six occasions he sent a gentleman to conduct me to the Powderhouse, outside the town, where he often stayed. He took pleasure in showing me guns and other things of that nature, regarding which he asked my opinion; and, among several presents which I made to him on my arrival, he was specially pleased with a very curiously and richly decorated pistol. When passing Aleppo, the French Consul had given it to me, its fellow having been unfortunately lost. It was a present which the nation intended to make to the pasha, who would have been able to boast the possession of a pair of the most beautiful and best made pistols in all Asia.

The Viceroys of Goa do not permit anyone, whoever he may be— not even their own children—to sit at their table; but in the hall where they take their meals there is a small space partitioned off, where covers are laid for the principal officers, as is done in the Courts of the Princes of Germany. On the following day I went to pay a visit to the Archbishop, and I reserved the day after for the Inquisitor. But when I went to his house he sent one of his gentlemen to say that he much regretted that he was unable to see me that day on account of the dispatches under preparation for Portugal, for which were two vessels that were about to sail waited. Nevertheless, if it was in reference to a matter of conscience, he would leave everything in order to speak to me. Having informed the gentleman that I had only come to pay my respects, and proposing to withdraw at once, he begged me to tarry a moment; and after he had reported what I had told him to the Inquisitor, he returned to assure me, on the part of his master, that the latter was obliged to me, and that as soon as the vessel had started he would send to let me know, so that we might have our interview at leisure.

As soon as the vessels had left, the same gentleman came, on the part of the Inquisitor, to tell me that the latter would expect me at about two to three p.m. in the house of the Inquisition, for he dwelt in another, and both houses are very magnificent. I did not fail to be at the place indicated at the prescribed hour; and on my arrival a page appeared, who conducted me into the great hall where, after I had walked up and down for a quarter of an hour, an officer came to conduct me into the room where the Inquisitor was. After passing through two grand galleries and some suites of rooms. I entered a small chamber where the Inquisitor awaited me seated at the end of a large table, made like a billiard table, and both the table and all the furniture in the room were covered with green cloth brought from England.

As soon as I entered he told me I was welcome, and after I had presented my compliments he asked me what my religion was. I replied that I professed the Protestant religion. He then asked me whether my father and mother were also of the same religion, and I having replied that they were, he repeated that I was welcome, calling out to some persons close by to come in. At once a corner of the curtain was lifted and I caught sight of ten or twelve persons who were in a small chamber at the side. The first who entered were two Augustin Carmelites, and some other ecclesiastics, to whom the Inquisitor straight away explained who I was, that I had no forbidden books with me, and that, being aware of the order to that effect, I had left my Bible at Vengurla. We conversed together for more than two hours about many things, particularly regarding my travels, all the company assuring me that they enjoyed hearing my account.

Three days afterwards the Inquisitor invited me to dine with him at a fine house which is situated about half a league from the town, and belongs to the Barefoot Carmelites. It is one of the most beautiful buildings in India, and I shall relate in a few words how these monks acquired possession of it. There was in Goa a nobleman whose father and grandfather had made much by trade, who built this house, which might be regarded as a splendid palace. He did not wish to marry; and, caring for nothing but religion, was frequently with the Augustins, for whom he manifested such affection that he made a will by which he bequeathed them all his wealth, provided that on his death they would inter him on the right side of the great altar, where they were to prepare for him a splendid tomb. According to common report this gentleman was a leper—a report which some persons diligently spread, seeing that he had given all his goods to the Augustins. It was said that the place on the right side of the altar was reserved for a Viceroy, and that it was not proper to place a leper there, to which the public generally and some even of the Augustins assented. Some Fathers of the convent having visited him and begged him to select some other place in the Church, he was so annoyed by the suggestion that he never returned to the Augustins, and went to his devotions with the Barefoot Carmelites, who received him with open arms, and accepted the conditions which the others had refused. He did not live long after he had made friends with these monks, who buried him with magnificence, and succeeded to all his property, including this superb mansion, where we were splendidly entertained with music during the repast.

I remained at Goa from the 21st of January to the 11th of March (1648), on the evening of which day I quitted it, after taking leave of the Viceroy. I also begged permission for the departure of a French gentleman named du Belloy, which was granted me; but by his imprudence, this gentleman, who had not told me why he was at Goa, had a very narrow escape of being brought back, and I too of being carried along with him, before the Inquisition. This is the way he came to India, and his history as he told it to me: He had left his father's house in order to visit Holland, where, having spent more than he should, and not meeting anyone who would lend him money, he resolved to go to India. He enlisted under the Dutch Company as a common soldier, and arrived at Batavia at the time when the Dutch were fighting with the Portuguese in the island of Ceylon. As soon as he had arrived he was included among the recruits who were being sent to that island, and the General of the Dutch troops, seeing a reinforcement of brave soldiers commanded by a French captain named St. Amant, full of courage and experience, resolved to lay siege to Negombo, one of the towns in the island of Ceylon. Three successive assaults were made upon it, in which all the Frenchmen bore themselves bravely, especially St. Amant and Jean de Rose, who were both wounded.

The Dutch General, recognizing in these two men of courage, promised them as a reward that if Negombo were taken one of them would be made Governor of it. The place having at length been taken, the General kept his promise to St. Amant, but when the news was sent to Batavia, a young man who had only recently arrived from Holland, a relative of the General, was appointed Governor of Negombo, to the prejudice of St. Amant, and came with orders from the Council at Batavia to displace him. St. Amant, finding himself thus treated, deserted with fifteen or twenty soldiers, the majority of whom were French, among them being MM du Belloy, des Marests and Jean de Rose, and joined with them the Portuguese Army. This small band of brave men, however, gave courage to the Portuguese, who advanced to the attack of

Negombo, whence they had been driven, and they took it at the second assault.

At this time Dom Philippe de Mascarenhas was Governor of the island of Ceylon, and of all the places dependent on Portugal. He lived in the town of Colombo, and having received letters from Goa informing him of the death of the Viceroy, and conveying an invitation from the Council and all the nobility to take the vacant place, before leaving he desired to see St. Amant and those he had brought over with him and reward them. Dom Philippe was a gallant gentleman, and when he had seen them he resolved to take them with him to Goa, either because he thought he would have there the best opportunity of promoting them, or because he wished to have with him a body of resolute men on account of the Malabaris, who were lying in wait for him with about forty vessels, whereas he had but twenty-two. When near Cape Comorin the wind became so contrary, and so violent a tempest arose that the whole fleet was dispersed, and many vessels were unhappily lost. Those who were in that of Dom Philippe exerted all their skill to bring it to land, but seeing they were unable to accomplish their object, and that it was breaking up, St. Amant, with five or six of his companions, including des Marests, du Belloy, and Jean de Rose, threw themselves into the sea with cords and pieces of wood, and managed so well that they saved Dom Philippe, and they themselves also escaped with him.

To shorten this long story, on their arrival at Goa, Dom Philippe, after he had made his entry as Viceroy, appointed St. Amant to the post of Grand Master of Artillery and Inspector-General of all the fortresses belonging to the Portuguese in India. Subsequently he arranged his marriage to a young girl, with whom he received a fortune of 20,000 ecus. Her father was an Englishman, who had quitted the Company's service and had married the illegitimate daughter of a Viceroy of Goa. As for Jean de Rose, he asked the Viceroy to send him back to Colombo, where, with his permission, he married a young mestive (half-caste) widow, who brought him a large fortune. Dom Philippe, who had a very high opinion of des Marests, having witnessed his gallant deeds, and the many wounds which he received at the siege of Negombo, appointed him captain of his bodyguard, which was the best office at Court. It may be added that he was especially indebted for his own life to him, des Marests being the one who saved him from the wreck by taking him on his shoulders. Du Belloy asked to be permitted to go to Macao, and leave was granted to him. He had heard that some of the nobility retired thither after having acquired fortunes by trade, that they received strangers well, and that they loved gambling which was du Belloy's strongest passion. He remained two years at Macao, greatly enjoying himself, and when his cash ran low these nobles willingly lent him some.

One day, after winning about 6000 ecus (1,350 Pounds) and going back to play, he had the misfortune to lose all, and a considerable sum besides, which his friends had lent him. When he realized his loss, and that no one was willing to lend him more, he began to swear at a picture representing some holy subject, which was in the room, saying, in the rage which the majority of players feel, that this picture which was before his eyes was the cause of his loss, and that if it had not been there he would have won. Forthwith the Inquisitor was informed, for in all the towns in India which belong to the Portuguese there is one of these officials whose power, however is limited, for he has only authority to arrest the person who has said or done anything against religion, to examine the witnesses, and to send the offender with the informations by the first ship starting for Goa. There the Inquisitor-General has the power to acquit him or condemn him to death.

Du Belloy was accordingly put on board a small vessel of ten or twelve guns with his feet in irons, while the captain was warned to watch him well, and that he would be held personally answerable for him. But as soon as they got to sea, the captain, who was a gallant man, and knew that du Belloy was of good family, ordered his irons to be removed, and even made him eat at his table, taking care to supply him with clean linen and clothes necessary for the voyage, which lasted some forty days.

They arrived at Goa on the 19th of February 1649, and the vessel had scarcely reached port when St. Amant came on board on the part of the Viceroy, both to receive letters and learn what was going on in China. His surprise was great on seeing du Belloy's condition, and learning that the captain would not allow him to land till he had delivered him to the Inquisitor. Nevertheless, as St. Amant at that time possessed great authority, by force of his entreaties he obtained permission from the captain for du Belloy to go with him to the town. Du Belloy purposely again put on his old clothes, which were all in rags and full of vermin, and St. Amant, who knew that it would not do to play with the Inquisition, went first to present him to the Inquisitor, who, seeing this gentleman in so poor a condition, took pity on him, and allowed him the run of the town as his prison till he should see what the advices regarding him were, on condition, however, that he should present himself when required to do so. After these proceedings St. Amant brought du Belloy to my lodging, just as I was on the point of going out to visit the Bishop of Mire (i.e. Myra in Lycia), whom I had formerly known at Constantinople when he was guardian of the Franciscans of Galata. I asked them to await my return to dine with me which they did, after which I offered board and lodging to M. du Belloy, who stayed with me, and I ordered three suits of clothes and whatever linen was necessary for his use.

I remained for eight or ten days longer at Goa, during which time it was impossible for me to induce M. du Belloy to put on his new clothes. But he would never tell me why, while from day to day he promised me to wear them. Being on the point of departure I told him I was about to take leave of the Viceroy and he besought me earnestly to try to obtain permission for him to go with me. I did so willingly and with success. We left the same evening in the vessel by which I had come, and immediately M. du Belloy began taking off his old clothes and putting on a new suit, threw his old ones into the sea, and continued swearing against the Inquisition without giving me any reason, for I was then unaware of what had passed. In my amazement at hearing him swear in this manner, I told him that he was not yet out of the hands of the Portuguese, and that he and I, with my five or six servants would never be able to defend ourselves against the forty men who rowed our boat. I asked him why he swore in this way against the Inquisition, and he replied that he would tell me the whole story from beginning to end; this he did when we reached Vengurla, where we arrived at eight 'o clock in the morning. On landing, we met some Dutchmen with the Commander, who had come down to the seashore to eat oysters and drink Spanish wine. They asked me at once who it was I had with me. I told them that he was a gentleman, who came with the French Ambassador to Portugal, and embarked for India with four or five others, who were still at Goa, and that, as neither his residence in the town nor the mariners of the Portuguese were pleasing to him, he asked me to help him to get back to Europe.

Three or four days later I bought him a country mount, i.e. an ox, to enable him to travel to Surat, and I gave him an attendant to serve him, with a letter to the Capuchin, Father Zenon, begging the Father to give him, through my broker, 10 ecus a month for his expenditure, and to obtain from the English President permission for him to embark on the first opportunity. This, however, did not come about, for Father Zenon took him back to Goa when he went thither on the business of Father Ephraim his comrade, of which I shall speak in the next chapter. Father Zenon thought, no doubt, that du Belloy, by showing himself to the Inquisition and asking pardon, would obtain it easily. It is true that he did obtain it, but only after two years spent in the Inquisition when he came out wearing a brimstone-coloured shirt with a great St. Andrew's cross on the front of it. He had with him another Frenchman called Maitre Louys de Bar-sur-Seine, who was treated in the same fashion, and they both had to go in procession with those who were led to torture. M. du Belloy had made a mistake in returning to Goa, and did much worse in showing himself at Vengurla where the Dutch, who had learnt by the advices they had received from the Commander at Surat that he had previously escaped from their service, seized him immediately, and placed him on a vessel which was going to Batavia. They said they had sent him to the General of the Company to be disposed of as that officer should think proper. But I know on good authority that when the vessel was a short distance from land they put this poor gentleman into a sack and threw him into the sea. This, then, was the end of M. du Belloy but that of M. des Marests had nothing tragical about it, as will be seen from his history, which I shall relate in a few words.

M. des Marests was a gentleman of Dauphine, from the neighbourhood of Loriol, who, having fought a duel, and killed his man, fled into Poland, where he performed some gallant acts, which secured for him the esteem and affection of the General of the Polish Army. At this time the Grand Seigneur kept two Polish Princes as prisoners at Constantinople in the Castle of the Seven Tower and the General, knowing the valour and skill of des Marests, who was enterprising, and a good engineer into the bargain, proposed to him to go to Constantinople to see if by any means he could manage to get the Princes out of prison. Des Marests accepted this commission very willingly, and would no doubt have had the good fortune to succeed if he had not been discovered by certain Turks, who accused him of having been seen examining the Seven Towers with too much attention, and, with pencil in hand, making a plan in order to accomplish some evil design. This had been sufficient to cause the destruction of this man if M. de Cesi, the Ambassador of France had not so arranged that the matter was promptly arranged by a present (this in Turkey is the most sovereign remedy in such troublesome matters), and by representing that he was a young gentleman who was travelling for his pleasure, and proposed going to Persia, by the first opportunity .It was not, however, the intention of the Sieur des Marests to go further, and he was waiting his opportunity to return to Poland after having done all that was possible to get the Princesout of prison; but to escape from the hands of the Turks he was obliged to say that he was going to Persia, and to act moreover so that in fact he did go thither.

The Grand Seigneur had resolved never to give their freedom to these Princes, but they were lucky enough at length to find means of winning over a young Turk, son of the Captain of the Seven Towers to whom his father generally entrusted the keys of the prison. On the night selected for their flight this young man pretended to lock certain doors, but left the padlocks open, and took the keys to his father; but he did not dare to do the same to the two principal doors—at one of which the captain with the main guard was stationed—for fear of being discovered. The young man, who was entirely devoted to the Princes had well considered his plans and made timely provision of rope-ladders in order to get over two of the walls. But for that purpose it was necessary to have same correspondent outside, and also someone inside who shared this important secret.

As the severest rigour was not observed towards the Princes they were allowed to receive some dishes from the kitchen of the French Ambassador, and the groom of the kitchen, who was in the plot, sent them on different occasions some pastry filled with ropes, of which they made ladders to aid them in their escape. The matter was so well planned and so well carried out that it succeeded, and the young Turk followed the Princes into Poland, where he became a Christian, and received an ample reward in appointments and money. The others who had aided in the escape of the Princes were rewarded in like manner, and the latter, when they reached Poland, made ample acknowledgement of the services which had been rendered to them by each person.

In due course M. des Marests arrived at Ispahan and first addressed himself to the Rev Capuchin Fathers who brought him to my lodging, where I offered him a room, with a place at my table. He made some stay at Ispahan, during which he became acquainted with the English and Dutch, who showed a high regard for him, as he indeed well deserved. But, it happened one day that his curiosity made him undertake too rash an adventure, and he nearly brought destruction upon himself and, with himself, upon all the Franks at Ispahan. Near the caravansarai where we lodged is a large bath to which men and women go by turns on certain days, and the Queen of Bijapur during her sojourn at Ispahan on her return from Mecca, was very fond of going to converse with the wives of the Franks, because the garden of her house adjoined the bath where they generally went.

The Sieur des Marests, eagerly desiring to see what passed among these women satisfied his curiosity by means of a crevice which he had observed in the roof of the bath, where he went sometimes; and mounting from outside upon the roof which was flat, and such as I have described in the account of the Seraglio and of Persia—by a hidden way which adjoined the caravanserai where we were dwelling, he lay down on his stomach and saw through this crevice, that which he so much desired to behold without being himself perceived. He went in this way, ten or twelve times and unable to restrain himself from telling me one day, I warned him against returning, and told him that he was risking his own destruction. And with himself the destruction of all the Franks.

But instead of profiting by my advice, he went again two or three times, and on the last occasion he was discovered by one of the female attendants of the bath, in charge of the sheets, who for the purpose of drying them upon the poles which project from the roof, had ascended by a small ladder which led to the top. Seeing a man stretched out there she seized his hat and began to raise an alarm; but the Sieur des Marests, to extricate himself from so dangerous a scrape, and to hinder the woman from making more noise, made a sign to her to be silent, and promptly placed in her hands two tomans which by good luck he had with him out of the money I had given him for his expenses.

When he returned to the caravansarai I saw he looked scared, and concluding that something unpleasant had happened to him, I pressed him to say what it was. With some reluctance he at length admitted that he had been discovered by the woman but had tried to silence her with money. He no sooner made this confession than I told him he must at once take flight, and that the danger was very much greater than he supposed. The Dutch Commander, whom it was desirable to inform of what had occurred, in order that a quick remedy might be applied to an evil of which we feared the immediate results, advised his departure at once, and we gave him a mule and as much money as he required to enable him to reach Bandar, and to embark there on the first vessel sailing for Surat.

I gave him a letter of recommendation to the English President. who was a friend of mine, and asked him to advance him up to 200 ecus if he should require them. I spoke very well of him in my letter and I mentioned the offer which the Dutch commander had made him at Ispahan, to send him to Batavia with letters to the General, who would certainly employ him according to his merit; and, as a matter of fact at this time, the Dutch being at war with the Portuguese in the island of Ceylon, a man of courage and intelligence like M. des Marests would be very useful to them. He was therefore strongly pressed to accept employment from them. They showed him great kindness and attention, and made him presents during his sojourn at Ispahan. But at length he told them that, not being of their religion, he felt some scruple in serving with them against the Portuguese, and that this was the only reason that prevented him from accepting the offers which they so kindly made him. The letters which I gave him for the English President contained an account of all this, but the Sieur des Marests preferring to serve the Portuguese, the President who wrote in his favour to the Viceroy, by whom he was much liked, laid stress upon the offer by the Dutch, in order to render this gentleman's services more acceptable.

The Viceroy also gave him a good reception, and when the Sieur des Marests made known to him that he desired to go to the island of Ceylon and take service in the Portuguese Army, he left by the first opportunity with very favourable letters from the Viceroy for Dom Philippe de Mascarenhas, who was still Governor of all the places which the Portuguese possessed in the island and its neighbourhood. He arrived three days after they had lost Negombo and when the Portuguese retook the place, as I have above said, the Sieur des Marests was one of those who received most wounds and acquired most glory. It was he also who did most to save Dom Philippe from the shipwreck, and Dom Philippe when he became Viceroy thought that he deserved no less a recompense than the office of Captain of his Guards in which he died three or four months afterwards. He was deeply regretted by the Viceroy by whom he was much loved, and he left all his property to a priest with whom he had established a very close friendship, on condition that he paid me 250 ecus which I had lent him; this I had nevertheless much difficulty in obtaining from the priest.

'Some of them worship Apes'

Jean de Thevenot

The Town of *Goa* (with its Isle of the same name,) which Goa is likewise called *Tilsoar*, borders upon *Viziapour*, directly Southward; it lies in the Latitude of fifteen degrees and about forty minutes upon the River of *Mandoua*, which discharges itself into the Sea two leagues from Goa, and gives it one of the fairest Harbours in the World; some would have this Countrey to be part of *Viziapour*, but it is not; and when the *Portuguese* came there, it belonged to a Prince called *Zabaim*, who gave them trouble enough; nevertheless, *Albuquerque* made himself Master of it in *February* One thousand five hundred and ten, through the cowardize of the Inhabitants, who put him into possession of the Town and Fort, and took an Oath of Allegiance to the King of Portugal.

This Town hath good Walls, with Towers and great Guns, and the Isle itself is Walled round, with Gates towards the Land, to hinder the Slaves from running away, which they do not fear (towards the Sea) because all the little Isles and Peninsules that are there, belong to the *Portuguese*, and are full of their Subjects. This Isle is plentiful in Corn, Beasts and Fruit, and hath a great deal of good water. The City of Goa is the Capital of all those which the *Portuguese* are Masters of in the *Indies*. The Arch-Bishop, Vice-Roy and Inquisitor General, have their Residence there; and all the Governours and Ecclesiastick and secular Officers of the other Countries (subject to the Portuguese Nation in the Indies) depend on it. *Albuquerque* was buried there in the year One thousand five hundred and sixteen, and St. *Francis of Xavier* in One thousand five hundred fifty two. The River of *Mendoua* is held in no less veneration by the *Bramens* and other Idolaters, than Ganges is elsewhere, and at certain times, and upon certain Festival days, they flock thither from a far, to perform their Purifications. It is a great Town, and full of fair Churches, lovely Convents, and Palaces well beautified; there are several Orders of Religious, both Men and Women there, and the Jesuits alone have five publick Houses ; few Nations in the World were so rich in the *Indies* as the Portuguese were, before their Commerce was ruined by the Dutch, but their vanity is the cause of their loss ; and if they had feared the Dutch more than they did, they might have been still in a condition to give them the Law there, from which they are far enough at present.

There are a great many Gentiles about *Goa,* some of them worship Apes and I observed elsewhere that in some places they have built Pagods to these Beasts. Most part of the Gentiles, Heads of Families in *Viziapour,* dress their own Victuals themselves; he that do's it having swept the place where he is to dress any thing, draws a Circle, and confines himself within it, with all that he is to make use of; if he stand in need of any thing else, it is given him at a distance, because no body is to enter within that Circle, and if any chanced to enter it, all would be prophaned, and the Cook would throw away what he had dressed, and be obliged to begin again. When the Victuals are ready, they are divided into three parts. The first part is for the Poor, the second for the Cow of the House, and the third portion for the Familie, and of this third they make as many Commons as there are Persons ; and seeing they think it not civil to give their leavings to the poor, they give them likewise to the Cow.

'A thousand insults and indignities'

Carre Barthelemy

Thurday, 22 December (1672) I arrived at Bande *[Banda] (Banda is about six miles below the town of Sawantwadi, on the right bank of the river Terekhol, some twenty miles from the sea.)* The church mentioned by Carre may also have been on it in the evening, and learning that there was a church under the Bishop of Bycholin *[Bicholim] (Bicholim, which was then in the Bijapur kingdom but is now in Portuguese territory, lies eight miles north of Goa.)* I went to it and was courteously received by three Canarin priests, who serve this church. It is finely situated on an eminence about a cannon-shot away from the town. Banda is an extensive town, and lies in a lowland covered with large trees, which hide most of the houses. It is watered by a good river, full of fish, and is under the rule of one of Shivaji's governors, a very powerful man. *(Shivaji had conquered Sawantwadi in 1662.* He always has a force of cavalry and several companies of infantry to oppose any designs or enterprises of the governors of the king of Bijapur in the neighbouring districts.

By travelling all the next day, 23rd, I reached the town of Bicholim in the evening. I stayed with the bishop, M. d'Hyerapolis, who lives here as a rule. *(It seems fairly certain that the Bishop of Bicholim was the one mentioned by Manucci as Dom Matheus of Canarese race, who had an interview with Shah Jahan. He was educated and ordained a priest in Goa, then went to Rome to study at the newly founded College of the Propaganda, and having taken the degree of Doctor of Theology returned to India where he became prior of a church in old Goa.)* He has a fine church and seminary which he was having much trouble in keeping up, owing to the persecutions, not only of the Moors and enemies of our Holy Faith, but also of the Portuguese at Goa, who disliked him so much that there was no indignity or insult that they have not inflicted on him, without consideration of his position. This saintly prelate has suffered all this injury with angelic patience and humility. In the evening after prayer this good bishop took me aside for a private conversation. He told me of all the insults continually received from those Portuguese, who had conceived such a hatred against him that they had tried several times to kidnap him in order to bring him before the Inquisition at Goa. They proposed to send him to Portugal by the first ship for punishment, because *(said these Portuguese)* he had come from Rome, and been sent by the Holy College of Foreign Missions with the authority of the Pope, but without the permission of the king of Portugal whom they alone recognized as the supreme spiritual and temporal head in India. *(The Pope by bulls granted in the sixteenth century, establishing various sees in India, had granted to the king of Portugal the right of nominating high ecclesiastical appointments within his dominions from the Cape of Good Hope to China; but in the seventeenth century the Pope, through the Congregation of Propaganda, sent out missionary Vicars-Apostolic independently of Portugal. From this arose a dispute as to their jurisdiction, which lasted to the nineteenth century.)*

However, these Goa Portuguese, having failed in spite of all their tricks to seize the holy bishop, tried a ruse invented by the worst enemies of this prelate, whose name I do not dare to give, so powerful are they and feared today by every one. They imagined they had to deal with a miserable Indian who lacked *(as the majority do)* honour and sense, and was quite ignorant; so that they would not fail to draw him into their trap. They sent an honourable embassy from Goa to inform him that it was intended to recognize his position and to render him all the honours due to his episcopal dignity. But, to obtain these favours, he was told to request the Viceroy at Goa to grant him liberty to go to Goa and exercise his episcopal functions there for a few days, after which he would be permitted to return to his bishopric at Bicholim and live peacefully among the people of his own nation. The prelate, however, had been warned of the designs of his enemies. He sent a reply to Goa worthy of his dignity, to wit, that he was astonished to receive such a ridiculous proposal; that he had never shown any desire, far less sought, for recognition of his position from Goa, because the bulls and powers he had received, on his leaving Rome, from the Holy Father were sufficient authority and recognition for his high office in the country of his birth; and that he did not need the approbation of the Portuguese; so that, if they or their Viceroy wished to see him, it was for them to send a request to that effect, which he would know how to answer worthily to the best of his judgment. The Portuguese were very irritated at this unexpected reply, and they determined to spare no efforts to ruin or drive out this upright man. They therefore posted men in all their aldeas and dependencies, with instructions to try to seize the bishop and bring him to Goa. Being warned of his plan, he was obliged to stay in Bicholim, without even the liberty of going to see his mother and relations, who live near Goa. *(This was at Navelim village on the island of Divar at Goa.)* He had not seen them for twenty-two years since he had gone to study at Rome (in 1650), where he was ordained by his Holiness for this high dignity which he executes as a true apostle amid continual crosses and persecutions by those who call themselves Christians. They even had the cruelty to prevent his good mother and relations from visiting him, saying they were Goa Christians, and behaving as if Christians from Rome were, in their opinion, excommunicated.

The holy bishop told me all these things in such a charitable way that, far from complaining of the continual insults and ignominy he had suffered, he tried to find excuses for the Portuguese as best he could. He was always glad to help them when they wanted anything from him. This he made clear when a large number of young Goa Portuguese were sent to him for instruction for the priesthood. With true charity and apostolic zeal he kept and fed them four or five months in his seminary for religious instruction at his own expense, though he was very poor, as he had only a small pension from Rome and the charity he received from some Frenchmen settled in India. These Portuguese young men, however, after having received holy orders, their keep, and every kindness from the bishop, returned to Goa without showing any gratitude to their prelate and benefactor. One day I asked one of these new priests why he had shown so little recognition of all the benefits he had received. He told me it was out of fear of the ecclesiastics in Goa who absolutely forbad any alms or charity to be given to the bishop under pain of their displeasure, so that, if anyone wished to do something for the Church at Bicholim, it would have to be done secretly.

The town of Bicholim is situated in a quite pleasant extensive area, nearly surrounded by large palm-trees, and is inhabited by Moors, Hindus, and some Canarin Christians. It belongs to the King of Bijapur, who keeps a loyal governor and troops there, to stop attacks from Shivaji's generals, who resented his having this town *(Bicholim had been taken by Rustam Zaman, the Bijapur commander from Shivaji in 1666.)* The bishop house is about a cannon-shot from the town on a high hill. On one side of it runs the river, which is well-shaded and is bordered with delightful gardens and fields. On the town-side, behind his house, there are many palms and other fruit-trees forming a little ornamental wood, which the young priests of the seminary use for walking in.

I have known the prelate for four years, and he could hardly express his joy in seeing me again. He wished me to pass Christmas with him. I had great difficulty in excusing myself, but he finally allowed me to leave, when I explained to him that I had important business in Goa, as I wished to see if I could not rescue our Frenchmen who had taken refuge there, and also to arrange the best way of getting safely to St. Thome. So I got ready to go to Goa, after promising the good bishop that I would return to him when the festivals and my business there were over.

Saturday, 24 December. I left Bicholim in the morning and after three hours' journey on the road I arrived within three leagues of Goa on the banks of a large river. This divides into several branches, which form many small fertile and inhabited islands belonging to Goa. I here took an almadia, a small, long and very narrow boat, in which I passed amidst all these islands. I found them delightful, being ornamented by castles, churches, villages, and country houses from which their seigneurs derive large revenues.

At noon I arrived at the city of Goa and lodged with the Carmelite Fathers, who have a magnificent house here in the best situation of the town. Its Superior, the Reverend Father Corneille, a Frenchman, received me with great honour, and to lose no time I immediately visited the French agent here, Senhor Antonio Martin, the richest and most powerful Portuguese merchant in Goa. He gave me fresh news of the state of affairs of our Viceroy at St. Thomas, which he had just received from Senhor Dogo Martin, his brother, who was at Golconda. He also instructed me in a most obliging manner as to the precautions I ought to take for my journey to St. Thome.

Sunday, 25 December, Christmas Day. In the morning, after having prayed in the Carmelite Church, I went to the Cathedral where I hoped to hear a good sermon, and to see the Viceroy in his splendor and all the fine folk of Goa but I was much surprised at finding hardly anyone in the streets and no worshippers in the church of Saye *[Cathedral]*, or scarcely any priests to celebrate High Mass. After twelve o'clock I returned to the church and found the doors shut. I went to the Augustinians, the Paulists, the Dominicans, and the Franciscans, without getting my sermon; so I rang the bell at some convents to ask the porter when and where there was a preacher. They all informed me very rudely that there were no sermons that day, and that I had no business to ring the bell, at a time when the priests were at rest. I was, therefore, obliged to apologize to these good brother-porters and to ask them to excuse me, as I was a stranger and did not know the habits of the Indian-Portuguese. I returned, scandalized at not finding any services or sermon, and not even a church open for prayer on Christmas Day in this large city of Goa, formerly so flourishing and celebrated for its divine worship and the propagation of our Holy Faith.

When I returned to the Carmelite Fathers, I did not fail to express my astonishment at this to the Father Superior, who being French, knew well with what solemnities and crowds of worshippers we celebrate Christmas in our churches in France. He laughed at hearing my complaints of the want of devotion I had found that day in Goa; and told me that I must not be surprised, as it was the custom of the Portuguese. They sat up on the night of Christmas Eve for the Midnight Mass, and considered that God owed them a day's rest after this effort, and therefore passed Christmas Day in repose or in feasting in their houses—laity as well as priests—which was the reason why so few people were in the streets and the churches were shut. He also told me that high-born ladies, if they were zealous and pious, and wished to hear Mass on that day, had an altar raised in their bedrooms and brought in a priest to say Mass at the foot of their beds. They stay in bed all day, in case of an indisposition which they feared might result from the hard work they had undergone in keeping awake in order to attend Midnight Mass. In this state they received visits from relations and friends, who came to pass the day in feasting with the doors shut. 'What!' I exclaimed to this Father, 'are these the Christians who treat all other Christian nations as heretics and ignorant, compared to themselves. I would not be surprised if they celebrate in the same way the greatest festivals of our Church, or if they reform to the same extent the beautiful customs and practices which we employ to encourage devotion in our churches in Europe. No. I am no longer surprised to see them living in this fashion, as they will not recognize the authority, the bulls, nor the bishops coming from His Holiness, because forsooth the king of Portugal did not send them, nor ratify their missions.' 'These Portuguese,' I said to the Carmelite, 'are like certain Armenian priests whom I met when I was travelling in Persia. One day I had a dispute with them, as to their not submitting to, or recognizing, the authority of the Pope. I told them there could be no priests in God's church other than those sent by the Holy Father. This infuriated the Armenians against me. I asked them who had ordained them as priests. They replied, their bishop. 'But who created these bishops?' I asked. 'Our patriarchs,' they said. 'And who creates those patriarchs?' I continued. 'Who had given them this power and authority to consecrate bishops and ordain priests?' 'The Grand Seigneur [*the Sultan of Turkey*],' they replied. 'Really.' I told them, 'it is a most surprising thing that the Sultan, who follows the vile religion of Muhammad, and does not recognize any other should be able to create patriarchs bishops, and priests, in the Church of God!' (*The appointment of Armenian Patriarchs by the Sultan of Turkey was started by Muhammad II after his capture of Constantinople.)*

'Thus most of these Indian-Portuguese are so stupid and ignorant that they imagine the King of Portugal should consecrate the bishops and priests for missions in India, and that they cannot go there without his permission and royal patents, so the result is that they will not suffer any other ecclesiastics here. Whatever may be their quality or condition, I should much like to know who is responsible for our French ecclesiastics being so maltreated by them, and why they are so persecuted by them, wherever they have the upper hand over them. Why have these Portuguese so little respect, or deference for the episcopal dignity, for the humility of the monks, and for the doctrine and zeal of our French ecclesiastics, who come to these oriental lands only in a spirit of charity and a true fervour for the spread of the holy Church of Jesus Christ? What have they not done in these last years to the Bishop of Eliopolis *(Heliopolis was an ancient city of Egypt, five miles east of the Nile, at the apex of the Delta)* to compel him to seek the Goa Viceroy's permission before going on a mission to Siam! What have they not done lately in China to yet another holy French bishop, M. de Beritte! They persecuted him in such a way that one can hardly read letters, which I have seen, without deep compassion. *(He was Mgr. Lambers de la Motte, who was consecrated titular Bishop of Bervthe [Beirut] in 1660.)* The Portuguese were jealous of the success of his mission, gave him a tempestuous time, and raised the country people against him, treating him as one who had led them astray, and taught a wicked and false doctrine. Things came to such a point that this holy man was condemned to four hundred strokes with a stick which he suffered like a true apostle, for the defence of the Church of Jesus Christ. What should one say of the treatment inflicted last year on M. Dechevroeuil, one of our worthy priests in China? *(He was Louis Chevreuil, one of the original members of La Societe des Missions Etrangeres in Paris [1660], who worked in Indo-China.)* They did not content themselves with driving him out and forbidding his ministry, but they sent him tied hand and foot, in a Portuguese ship from Macao, with orders to throw him into the sea. The ships officers were so horror-struck at the proposed cruel murder of such a worthy priest that they wanted to land him on some desert isle; but God prevented this, as they could not find one. So they brought him to Goa, where the Portuguese kept him several months under their Inquisition. They were finally obliged to set him at liberty, as they could find nothing against him, except a patience, a humility, a teaching, and virtues, which abashed even them. What have they not done to a good Capuchin priest, Father Ephraim of Nevers, to prevent the establishment of his mission at Madraspatan, now called Fort St. George! They inflicted a thousand insults and indignities on him. They held him prisoner for a long time in their town of St. Thome, before they themselves were driven out by the Moors. They then sent him to Goa like a criminal and kept him two years under the Inquisition. This good old man no doubt would have died of misery and affliction, had God not sustained him with celestial consolations—the sole help and sustenance of those who devote their lives to apostolic work. *(Father Ephraim de Nevers was the head of the Catholic Mission in Madras from 1642. A long account of the trick by which he was induced to go from Madras to St. Thome in 1649, his arrest and imprisonment there, and his trial by the Inquisition in Goa in 1650-51 is given by Manucci.)*

'Let us now try to discover the reason which have led to such injustices and bad treatment inflicted by them on all European ecclesiastics when they come to the East. *(Manucci also complains of the persecution suffered by non-Portuguese missionaries in India from 'the Portuguese and local Christians, who admit no arguments but what the Portuguese tell them'.)* Let us ask them what induced these outrages. They will all answer that it is because the priest have no brevet, or permission, from the King of Portugal, whom they consider, as an article of faith, to be the spiritual and temporal head of all *(Portuguese)* India. But it is not really that. No, no; this is not the reason that incites them to such cruel behaviour. There are many other more urgent motives that induce this conduct. To speak frankly, it is that they do not want people of honour or decency, or one of probity and high virtue like our French priests. They cannot endure,'

I said, 'that these enlightened persons should learn of their ignorance, manner of living, indulgence in trading, and the abuses and impieties they commit in this country, fat from the bright light of our doctrines. This is what offends them, and makes them act like madmen against Europeans, and particularly against the French, because they alone send missionaries to these fields full of thorns and brambles, where they already begin to sow the seed of the Holy Faith in spite of the envy and persecutions of these Portuguese.'

This is what offended a certain priest, Father Emanuel de Cabral, Superior of the Madre de Deos at Goa *(The Madre de Deos convent was one belonging to the Recollects at Goa; Manucci.)* with whom I left Persia [*in the* St. Francis] last September. One day I had a talk with him touching our religion, and he flew into a furious rage with me over it. Seeing that he treated me as a heretic, because I once used a phrase to him in Latin, which he did not understand, I felt obliged to lead him on and expose his ignorance. I asked him if he was really a monk, and he replied that his dress showed that sufficiently, but all the same his actions did not do so. 'They you say the Holy Mass?' I asked him. 'Certainly,' he replied. 'You will oblige me by showing your breviary,' I said. This Father imagined that I thought he had not a breviary, as I had never seen him reading anything but a Portuguese book, which dealt only with games such as manilla, diamonds, spades, clubs, hearts, canal, and what is called 'the book of kings' by the French Academy. He summoned a Kafir servant, gave him the keys of a large chest, and told him to fetch his new breviary that he kept there for fear of wearing it out. 'There,' said this Father, presenting it to me on its arrival, 'see if I have not got a breviary,' 'Yes,' I replied, 'I do see it but no doubt the reason you use it so little is that it is full of heresies.' 'Heresies in my breviary,' he cried angrily, 'ah! By St. Anthony this Frenchman is a Jew,' and he promised me nothing less than a narrow cell in the Inquisition as soon as we should arrive in Goa. However, to confound him absolutely, and to explain my reason for affronting him by treating his breviary as heretical, I took the book and found in it the same words I had quoted to him in Latin. I made him read them before all the company and asked them whether they were not heretical. He swore by St. Antony that they were not, but that they were the prayers he had to recite every day. 'I am astonished then, my reverend Father,' I said to him, 'that you treated me as a heretic with so much anger, when I quoted this passage, which is in your breviary, and which you do not understand in Latin, though it ought to be familiar to you.' He did not know what to answer and his ignorance and stupidity were thus tacitly shown up. *(It has been suggested to us by Father Romanus Rios that the incident was really due to the Portuguese father not understanding the French pronunciation of Latin by the Abbe, and so failing to recognize the quotation from the breviary.)* I was surprised to see that the other Portuguese with us appeared to fear and respect him, and wanted to change the conversation to cover the chagrin that I had caused him. But it was in vain: he wished to wreak his anger on me and to such a point that, if the officers of the ship had listened to him, they would have thrown me into the sea. 'No,' he said, of all the European nations that have come to India, we have no worse enemies than the French. The English and Dutch have had wars with us, which did not last very long. *(The Father here apparently refers to the English and Dutch opposition in India to the previous Portuguese supremacy there.)* But the French wage a continual one against us, ever since they came to India, with their bishops, their monks, and their missionary priests, who try to upset our ministries and ecclesiastical duties.' I had a great desire to pursue my advantage with this Father all along the line, but the other Portuguese prevented me. I would have shown him that, instead of complaining as he had done, all the Portuguese priests in India had every reason to be thankful and pleased with our French ecclesiastics, who came to the East only to perform the Church work that the Portuguese would not do, because of their other occupations and employments. These had more attraction for them than religious matters, of which I have had too many proofs in the short time I have been in India.

Have I not spoken in my first journal of a Portuguese priest who was returning from Persia, where he had been a Superior for six years? What progress had he to report for these six years' mission? Had he any certificates and registers of those whom he had converted to the faith of

Jesus Christ? I asked one day to see them, but he could show me nothing. However, he had plenty of other proofs that he had not wasted his time in his Persian mission; he had half a shipload of rich and exquisite merchandise from Persia, which he was taking to Goa. Have I not seen others openly dealing in Persian women and wine, which they sent to the fidalgos at Goa and other Indian towns, under commissions to buy this merchandise, that ill become men of their calling. I have also written of two Portuguese monks, whom I met some years ago at Cannanore on the Malabar coast. They were so occupied with Hindu heathen traders that in my presence they refused to help a large number of poor Christians, who ran after them, begging for the Sacrament of Penance, as they had been without priests for over a year. I was so exasperated at this lack of charity from the Portuguese Fathers, at the grief they caused to these poor Christians, that I resolved to stay some days amongst them to help them and administer the Sacrament, which these monks had so unkindly refused. But, without going so far, take the case of the priest who was returning to Portugal by land, and whom I met some months ago *(in July 1672)*. He asked me for advice, how to pass safely with a quantity of precious stones, which he had with him. This he told me was the profit which he was brining back from his Chinese mission, where he had been for twenty-two years. Moreover one now sees only misery and poverty among the ordinary inhabitants of their towns; and there remain none of those rich merchants who formerly had ships and agents trading profitably all over the East. You must indeed go into the Portuguese convents if you still want to find riches and treasures: there you will see brokers, merchants, and other country people, who trade only with Portuguese priests. All the commerce of that nation is thus in their hands. One cannot say this of our priests or French ecclesiastics, wherever they may be in India. They set a high example of virtue and probity in their regular mode of life, and carefully restrict themselves to practising their charity, patience, and humility.

Monday, 26 December. I visited this large and once flourishing city of Goa. I could hardly find any shadow or vestige of its former splendour. I saw the once magnificent palace of the Viceroy in the middle of the town; it is low-lying, with the harbour and the river on one side and a big open square of the town on the other. It contains nothing remarkable except the picture gallery where one still sees the portraits of the ambassadors sent by the Indian kings and princes to do homage to the Viceroy of Goa. The rest of the palace, except the Viceroy's quarters, is not in good order, and manifests only its antiquity. Near the palace, outside the town on the bank of the river, is the arsenal, where formerly they made the guns and other instruments of war, which for a time kept all these countries in subjection to the Portuguese yoke. Now it seems to be mere warehouse of cables, rigging and other naval gear; but once it could rightly be called the sole arsenal in the East. The kings and princes in this country had then no defences for their forts and territories, except the artillery they took from the Portuguese, whom they drove in such a shameful way from all their principal possessions, though they seemed to have settled themselves there for good. One could see this from their fine buildings in Hormuz, Bandar Abbas, Muscat, and other places in the Persian Gulf, and in the Red Sea, as well as in Cochin, Calicut, Barcelor [Basrur], Cannanore, Ceylon, Golconda, Bijapur, on the Coromandel coast, in Bengal, and in many places in the East as far as China. The factories had so exhausted the arsenal that I could see nothing but empty places, where such artillery had formerly been made.

The royal Feytor's house is near this place. He has the administration of all the revenues of Goa, from which he pays the officials both of the town and of the marine. All this part is on the bank of the river in a low and unhealthy position. The town also is in a hollow extending between high mountains, which obscure it for the best part of the day from the sun. There are two high hills on the east and the west, which are the best and most healthy spots. On them are two magnificent monasteries, the finest ornaments of this town: the Carmelites to the east; and the Augustinians to the west. They are like two magnificent palaces and face one another. The other churches are the cathedral and four more parish churches in the town; also the monasteries of St. Francis, St. Dominic, the Theatins, and the Paulists. The last named have three houses, St. Paul, the Good Jesus, and St. Roch. That of St. Paul, from which the

Paulists derive their name, was their principal house, where formerly they had a large college with boarders and a seminary in which Hindus and heathens were taught the Catholic faith. Now, all these things having been abolished, they have abandoned this house, as there are scarcely enough monks to serve the other two. They now live as simple citizens, having nothing to do but to give advice on any important questions, as they are very expert and clever in such matters. The other churches, both of the parish priests and of the regulars, are ill-served; and in most of them the Mass and divine service are no longer sung for want of priests and monks. These diminish in numbers, as their revenues are confiscated; and they have been obliged to abandon many fine churches both in and outside the town, where one sees only the vestiges of the former splendour of the Portuguese. The Paulist Fathers, the Dominicans, and the Augustinians alone still maintain some remnant of *éclat*, as they have not lost the power and means to uphold their rights and to draw their rents and revenues.

Thus it seems that this grand town, once so rich and called the Treasury and Queen of the East, is now at its gasp. One sees no longer the splendour, magnificence, and those fêtes, which drew all the Eastern people here to seek the friendship and goodwill of the Portuguese. Indian ambassadors, laden with rich presents, no longer come to Goa; nor do kings and princes send their daughters to serve as slaves to the wives of its Viceroys. The Portuguese ladies now can longer go out in carriages or palanquins of gold, enriched with precious stones and other valuable ornaments. They are no longer worshipped by troops of slaves, who bowing to the earth present them with incense and perfumes in golden vases, as if they were little human goddesses. No, they have brought the just anger of the Almighty on themselves by this luxury, these honours, and the idolatry, which they exacted with such overweening pride. Yet they still keep this pride in their misery and degradation. Everything changed very suddenly. First the great trade and commerce, which so enriched this town, ceased: and then all the treasure and immense wealth, which they had collected, vanished like smoke. The noble families that upheld this splendour also disappeared. Others came from Portugal so impoverished that the little they had on arrival lasted only a moment. This is not surprising, as formerly only men of honour and capable of governing were sent out, whereas today Portugal sends only people taken out of jail or from the scaffold, and outcasts exiled here, who are more inclined to dissipate than to try to amass wealth. I am not, therefore, surprised that they have reduced the town to such a state that the inhabitants can hardly make a living. The only people who seem to flourish are the principal officers, who share the balance of the revenues among themselves, and those (such as the priests and some fidalgos) who have preserved some effects and lands in the country. Their present Viceroy, Dom Luiz de Mendoza Furtado, is a man who passes a tranquil life in pleasures and revels with his women, and is so besotted with them that he will hardly let them out of his sight. He has found a splendid way of enriching himself without much trouble, which is to confiscate all the wealth of those who have managed to save something. The Portuguese formerly believed that it would be a sacrilege, and attract the curse of the Almighty, if Hindus or heathens were allowed to live here, so it was peopled only by Christians, Portuguese as well as half-castes, and native Christians. But this Viceroy's predecessor *(the Conde de San Vincente, who died in 1668)* considered that the town was going to rack and ruin for lack of inhabitants and traders, so he permitted the entry of Hindus and merchants of the country to try to re-establish commerce.

The outskirts are very beautiful and pleasant, with several castles on fertile hills, forts on the river banks, and many charming islands, well peopled and abounding in rice, grain, and fruit. There are also some country-houses, which are fine only on the outside, as their lands and revenues diminish daily for want of people who can work them properly and keep them up, as formerly.

Tuesday, 27 December. This morning I received a visit from some Portuguese naval officers. I knew them very well, and I soon discovered the reason for their coming. After some conversation they came to the point, and informed me that the Viceroy had heard of my arrival in Goa wished to see me to hear all the news from Europe. Thereupon I replied

that I had every intention of paying my respects to him, having a request
to make about the Frenchmen who were in their fleet and in his service
here; that I hoped he would kindly liberate them, and let me send them
back to the service of their own nation; and that I had postponed my
visit, as I believed he would not be able to see me sooner, having heard
that he had refused an audience to two Englishmen, who had come from
Bombay to treat with him on some urgent matters *(These envoys were
James Adams, a member of Aungier's council at Bombay, and Samuel
Walker, secretary of the Council. Aungier sent them at the end of November
to negotiate a proposed treaty of friendship with the Viceroy. But the Viceroy
advised the Prince Regent of Portugal not to agree to them)* and whose visit
he had postponed until after the fetes. 'That is quite true,' said one of the
fidalgos, 'but our Viceroy makes a great difference between you and
these Englishmen, for they have come here to discuss an affair with
which the Viceroy would much rather dispense, namely the rights and
pretensions which the English set up to some farms and aldeas that really
belong to us *(This seems to refer to the objection of the Portuguese to Cooke's
taking possession of Mahim and other parts of Bombay, which they claimed
to be not included in the cession under the treaty of 1661.)* This audience
will be postponed as long as possible, and even avoided, if that can be
done, but as far as you are concerned, you can visit the Viceroy when you
please, and he will be delighted to receive you.' One of them even
whispered in my ear that I was awaited with impatience, as he hoped I
would help him regarding General Dom Antonio de Mello de Castro,
who had been arrested for matters of which he knew I was cognizant, as
I was with their fleet in Persia and at Muscat in the last campaign. In
regard to the French whom I hoped to retrieve from him these officers
believed that I would get no satisfaction from the Viceroy, and that he
would set none of them at liberty. He had made them into a company,
and given the command to a French gentleman called the Cadet de la
Vertierre. He had deserted from our Viceroy's squadron, in which he
was a volunteer, and had escaped to Goa. There he was received with
honour and given the command of this French company, of which the
Portuguese Viceroy was very proud. He intended to send it with the
fleet, which was shortly returning to the Persian Gulf.

On hearing all this from these gentlemen, I almost lost the wish to visit the Viceroy, for I did not want to mix myself up with the Antonio de Mello affair. I had never said anything that could prejudice him, as I had received every courtesy and many proofs of his affection and goodwill towards our nation. I could not, however, bring myself to leave Goa without doing my utmost to accomplish the principal purpose that had brought me here. I felt obliged to approach the Viceroy on the subject of our Frenchmen, having the utmost displeasure in finding them thus dispersed and vagabonds all over India, at a time when out own Viceroy and Company were in extreme need of their help against two powerful enemies, the king of Golconda and the Dutch who (*the former by land and the latter at sea*) were waging a cruel war against us.

At noon I went to the Viceroy's palace and was immediately shown into a room, where the Viceroy wished to speak to me in private. He at first received my compliments very graciously and no one could have been more civil than he was, as long as our talk was on European affairs and other indifferent topics. But when I made my request, and told him I had been ordered to collect all the French and send them to Surat for embarkation in ships that were being dispatched to help our Viceroy at St. Thome, he appeared thunderstruck, hardly knowing how to answer me. I noticed that he changed colour and because flushed when I said the words 'our Viceroy'. This at once showed me his Portuguese jealousy, and it was evinced still more by some words which escaped him, as he was considering my proposals. 'What!' he said, 'a French Viceroy at St. Thome?' Then, recovering himself, he said, 'Don't you know that St. Thome was built by the Portuguese and belongs to them?' 'Yes,' I replied, 'but your Excellency well knows that our French found in possession of it only Moors, who refused them provisions though asked with civility to supply them for cash down. We could not stand the insults and jeers of these Moors, who treated us like dogs, on our arrival, so we were obliged to chastise this scum, who are enemies of our religion. We drove them ignominiously from the town, which they had not the courage to defend, though they had strongly fortified it during the eleven years that had elapsed since they expelled the Portuguese [*in*

1662] and became its sole possessors. The town is dedicated to God and to the great apostle St. Thomas, who has honoured it by many miracles. *(According to tradition, St Thomas suffered martyrdom, or at any case was killed near the town, and had been buried there. Several miracles at or near that place were also ascribed to him.)* Therefore your Excellency ought to feel that it is much more honourable to the Portuguese for it to be in the hands of the French, who are good enough Christians, instead of under the domination of the Moors, who are the sworn enemies of our Faith.' 'Yes,' replied the Viceroy, 'that's all very well, but the Portuguese ought to have been with the French in this capture. They would afterwards willingly have waived their claims in favour of the French; but the latter having taken it without warning or any notice of their plans, we cannot now cede our rights and pretensions to that town. We should have retaken it easily, as we are going to seize Muscat and the other towns we have in the East, now that are at peace and Portugal is more powerful than ever.' He made me other boastful speeches of this nature, and I could hardly maintain the gravity I was obliged to keep before him. We had some more talk on this subject, and I saw clearly that this Viceroy was far from being well-disposed to our nation, and was mad with jealousy at the idea of another Viceroy besides himself in India.

Feeling that our conversation was growing colder, and that I could do nothing to free the Frenchmen in his service, I took my leave of his Portuguese Excellency and withdrew, very sad at not having done what I so much desired. I stayed two more days in Goa to try to smuggle some of our French out of the town. I had got into touch with them, and they told me of their earnest wish to free themselves from the misery in which they were, and to return to the service of our nation. But the Viceroy, suspecting that I would try to persuade my people in that way, sent them all on board the ships, and kept such strict watch in the town and all the passages [*out of Goa*] that I could not execute any of my plans.

'The sharp dart of excommunication'

Alexander Hamilton

Goa, the Metropolis of *India*, under the Dominion of the Crown of *Portugal*, stands on an Island about 12 Miles long, and 6 broad. The City is built on the North Side of it, on a Champain Ground, and has the Conveniency of a fine Salt Water River, capable to receive Ships of the largest Size, where they lie within a Mile of the Town. The Banks of the River are beautified with noble Structures of Churches, Castles and Gentlemens Housess; but, in the City, the Air is reckoned unwholsom, which is one Cause why at present it is not well inhabited. The Viceroy's Palace is a noble Edifice, standing within Pistol Shot of the River, over one of the gates of the City, which leads to a spacious noble Street, about half a Mile long, and terminates at a beautiful Church, called *Misericordia*. The City contains many noble Churches, Convents and Cloisters, with a stately large Hospital, all well endow'd, and well kept. The Market-place stands near the *Misericordia* Church, and takes up about an Acre square, where most Things of the Product of the Country are to be sold; and, in the Shops about it, may be had what *Europe, China, Bengal,* and other Countries of less Note furnish them with. Every Church has a Set of Bells, that one or other of them are continually ringing, and, being all christened, and dedicated to some Saint, they have a Specific Power to drive away all Manner of evil Spirits, except Poverty in the Laity, and Pride in the Clergy; but, to those that are not used to nocturnal Noises, they are very troublesom in the Nights. The Vice-roy generally resides at the Power-house, about two Miles below the City, on the River Side, the Springs of Water there being reckoned the best on the Island, which is a Liquor very much esteemed by the *Portugueze*, except when they can get Wine or Spirits Cost free, and then they'll drink to Excess.

The Religion, established by Law, is the *Romish*, and here are the most zealous Bigots of it; and the Laws of the Church (but not of their Country) are rigorously observed, and there is a severe Inquisition Court to punish any whom the Inquisitors have the least Suspicion of, which aws both Clergy and Laity to such a Complacency, that I question if there is such a Pack of notorious Hypocrites in the World; and yet their *Indian Converts*, who go by the general Name of *Canarians*, retain so much of the ancient *heathnist* Superstition, that they abstain from eating Cows' Flesh, because of the veneration paid to that Beast, above others, by the *Gentows*, whose Offspring they are.

There are many *Gentows* dwell in the City, who cannot be bought to change their idolatious Superstition for the Religion of *Rome*, but they are tolerated, because they are generally more industrious than the *Christians*, especially in mechanical Employments and Agriculture; but the mercantil Part of them are very subject to the Infusts of the *Reynolds*, or *European Fidalgoes*, who will often buy their Goods, and never pay for them, which Custom has also crept into some Countries better polished than the *Portugueze*, only with some Restrictions, that they dare not use Force in taking what they have Occasion for, as the 'Portugueze do nor inflict corporal Punishments on their Creators, when they ask for their Money, for that it is dangerous for the poor industrious Merchant, either to refuse their Goods, or ask for their Money when it is due, for Fear of a Bastinado in either Café, and Sometimes worse Consequences, which Abuses make the Circulation of Trade very faint and weak.

The Clergy at *Goa* are very numerous and illiterate, and are a very great Burden on the State. Their Churches are richly furnished with fine Decorations and Images, and, as I said before, richly endow'd to maintain the Luxury of a great Number of idle Drones.

Their Houses are large, and their Outsides magnificent; but within (like their Owners Heads) they are but poorly furnisht, and their Tables very mean. Green Fruits and Roots, in their Seasons, with a little Bread and Rice go far in their Diet; and candied and preserved Fruits are their *Regalio* in all Seasons. They have Hogs and Fowl plenty, but use them sparingly; and the Church feeds most on Fish, but not miraculously, for the poor Fishers dare fell none till the Priesthood is first served, for that the Laity mostly eat stale or Stinking Fish. And the Soldiery, Fishers, Peasants and Handicrafts feed on a little Bit of Salt Fish, or *Atchaar*, which is pickled Fruits or Roots, and drink fair Water, when they can get it. This fine Spare Diet never loads them with superabundant Flesh on their Bones, and, without the Church, it is rare to find a corpulent Man among them. They are generally very weak and feeble, but whether that proceeds from the Diet, or from their too great Inclinations to Venery or from both, I am not Physician enough to determine.

Their Soldiers Pay is very small and [they are] ill paid. They have but *six Xerapheens* per Month, and two suits of Calico, script or chequered, in a Year. Their two Suits may amount to forty *Xerapheens*, and a *Xerapheen* is worth about sixteen Pence half-Peny Ster. Out of their *Xerapheens* in Money that they are to receive, their Captain, who is Barrack-master and Victualler to his Company, detains five, and the other one is paid in small Money to discharge the Accounts of the Shoemaker, Taylor, Barber, Weatherman and Tobacconist, for that Frugality is no great Virtue among them, tho' Theft is, and really they are very dextrous in that Art, as well as in Murder, for if they are detected in committing such innocent Crimes, the very next Church is a Sanctuary for them, and neither divine nor human Laws can affect them after they get in there.

This Nation was famous in the Fifteenth Century for their Navigation and Discoveries into the *East Indies*, where, by Friendship or Force, they made Settlements all over its Sea-coasts. Their Settlements were thick set between *Mozambique and Japan*; and, as a Monument of their Grandeur then, their Language goes current along most of the Sea-coast at this Time. Their insolent Pride and War with the *Dutch* have brought them to the Poverty and Contempt they are in, as I shall remark in their proper Places.

The *Muskat* War, (that has lasted since the *Arabs* took that City from them) tho' the longest, has done them least Harm, for it obliges them to keep an *Armada* of five or six Ships, besides small Frigats and Grabs of War, which gives Bread to great Numbers of People, who otherwise would be much more burdensom to the State, by crowding into Churches. The *Arabs* and they have had many Encounters, but no great Damage done on either Side. I was Witness to one Engagement near *Surat* Bar, but it was not bloody.

They also have had several Wars ashore, but the most dangerous to the City of Goa, was that with *Sevajee Raja*, who got Footing on the island about the Year 1685. He raised some Batteries against the Town, which would have annoyed it very much, had not a *Portugueze* Heroine, in a Sally, got into a Redoubt of the Enemy's and cut them to Pieces, which struck such a Terror into *Sevajee's* Army, that they quitted their Posts and fled. The Lady was alive *in Anno* 1705 and received the Pay of a Captain all her Days after that noble Exploit. She was called *Donna Maria*. She came to India in Man's Apparel, in Quest of a Gentleman that had promised her Marriage, and then deserted her, and went, in Quality of Captain, to *India*; but she found him, and challenged him at Sword and Pistol, but he rather chose to make the Quarrel up amicably by Marriage.

I have stood on a little Hill near the City, and have counted about eighty Churches, Convents and Monasteries within View; and I was informed, that, in the City and its Districts, which stretch about 40 Miles along the Sea-coast, and 15 Miles within Land, there are no fewer than 30,000 Church Vermin, who live idly and luxuriously on the Labour and Sweat of the miserable Laity, so that every Body that has Sons and Substance, strives to buy Places for them in the Church, because neither military nor civil Preferments can be expected from the State, or if by merit they chance to raise themselves, yet the Tyranny and Opperations of the domineering Clergy is insupportable; for Instance, I knew a Gentleman that bought a Parcel of fresh Fish, and Priest coming soon after to the Fishers, and finding that none was left for the Church, he demanded the Gentleman using some tart Language to the Priest, that offended him, he let fly the Sharp Dart of Excommunication, that pierced him so deep , that it cost him above *7 L. Sterl.* to take it out again, and beg his Pardon on his Knees before the Archbishop, before he could be absolved.

In a fine stately Church dedicated to *St. Paul* the Apostle, lies the Body of *St. Francis Xavier a Portugueze* Apostle, and a *Jesuit* by Trade, who died in his Mission to *Japan* in the fifteen Century; and, about fifty Years after, as a *Portugueze* Ship was going to, or coming from *China*, being near an Island on that Coast, called after *St. Juan*, some Gentlemen and Priests went ashore for Diversion, and accidentally found the Saint's Body uncorrupted, and carried it Passenger to *Goa*, and there, with much Veneration and ecclesiastical Ceremony, it was deposited in an Isle of *St. Paul's* Church, where it lies still, and looks as fresh as a new scalded Pig, but with the Loss of one Arm for, when the Rumour of the Miracle reached *Rome*, the sovereign Pontiff ordered his right Arm to be sent, that he might find out if there was any Imposture in it or no, or perhaps make him fadge in a *China Bonzee* into his Calendar, under the Name of a *Christian* Saint. Accordingly his Arm was fairly cut out off by the Shoulder, and sent to Rome to stand its Trial. When his Holiness had viewed it, he called for Pen, Ink and Paper to be brought on a Table, and the Arm set near them. After a little conjuration, in full view of the sacred College, who were there present, and no Body else, the Saint's Hand took hold of Pen, and dipt it in Ink, and fairly wrote *Xavier*.

I take it to be a pretty Piece of Wax-work that serves to gull the People of their Money, for many visit it with great Veneration, and leave something as its Shrine for the Maintenance of Candles and Olive Oyl, that continually burn before it: And a Priest attends weekly to shave his Head and Beard; but none but that Priest has the Honour to come within the Iron Rails that are placed about the Crops, four or five Yards distant from it. Now if any should question the Truth of *Xavier's Story* at *Goa*, they would be branded with the odious Name of an obstinate incredulous Heretick, and perhaps fall in the Hands of a convincing Inquisition.

But, if any incredulous Heretick should be squeamish, and cannot swallow the Story of *Xavier* without chewing it, I will tell them of another that doubtless will go gliby down. At a certain Time, but God knows when, a Ship of *Portugal* coming to *India*, got the Length of *Cabo de Bona Esperanza*, and then met with such a violent Storm, that drove the Ship for violently before it, that it was past the Pilot's Skill to keep her Rights in her Course; and who should come to their Assistance in that critical Juncture, but *Senhor Diabolo*, who took the Helm, and managed it very dexterously: And the Virgin *Mary*, to shew her kindness, and still in Navigation, Stood a whole Night on the Forecastle, directing the Devil how he should Steer, and behold, to the great Admiration of all concerned, the ship was high and dry in the Morning, in a Valley on the South Side of the River of *Goa*, about a Mile within the Land. The ship sailed very well, for that one Night she ran, according to a moderate Computation,1500 Leagues. And, in Commemoration of this Miracle, there is a fine Church built where the ship anchored for Safety, and the Structure is just the Length, Breadth and Height of the Ship. The Church I have often seen as I past up and down the River. And this Story is so firmly believed at *Goa*, that it is dangerous to make any Doubt of it.

Of all the churches in or about *Goa* none is honoured with Glass windows, but one in the city dedicated to *St. Alexander*, for the rest are all served with clear Oyster-Shell Lights, that are far inferior to lights of glass. And all their stately Houses are furnished with Oyster Shell lights.

The Country about *Goa* is steril in Corn, but it produces some excellent Fruits. The *Goa Mango* is reckoned the largest and the most delicious to the Taste of any in the World, and I may add, the wholesome and the best tasted of any fruit in the world. Their *Jambo Malacca* is very beautiful and pleasant, and they have very good Pine Apples and Melons.

The little trade they have, is mostly from their Arrack, which is distilled from *Toddy* of the Cocoa-nut tree, which grows in great Abundance in the Territories of Goa. The *English* are their best Customers, for they buy great Quantities yearly for Punch. It is sold by the *Candy*, or two Casks, about 45 Gallons each, for 25 *Xerapheens* per Cask, but I have bought it for 20, when there was no great demand for it. They also make a great Deal of Salt in Ponds made in low Grounds, where they may convey the Water at the Spring Tides. It may be bought for a Crown the Tun, and sometimes cheaper.

The River's Mouth is guarded, and the Entrance defended by several Forts and Batteries, well planted with large Cannon on both sides. On the Island is the Black Fort, which stands within half a Musket shot of the Bar, which is shut up by the South-South-West Monsoons, from *April to September*, when is St. *Anthony's* New-Moon, as they call being the first New-Moon in *September*. The Freshens coming down from the Mountains, tains, carry off the Sands, which choke the Mouths of the Rivers along all the Coasts of *India*. And, without the black Fort, is a Battery built close to the Sea on a little Promontory, called *Nos Senhor de Cabo*, about a Mile without the black Fort. And, just over that Battery, on a little Hill about 40 Yards high, is a fine Monastery, always kept as white as Snow, and may be seen a good Distance off at Sea. The Monastery has a large pleasant Garden towards the Land, and an Orchard of excellent Fruit Trees. And, on the Opposite of *Nos Senhor de Cabo,* is a Fort built on the Face of a little Hill, which commands that Side of the River. And, without that, is the *Aguada*, fortified with a Fort on its Top, and several Batteries at the Foot of its high Grounds, which are also about 40 Yards high. In the Castle is placed a large Lantern for a Light-house, to shew Shipping the Way into the Road about the Beginning of *September*, when thick Clouds obscure the Land, that it cannot be well known at Sea. All Boats that are bound to the City, are obliged to call *Aguada*, to give an Account from whence they came, and what their Business is; and if any presume to pass without calling there, they are sure of a Shot fired from a Battery at them, to put them in Mind of their Duty. Two Leagues to the South of *Aguada* are the *Marmagun* Islands, being five in Number, and run a League into the Sea. The two innermost are fortified, to command the Entrance of the River of St. *Lorenzo*, which is a Branch of *Goa* River, parting about five Leagues from their Mouths, and compose the Island called *Goa* Island.

'Reduced to a miserable condition'

Gamelli Careri

Gemelli next visited Goa, the metropolis of Portuguese India. Here he saw most plainly the evidence of the decline of Portuguese power in India, which he attributed chiefly to the hostility of the Dutch, and to the fact that the conquest of Brazil diverted the greater portion of Portuguese energy to the New World. The effect of these causes was visible in the decline of Goa from its former greatness, manifested by the compass of its walls, which extended full four leagues, with good bastions and redoubts, a world too wide for the city of some 20,000 inhabitants that Gemelli visited in 1695.

He found its trade declining, and its wealth and grandeur impaired 'to such a degree that it was reduced to a miserable condition'. The commencement of the decline of Goa was supposed to have been indicated seventy-four years before Gemelli's arrival by a crucifix on a hill in Goa which 'was found with its back miraculously turned towards Goa, which city from that time has very much declined'. There was another miraculous crucifix in the church of St. Monica's Augustinian nuns, one of whom had died in the monastery 'with the reputation of sanctity, she having the signs of our Saviour's wounds found upon her, and on her head, as it were, the goring of thorns, whereof the archbishop took authentic information'.

But, of course, the greatest object of religious veneration at Goa was the body of St. Francis Xavier at the church of Bom-Jesu. Gemelli, as a great favour, was allowed to view it, although for nine years past the Jesuits had allowed it to be seen only by the Viceroy and some other persons of quality. It was in a crystal coffin, within another of silver, on a pedestal of stone; but they expected a noble tomb of porphyry stone from Florence, ordered to be made by the Great Duke. Gemelli tells us that 'since, with the Pope's leave, the saint's arm was cut off, the rest of the body has decayed, as if he had resented it'. It was on account of this supposed resentment that the Jesuits were unwilling to show the body to everybody who wanted to see it.

Of the European nations in India, Gemelli evidently much preferred the Portuguese to the Dutch and English, which preference is natural enough, as he was a zealous Roman Catholic. He specially commends Portuguese politeness. 'Courteous,' he remarks, 'is the Portuguese nation,' and elsewhere he speaks of 'the Portuguese civility, which in all places I found they practised more towards me than towards their own countrymen'.

One good story he tells that shows how the Portuguese occasionally abused their knowledge of the ceremonial law of etiquette, and how an Indian prince outwitted them. The son of an Indian king about to visit a Portuguese Governor got an inkling that an attempt would be made to sit upon him by giving him no chair to sit upon: so he gave to two slaves instructions of such a kind that he both avoided the affront and effectually turned the tables on the Portuguese magnate. 'Being come into the Governor's room, and seeing no chair brought him, he caused his two slaves to squat down, and sat upon them. The Portuguese admired his ingenuity, and presently ordered chairs to be brought. After the visit the two slaves stayed in the Governor's house, and their master being told of it by the Governor's servants, that he might call them away, he answered he did not use to carry away the chairs he sat on.'

The Indian prince's ingenuity in converting his slaves into chairs rivals that of the Highland chief who won a bet with an English lord by turning his tall retainers into candlesticks, as related in Scott's *Marquis of Montrose*.

'Great lovers of fine titles'

Jacobus Canter Visscher

It [Goa] is considered by the Portuguese, as you know, the capital of the Indies and here a viceroy sent from Portugal has his seat of government and holds his Court. It is sufficiently strong on the sea side and the moles are protected by forts and dykes, but it has nearly fallen into decay within and is destitute of inhabitants, excepting the ecclesiastics who have a convent here, the artisans and the poor people. The upper classes have retreated to the environs of the town on account of the insalubrity of the climate and the river banks and islets are adorned with nourishing farms and plantations of cocoa and other fruit trees on the profits of which they subsist. The whole island of Goa is furnished with such like farms as is also the case with Salsette in the north where the Jesuits play the master and other places. It would be considered a disgrace by the Portuguese Fidalgos to follow any trade but the Jesuits look on such employments as honorable and they are in fact the chief traders of these parts.

We need be under no apprehension that the Portuguese will cause any injury to our commerce here for they are devoid of any knowledge of business and what with their indigence and their fraudulent conduct which has destroyed all confidence in them, they are held very low in public estimation throughout the Indies. But they are great lovers of fine titles. High offices and generals are all the talk among them. An office which with us would be filled by a small tradesman must needs require a general with them. For each ship of war they have a Capitano di Marre Guerre and a levy of captains, lieutenants and ensigns besides. It would be a great mistake however to suppose that their pay is proportionate to their titles. A captain receives less than one of our Serjeants and the

Resident of Panoor assured me that he had only twenty golden funams or shillings per month from the king for his maintenance, yet these gentlemen like to cut a figure. Not satisfied with having one umbrella carried over his head, a man of high rank requires two or three ornamented with hanging fringes and silver buttons. The bearers must be Kaffres clothed in red coats and these are accompanied by other Kaffres bearing long swords called Espingardes who act as bravoes for their masters. For as their incomes are so slender and their state so imposing, these signors often betake themselves to schemes of plunder and assassination and every year they despatch an expedition against their hereditary enemies, the Arabs, in the hope of obtaining booty of which however in these days they do not gain much.

There is no place in the world where law is less regarded than here. Scarcely any enquiry is instituted into cases of murder. Moreover, the Fidalgos or noblemen cannot be punished for crime in the Indies but must be sent to Portugal for trial and this is rarely done. Their vice and dissipation are excessive. They surround themselves with troops of Bayaderes or dancing girls, row with them in their *Oranbaien* on the rivers and spend their time with them in all sorts of amusements These Bayaderes are for Hindoos very pretty. In their dances they move not their feet alone but all their limbs. They attire themselves very gaily with bracelets and golden ornaments and exercise great fascination over the pleasure-loving Portuguese. The Portuguese ladies are not better conducted than their husbands. When a man of any rank travels abroad, he does not leave his wife at home but takes care to shut her up in a convent. Indeed, the jealousy of the husbands goes so far that they remark if any man speaks to their wives and not unfrequently death is the penalty he incurs.

The Viceroy here is the highest in command. He remains for three years only unless the Portuguese sovereign should prolong the term. He has two residences—one in the city called the Casa di Pulvere and the other where he commonly sojourns outside the walls. He holds audience every morning, standing under a canopy and takes his meals alone. His Court circle is considerable and he makes a good sum out of the presents which the inhabitants, according to custom, must offer at his coming and going. In the interregnums between the departure of a viceroy and the arrival of his successor, the Archbishop or Primate takes the reins of Government and then the Clergy have their turn in the appointment to offices.

The Ecclesiastics here are innumerable. Hindoos and natives of Canara as well as Europeans so that there are much fewer soldiers than priests. The reason why so many natives enter the priesthood is that they may be spared the insults of the Portuguese who treat all black men as if they were slaves. The Portuguese trade in the Indies is of little value. It makes a great noise when two ships from the mother country arrive together in the year at Goa and these come more for the purpose of providing the inhabitants with necessaries than for commercial enterprise. Each has on board more than forty Ecclesiastics of various orders. Tobacco is charged with heavy imposts, the produce of which is assigned especially to the Queen for her private purse. It is nevertheless an article of great consumption, being not only used by the Portuguese in all parts of India but exported also to foreign nations in Europe, the Dutch taking no small share of it. The most profitable trading voyage of the Portuguese is that to Mozambique. Here they sell linen and other commodities and purchase in exchange many slaves or Kaffres whom they convey to Goa where they fetch a good price.

They carry on commercial transactions with China likewise where they possess an island called Macao. The Macao merchants have for some years kept up a brisk intercourse with Batavia, the Chinese junks having kept aloof. But not more than one or two ships visit Goa during the course of the year and these part with most of their cargo, consisting principally of Chinese luxuries as silks, tea, sweetmeats and sugar at Cochin and Ceylon. There is no nation in the world so fond of sweetmeats as the Portuguese. They always hand them about on their social visits. But for wine, beer and strong liquors in general they have no taste. Intoxication is of rare occurrence among them. The Dutch on the contrary drink to such an extent as to expose themselves to the reproaches of the Portuguese and the Natives who commonly call us Hollandeses bebidos or Dutch drunkards. The English are liable to the same imputation. They are greatly attracted by the Persian wines and by Punch which is made of the arrack of Goa. I must remark by the way that though in England they talk a great deal about the Protestant religion, the English in India allow themselves to be very much mixed up with members of the Romish communion, generally having their children baptized by the Priests and marrying Roman Catholic wives. Having thus far extended my account of the Europeans at Malabar and the neighbouring places which I trust you will not find tedious I shall now conclude &c.

'My object all the time was the Inquisition'

Claudius Buchanan

Dr Buchanan's next letter to Mr Brown is dated Goa 25th January from the great hall of the Inquisition. It contains an account of his bold and interesting visit to that metropolis of the Roman Catholic religion in the East and is similar to that with which the public in general is already well acquainted. Instead therefore of repeating that admirable narrative in which the ardour of Christian research and of Christian courage and benevolence are strikingly displayed, a sketch of this enterprising expedition only shall be given which occurs in a letter to Colonel Macaulay.

'On my arrival at Goa I was hospitably entertained by Captain Schuyler. He and Colonel Adams introduced me next day to the Viceroy who affects great pomp, rails at the French and is a true Frenchman at heart. Next day Major Pareira went up with me to old Goa. The Archbishop received me cordially. I professed a purpose of remaining some days there. This it seems was unusual and it occasioned some discussion and difficulty. At last I was received by one of the Inquisitors…the second Inquisitor Josephus a Doloribus, the chief agent of the Inquisition and the most learned man of the place. By this *malleus hereticorum* was I received in his convent of the Augustinians in a suite of chambers next his own. He was extremely communicative. All the libraries were opened and were extensive and valuable beyond my expectation. That of the Augustinians alone appeared to be larger than the library of the college of Fort William.

'My object all this time was the Inquisition and I gleaned much information imperceptibly. I disguised my purpose for the first three days and the Inquisitor referred me to various books and documents elucidating the very subject I wanted to investigate so that on the fourth day I attacked him directly on the present state of the Inquisition. I had already discovered that it was abolished in 1775 by the court of Portugal on account of its inhuman rigour, that in 1779 it was restored on the accession of the present Queen and that it has been in operation ever since. On its restoration, its rigour was qualified in some points. It was not to have a public Auto da Fe but it was permitted to have a private one annually. The dungeons and torture remain the same. It has power to incarcerate for life and there are now victims in its cells. The tribunal is supported in its ancient pomp and its establishment is full. In fact it is the only department which is *alive* in ancient Goa.

'Josephus a Doloribus was alarmed when he discovered the real drift of my inquiries. I told him that he had now said so much he might as well tell me all and that I should not leave Goa till I had seen the Inquisition. He at last consented to shew me the great hall. I accompanied him clothed in the solemn robes of his office. When I had surveyed the place awhile in silence, I desired that he would now let me go below and visit the dungeons. He refused and here our first contest began. I told him that if he did not open the dungeons and let me count the captives and inquire into the periods of their imprisonment and learn the number of deaths within the last year, I should naturally believe that he had a good reason for the concealment and that the ancient horrors of the Inquisition still subsisted. Whereas if he would now unbar his locks, I could only declare to the public the truth as it was and nothing would be left to imagination. He felt the force of this, but answered that he could not oblige me consistently with his oath or duty as an Inquisitor. I observed that he had broken that oath frequently during the four last days and that he had himself noticed in his own justification that the ancient regulations of the Church were in many instances obsolete. I then put the following question solemnly: "Declare to me the number of captives which are at this moment in the dungeons below." "That, Sir, is a question," said he, "which I must not answer."

'I was now in the hall where the captives were wont to be marshalled when they proceeded to the flames. I contemplated the scene awhile with mournful reflection and then retired. The alcaides and familiars of the holy Inquisition stood around me, wondering at my introduction into the hall and my conversation with the Inquisitor. I went into a neighbouring church and ruminated on what I had seen and heard. I resolved to go again to the Inquisition. The familiars, thinking I had business with the Inquisitor, admitted me. I immediately saw a poor woman sitting on a bench in the great hall. She appeared very disconsolate and was waiting to be called before the tribunal in the next room. I went towards the tribunal and was met at the door by Josephus a Doloribus who seemed to have lost his temper at this intrusion and exclaimed, "*Quid vis tu Domin?*" All our discourse was in Latin. I told him I wanted to speak with the chief Inquisitor who was then on the bench. I then looked at the poor woman very significantly and then at him. And what has this poor woman done? He was silent and impatient to lead me out.

'When we came to the head of the stairs, I took my last leave of Josephus a Doloribus and repeated once more in his ears what I had pleasantly pronounced before in our amicable discussions about the Inquisition: "*Delenda est Carthago.*"'

'Before I left Goa I communicated to him my intention... I first declared it to him in his own cell of addressing the Archbishop in a Latin letter which would probably be published on the four following subjects:

1. the Inquisition,
2. the want of Bibles for the priests,
3. the disuse of public preaching and instruction in his diocese,
4. the state of the public libraries

This letter I began and dated from the convent of the Augustinians, 25th January 1808. I shall probably print it before I leave Point de Galle.

'My visit at Goa has excited a very general alarm among the priests. The Viceroy wishes success to my endeavours. The English at Goa seemed to know little or nothing about the subject. The whole Catholic body there are awed by it and it was said that some would suffer in consequence of my visit for Major B and others of the Viceroy's household were known to furnish me with every information in their power. But at last I perceived that even B himself, the philosophic liberal learned B, was cowed and endeavoured to draw off.'

On quitting his friend Josephus a Doloribus whose favour and forbearance had perhaps been conciliated by the present of a small purse of moidores previously to his admission into the *santa casa*, Buchanan confesses in his letter to Mr Brown that his own mind was much agitated. 'I began to perceive,' he says, 'a cowardly fear of remaining longer in the power of the Inquisitors. My servants had repeatedly urged me to go and I set off about twelve 'o clock not less indignant at the Inquisition of Goa than I had been with the temple of Juggernaut.'

Dr Buchanan's great object in this as in all his researches was not so much the gratification of personal curiosity as the discovery of useful and important information with a view to the detection and the removal of spiritual and moral evils. The suggestion in the published extracts from his journal as to the propriety of an interference on the part of the British government with that of Portugal for the abolition of the dreadful tribunal of the Inquisition had been happily anticipated, but did not render his animated appeal upon that subject superfluous while his inquiries, relative to the moral and religious state of the Romish and Syro-Romish churches on the coast of Malabar, led to efforts to disseminate the Holy Scriptures, for the instruction and illumination of that numerous and long neglected body of Christians.

'In two hours,' continues Dr Buchanan in his letter to Mr Brown, 'I reached New Goa. The alarm of my investigations had gone before me. The English came to inquire what I had seen and heard and I told them all. I staid a day or two with them and embarked in a pattamar (an open boat) for Bombay.'

'Most regular and exemplary in their manners...'

Denis L. Cottineau de Kloguen

Pangi and the neighbouring villages

Pangi, the residence of the Viceroy, or Governor, ever since the administration of Emanuel Saldanha de Albuquerque, Count of Ega, who governed Portuguese India, from 1758 to 1765, as we have said, is now a very handsome town, about three miles west of Goa; all the houses, well-built, and having generally one story above the ground floor, are always kept white and clean, and have the doors and window frames painted green, and several of them have balconies; the streets are pretty broad, and some are paved; the Viceroy's palace is close to the water, and it is no higher than the other houses, and has not much external appearance; but it is large and has very fine rooms in the inside, both for the lodging of the Governor, and for the different public offices; the other public buildings, are a large and fine church, with good revenues, the custom-house, barracks, and a gaol; the number of communicants in the parish amounts to 2,000 and the number of strangers including Pagans and Mahometans, is supposed to be 6,000; so that the whole population may amount to about 9,000, besides the troops.

The village of Ribander is between Pangi and Pannely. It is much inferior to either, but has still several good houses and a large church; it is in this village that the chief civil and criminal court or tribunal of the colony is established, and which has, under its immediate jurisdiction, the whole island of Goa, and the other neighbouring islands; it receives appeals from the two other tribunals of Salsette and Bardes.

The village of St. Agnes, west of Pangi, is trifling. It is only remarkable for its Archiepiscopal palace, which we have already mentioned, and the artillery quarters and barracks.

The Goa clergy

The Goa clergy are very poor…They are in general most regular and exemplary in their manners, and the performance of their functions, by which it is evident that there must have been a very great reform among them, since near a century, if the accounts, which old travellers give, of the Goa priests of their times, be not false, or at least greatly exaggerated; they now all wear the clerical robe, or cassock, and the clerical cap, and are never seen out of their houses in any other dress.

They are far from being so ignorant as the English generally before them to be. They cannot, it is true, explain the Latin poets, and high-prose writers, as well as it is done at Oxford and Cambridge, and many of them perhaps cannot do it at all; but they can all explain not only their office, their philosophy and divinity, and other Latin church books, but likewise, the easy authors, as Cornelius Nepos, &c, with perhaps more facility than Englishmen in general; and they have much more facility chiefly in talking, and few among them are incapable of keeping up conversation in Latin. If some Englishmen cannot understand them, it is entirely owing to their own way of pronouncing that language, which is unintelligible to all other European nations; as for one who pronounces the Latin after the French manner, (which I do not, however, pretend to be the true pronunciation, no more than that of the Portuguese), he understands them perfectly. I have always been able to converse with all the Goa priests that I have found and we have always understood each other perfectly well; there is not the least possible doubt, that it would be the same case, if they had to speak Latin with Spaniards, Italians, Germans and even Scotchmen. Besides the Latin language, they all possess a perfect grammatical knowledge of the Portuguese, and an acquaintance with the country language, and are able to preach in both with equal ease; they know their philosophy and divinity, as well in general, as the mass of the French clergy; who have of all Catholic clergymen, been those who have escaped the reproach of ignorance, even from their enemies. But it must be owned that in history, geography, and the sciences, they are generally deficient, and know very little of the manners of other countries. As it is to be wished, on the one hand, that they should retain their honesty and simplicity of manners, and stick firmly to all their good habits, it should be likewise desirable on the other that they should study a little history, and the manners of other nations, which would divest them of many prejudices, and persuade them that many usages may be equally good, and, perhaps, better than those of Goa, and thus render them much more interesting in society. This would also have the good effect of clearing them in the eyes of foreigners, of the accusation of total ignorance, which they are too often, but most unjustly taxed with.

We have already sufficiently spoken of the monks, or regular clergy.

Inquisition

In the course of less than fifty years, all the inhabitants of Salsette embraced Christianity, and 28 parishes were erected therein. In this same year (1560) was founded the too celebrated tribunal of the Inquisition, against which so much has been written and said. Though we are very far from justifying its proceedings, we are at the same time obliged to declare, that many falsehoods and exaggerations have been advanced respecting it. It must be owned, it is true, first, that this tribunal, both in Spain and Portugal, greatly degenerated from its original institution; secondly, that many of its forms were extremely vicious and cruel; though it might be observed at the same time, particularly, as to the tortures it inflicted, that it had them in common with all the civil tribunals existing in the time it was erected; and thirdly, that the governors, powerful men, and the corrupted part of the clergy, took too often advantage of the vicious way in which justice was administered in that tribunal, to satisfy their private vengeance and hatred, as it evident in the case of Dellon, and of several other persons whom he mentions. But, on the other hand, it must be confessed, that the cruelties of that tribunal have been greatly exaggerated; whereas, we see in the first place, that the Inquisitions, during the greatest part of the time, sincerely desired to save the lives of their prisoners, and that at every Acto de Fe, of the great number of the accused and supposed convicts, very few suffered death, and almost all of these were strangled before they were burnt; secondly, that the greatest care was taken of the lives, health, and cleanliness of the prisoners, at a time when all the public prisons, in almost all Christian countries, were kept in a most wretched and inhumane state; thirdly, that the rigours of the Inquisition were never exercised but against Christians, and not even against individuals out of the Catholic communion, unless they relapsed, and that they never forced any one either to embrace Christianity or to become a Catholic. Thus much have we said to shew our entire impartiality, but by no means to approve the institution itself, nor to excuse it from all that has been advanced against it; it is merely to correct false and unwarranted statements, which can have no other effect than that of leading the readers into erronous opinions, and of propagating falsehood, a thing always very blameable, whatever may be the intentions of the authors of it.

Population

The whole Christian population under the Portuguese sway, and under the immediate dependence of the Governor of Goa, is reckoned to amount to 380,000, and the Pagan and Mahometans to about 100,000, making a total of 480,000; which, with the transient population, the small, but still kept up, introduction of slaves from Mosambique, and the new acquisition of Aldeas in the new provinces, may make in all half a million of souls.

Distinction of classes or castes

Although the Indians of Goa, in embracing Christianity, have not retained, like those of the Jesuit and Pondicherry Missions, all those distinctions of castes and ancient usages of Paganism, which have been considered indifferent to religion, they nevertheless keep up that distinction only in respect to marriages, which are most generally, though not always, contracted between members of the same castes; these castes may therefore be now considered as the different tribes into which the ancient Israelites were divided.

The first class or caste is that of the Europeans, or their children, born in the country, without the probable intention of remaining in it. This class is very small, and confined to the Viceroy, or Governor, and some of his Subalterns, as well as some officers of the army, a few seamen, the Archbishop, and a very few clergymen and monks, and lastly a few soldiers, who marry in the country, and whose children are immediately numbered in the second or mixed class.

The second class is that called the mistiss, or mixed class, very much similar to that called among the English, Indo-Britons, though it has a more extensive comprehension, than that term; for it includes even natives of pure European blood, but established in the country since the first generation; these families, although considered in Portugal on the same level with Europeans, and though all Fidalgos, or noble men, according to the use introduced into Portuguese India from the origin, are nevertheless comprehended by the Goanese into the mixed race, because, as they say: 'If there is no mixture of blood, there is a mixture of air'; these families, all very respectable, are not numerous. After these, come all those who are of the mixed European and Indian blood and who are much more numerous and the greater part poor. The second class, however, is still the smallest after the pure Europeans; those descended only from European parents, though after several generations, differ very little in complexion from the Portuguese of Europe; the others have a lighter or deeper shade, according to the proportion of Indian blood they have in them.

The third class or caste, is that of the Brahmins; they are held in high esteem and consideration, though excluded from the greatest privileges of the Europeans and their descendants, which consists chiefly in holding the most important situations, as those of Viceroys, Governors of Subordinate Colonies, Archbishops, Deans, &c.; since, however, representatives of the colonies have been sent to the Cortes at Lisbon, Brahmins, Chardos, and even Sudras, have been admitted as candidates, and some have been elected. The Brahmins are the less numerous Indian caste, but much more numerous, indeed, than the two preceding put together.

The fourth class or caste is that of the Chardos, who, like the Rajpoots and Parvos, in other parts of India, pretend to be of the Chatria, or royal and military caste, (though many authors maintain that that caste, as well as that of the Vaisias, is now extinct.) This caste in the colony of Goa, is more numerous than that of the Brahmins, and held in equal estimation, though inferior with respect to rank.

The fifth class is that of the Soodras or Sudras, which, as in other parts of India, forms by far the greatest part of the population. In this colony, the Sudras are more numerous than all the other Christian inhabitants, both of the superior and inferior castes. They are not so much respected as the Brahmins and Chardos; and formerly were not even admitted to holy orders, but that and all the other privileges of the two superior tribes, are now concealed to them, though they are not by far held in the same estimation.

The sixth class is that of the inferior Sudras, who follow the profession of fishermen and other viler occupations, called Corombis, Franzas, &c., and likewise the out-castes. They are similar to the Parias in the southern provinces of India, or to the coolies and other low castes in the north. They are, however, not treated with the same contempt as among the heathens; but they must remain in their own professions, and are not admitted to any place of trust whatsoever, which are held not only by the higher, but ordinary servants, who are all of the superior castes; though reduced by poverty to serve, in order to gain their livelihood.

The slaves of Mosambique may be considered as the last Christian caste. They are employed like the preceding. As to the Pagan Hindoos, it would be foreign to the plan of this sketch, to enter into any details concerning them; as their manners and distinctions of castes, are the same as those of the rest of Concan, which are sufficiently known from other English accounts.

The Mahometans, though generally everywhere throughout India, are in the proportion of one to ten Hindoos, are still in smaller proportion in this colony; there are besides them some few Parsees, chiefly at Pangi.

The members of the five superior tribes, very rarely marry out of their own castes, except the soldiers and some few Europeans of distinction, who may, but very rarely, enter into the bonds of matrimony with some descendants of pure European blood. It sometimes, however, happens that men of one caste take wives from the inferior ones, and the children in such cases retain the caste of their father; but never will a man of a superior caste give his daughter in marriage to a man of an inferior one; and generally such mixed marriages take place between a man and a woman of the caste immediately following that of the man in inferiority. Except in regard to marriages, the five superior castes agree in most things; they make not the least difficulty of eating together, and of concurring in all the other circumstances of civil life; they likewise make no distinction of food whatever.

General observations on the manners of the Goanese

All the ancient travellers expatiate, with what justice it is not easy to ascertain, on the corruption of manners of the inhabitants of Goa, on the profligacy and jealousy of the men, the no less immorality of the women, the frequency of murders, &c. It is certain that the authors of the life of St. Francis Xavier themselves, though Portuguese, give a dreadful account of the state of morals in Goa, at the arrival of that celebrated missionary, who, however, in a little time, operated a thorough change for the better, but matters may have afterwards again retaken their old way; yet, howsoever they may have been in the flourishing state of this settlement, it would be very unjust and contrary to truth, to think, that there are still remains of that ancient corruption of manners. On the contrary it would be difficult to find a community of the same number of individuals, pursuing a more regular, tranquil and moral conduct, than that of the present inhabitants of Goa; very seldom, indeed, does there happen any misconduct among the females, not only of the first respectability, but of the great majority of the population. If some of the young men behave, as too many of the other countries do, and which is difficult to suppose never to be the case in any place, they at least take great care to conceal the disorder in their conduct; quarrels are very rare, and murders, or even duels are still more so; the least regulated in their demeanours are the European soldiers who settle in the colony; except these and a few others, chiefly Europeans, I have been well assured that all, without exception, perform their annual confessions and receive their Easter Communions, a circumstance, which, whatever others may think of it, I have found in all the Catholic countries I have been in, to be a very great, if not, an absolute proof of the rest of the private conduct of the people being as it should be.

There are very few rich families in this colony, and no fortune exceeds an annual income of 20,000 rupees. If there be two or three amounting to what it is all that can be expected, all the others fall far short of it, and the vast majority, even of those accounted considerable do not exceed two thousand rupees; those of one thousand are still more numerous; and the income of those families, who are deemed in easy circumstances, though not rich, amount to between five hundred and six hundred rupees. It is supposed that a quarter of a rupee, or half Pardao, is sufficient for the decent maintenance of a single individual; but four fifths at least of the population are truly poor and miserable. Hence, as it is well known, a great part of all the castes, exercise the functions of servants, for which, many receive only one rupee, or at most two or three rupees a month. Many now go to Bombay, and to other parts of the Presidency where they find the exercise of their professions more profitable; the cooks, chiefly of all the Europeans and easy inhabitants at the Presidency, are almost all natives of Goa; they, however, seldom go to Bengal, Madras, or the Eastern Coast in order to keep near their native land, as much as possible they return to, visit it, some every year, some less often; many even marry in Goa, leaving their wives in the houses of their fathers-in-law, going every now then to see them, and bringing them a part of the fruit of their labour; some, who are fortunate enough, find situations in Bombay, and other stations of that part of India, as writers, and guardians of the sick in the hospitals.

The families, who remain in the colony, are given up to agriculture, or live upon their rents; they are a pretty good number exercising the profession of lawyers, and physicians; some are shop-keepers in the towns, but there are hardly any regular merchants. In every family, that can afford it, one of the boys at least, takes to the church, from indolence, which is perhaps the greatest reproach that can now be cast on the Goanese.

All the men wear the European dress, and use their black coats, much oftener than many British residents in India. It is sometimes very odd to see, in the middling class, men with cloth coats, waistcoats, short breeches, and shoes, without stockings. The poorest of the men, except the slaves, wear a shirt, jacket, and breeches, without hats or shoes. The women, in rich and easy circumstances, dress after the actual European fashion; some also of the latter, use the old Portuguese dress, consisting of a plain linen cap, long waistcoats, thick silk striped petticoats, made of those stuffs which are manufactured throughout Guzerat, and large and thick black veils over their heads, like the Mahratta Christian women, of the islands of Bombay and Salsette, which does not much differ from that of the Indians, having rings or bracelets in their ankles and wrists, and part of their legs bare. When they go to church, they wrap themselves up in a large piece of white linen as a veil and overall.

The food of the poorer sort, consists chiefly in rice, fish, plantains, other fruits, and some cakes of flour; they do not eat meat more than three or four times a year; they season their dishes with ghee, or clarified butter, after the manner of the Indians; curry is their principal dish, and rice congee is their only morning and evening meal; cocoanut water enters in almost every thing they eat.

Rich and easy families take their breakfast between seven and eight, after hearing Mass; it now chiefly consists of tea, bread, and butter, and sometimes coffee; some, however, keep to the old way of eating rice congee; between twelve and one, dinner is taken. The riches have soup, and boiled and roast meat, and always finish by rice and curry before the dessert, which consists of cakes and sweetmeats; they drink Madeira, Lisbon and other Portuguese wines; those less easy take no soup, but never omit the curry, and they drink urraca; they have a particular way of dressing rice, which is very much like the Turkish pilow; the use of sleeping after dinner is universal. At four they drink plain tea, some adding cakes and biscuits; the supper is taken at eight, and chiefly consists of fish curry and rice; very few eat flesh meat; they are all in general very fond of smoking, and many even among the women.

The only kind of conveyances for the rich, are palkies, or rather covered manchils and boats; as navigation can be carried on to almost every part of the colony, by means of the numerous rivers and streams.

Their only amusements consist in visits, playing at cards, and sometimes drafts and balls; the other great rendezvous, takes place only at church, on religious festivals. After the morning service, a small fair is held near the door of the church, consisting of articles of crockery, cutlery, small looking glasses, rosaries, sweetmeats and cakes; in every family there is on that day, a more plentiful and ceremonious meal.

These are the informations which I have been able to collect, concerning the history and present state of the colony of Goa.

'Intolerably dirty and disagreeable'

Richard F. Burton

The black Christians, like the whites, may be subdivided into two orders; first, the converted Hindoos; secondly, the mixed breed of European and Indian blood. Moreover, these latter have another distinction, being either Brahman Christians, as they ridiculously term themselves, on account of their descent from the Hindoo pontifical caste, or common ones. The only perceptible difference between them is, we believe, a moral one; the former are justly renowned for extraordinary deceitfulness and treachery. They consider themselves superior to the latter in point of dignity, and anciently enjoyed some peculiar privileges, such as the right of belonging to the orders of the Theatins, or regular clerks, and Saint Philip Nerius. But in manners, appearance, customs and education, they exactly resemble the mass of the community.

The Mestici, or mixed breed, composes the great mass of society at Goa; it includes all classes, from the cook to the government official. In 1835 one of them rose to the highest post of dignity, but his political career was curt and remarkably unsuccessful. Some half-castes travel in Europe, a great many migrate to Bombay for service and commerce, but the major part stays at Goa to stock professions, and support the honour of the family. It would be, we believe, difficult to find in Asia an uglier or more degraded-looking race than that which we are now describing. The forehead is low and flat, the eyes small, quick and restless; there is a mixture of sensuality and cunning about the region of the mouth, and a development of the lower part of the face which are truly unprepossessing, not to say revolting. Their figures are short and small, with concave chests, the usual calfless Indian leg, and a remarkable want of muscularity.

In personal attractions the fair sex is little superior to the other. During the whole period of our stay at Goa we scarcely ever saw a pretty half-caste girl. At the same time we must confess that it is difficult to pronounce judgement upon this point, as women of good mixed family do not appear before casual visitors. And this is of course deemed a sign of superior modesty and chastity, for the black Christians, Asiatically enough, believe it impossible for a female to converse with a strange man and yet be virtuous. The dark ladies affect the old Portuguese costume…; a few of the wealthiest dress like Europeans. Their education is purposely neglected—a little reading of their vernacular tongue, with the Ave and other prayers in general use, dancing, embroidery, and making sweetmeats, are considered satis superque in the way of accomplishments. Of late years, a girls' school has been established by order of government at Panjim, but a single place of the kind is scarcely likely to affect the mass of the community. The life led by the fair sex at Goa must be, one would think, a dull one. Domestic occupations, smoking, a little visiting, and going to church, especially on the ferie, or festivals, lying in bed, sitting en deshabille, riding about in a mancheel, and an occasional dance—such are the blunt weapons with which they attack Time. They marry early, begin to have a family probably at thirteen, are old women at twenty-two, and decrepit at thirty-five. Like Indians generally, they appear to be defective in amativeness, abundant in philopregenitiveness, and therefore not much addicted to intrigues. At the same time we must record the fact, that the present archbishop has been obliged to issue an order forbidding nocturnal processions, which, as they were always crowded with lady devotees, gave rise to certain obstinate scandals.

The mongrel men dress as Europeans, but the quantity of clothing diminishes with the wearer's rank. Some of the lower orders, especially in the country, affect a full-dress costume, consisting in toto, of a cloth jacket and black silk knee breeches. Even the highest almost always wear coloured clothes, as, by so doing, the washerman is less required. They are intolerably dirty and disagreeable—verily, cleanliness ought to be made an article of faith in the East. They are fond of spirituous liquors, and seldom drink, except honestly for the purpose of intoxication. As regards living, they follow the example of their white fellow-subjects in all points, except that they eat more rice and less meat. Their characters may be briefly described as passionate and cowardly, jealous and revengeful, with more of the vices than the virtues belonging to the two races from which they are descended. In early youth, especially before arriving at years of puberty, they evince a remarkable acuteness of mind, and facility in acquiring knowledge. They are equally quick at learning languages, and the lower branches of mathematical study, but they seem unable to obtain any results from their acquirements. Goa cannot boast of ever having produced a single eminent literato, or even a second-rate poet. To sum up in a few words, the mental and bodily development of this class are remarkable only as being a strange mélange of European and Asiatic peculiarities, of antiquated civilization and modern barbarism.

We before alluded to the deep-rooted antipathy between the black and the white population: the feeling of the former towards an Englishman is one of dislike not unmingled with fear. Should Portugal ever doom her now worse than useless colony to form part payment of her debts, their fate would be rather a hard one. Considering the wide spread of perhaps too liberal opinions concerning the race quaintly designated as 'God's images carved in ebony', they might fare respectably as regards public estimation, but scarcely well enough to satify their inordinate ambition. It is sufficiently amusing to hear a young gentleman, whose appearance, manners, and colour fit him admirably to become a band-boy to some Sepoy corps, talk of visiting Bombay, with letters of introduction to the Governor and Commander-in-chief. Still more diverting it is when you know that the same character would invariably deduct a perquisite from the rent of any house he may have procured, or boat hired for a stranger. Yet at the same time it is hard for a man who speaks a little English, French, Latin and Portuguese to become the lower clerk of some office on the paltry pay of 70£ per annum; not is it agreeable for an individual who has just finished his course of mathematics, medicine, and philosophy to sink into the lowly position of an assistant apothecary in the hospital of a native regiment. No wonder that the black Indo-Portuguese is an utter radical; he has gained much by Constitution, the 'dwarfish demon' which sets everybody by the ears at Goa. Hence it is that he will take the first opportunity in conversation with a foreigner to extol Lusitanian liberty to the skies, abuse English tyranny over, and insolence to, their unhappy Indian subjects, and descent delightedly upon the probability of an immediate crash in our Eastern empire. And, as might be expected, although poverty sends forth thousands of black Portuguese to earn money in foreign lands, they prefer the smallest competence at home, where equality allows them to indulge in a favourite independence of manner utterly at variance with our Anglo-Indian notions concerning the proper demeanour of a native towards a European.

The native Christian is originally a converted Hindoo, usually of the lower castes; and though he has changed for centuries his manners, dress, and religion, he retains to a wonderful extent the ideas, prejudices, and superstitions of his ancient state. The learned griff, Bishop Heber, in theorizing upon the probable complexion of our First Father, makes a remark about these people, so curiously erronous, that it deserves to be mentioned. 'The Portuguese have, during a three hundred years' residence in India, become as black as Caffres; surely this goes far to disprove the assertion which is sometimes made, that climate alone is insufficient to account for the difference between the Negro and the European.' Climate in this case had nothing whatever to do with the change of colour. And if it had, we might instance as an argument against the universality of such atmospheric action, the Parsee, who, though he has been settled in the tropical lands of India for more than double three hundred years, is still, in appearance, complexion, voice, and manners, as complete an Iranian as when he first fled from his native mountains. But this is par parenthèse.

The native Christians of Goa always shave the head; they cultivate an apology for a whisker, but never allow the beard or mustachios to grow. Their dress is scanty in the extreme, often consisting only of a dirty rag, worn about the waist, and their ornaments, a string of beads round the neck. The women are equally badly clothed: the single long piece of cotton, called in India a saree, is their whole attire, consequently the bosom is unsupported and uncovered. This race is decidedly the lowest in the scale of civilized humanity we have yet seen. In appearance they are short, heavy, meagre, and very dark; their features are uncomely in the extreme; they are dirtier than Pariahs, and abound in cutaneous diseases. They live principally on fish and rice, with pork and fruit when they can afford such luxuries. Meat as well as bread is holiday diet; clarified butter, rice, water, curry, and cocoa-nut milk are everyday food.

These people are said to be short-lived, the result of hard labour, early marriages, and innutritious food. We scarcely ever saw a man that looked fifty. In disposition they resemble the half-castes, but they are even more deficient in spirit, and quarrelsome withal, than their 'whity-brown' brethren. All their knowledge is religious, and consists only of a few prayers in corrupt Mahratta, taught them by their parents or the priest; these they carefully repeat three times per diem—at dawn, in the afternoon, and before retiring to rest. Loudness of voice and a very Puritanical snuffle being sine qua none in their devotional exercises, the neighbourhood of a pious family is anything but pleasant. Their superiority to the heathen around them consists in eating pork, drinking toddy to excess, shaving the face, never washing, and a conviction that they are going to paradise, whereas all other religionists are emphatically not. They are employed as sepoys, porters, fishermen, seamen, labourers, mancheel bearers, workmen and servants, and their improvident indolence renders the necessity of hard labour at times imperative. The carpenters, farriers, and other trades, not only ask an exorbitant sum for working, but also, instead of waiting on the employer, scarcely ever fail to keep him waiting for them. For instance, on Monday you wanted a farrier, and sent for him. He politely replied that he was occupied at the moment, but would call at his earliest convenience. This, if you keep up a running fire of messages, will probably be about the next Saturday.

The visitor will not find at Goa that number and variety of heathen castes which bewilder his mind at Bombay. The capital of Portuguese India now stands so low amongst the cities of Asia that few or no inducements are offered to the merchant and the trader, who formerly crowded her ports. The Turk, the Arab, and the Persian have left them for a wealthier mart, and the only strangers are a few Englishmen, who pass through the place to visit its monuments of antiquity.

The Moslem population at Panjim scarcely amounts to a thousand. They have no place of worship, although their religion is now, like all others, tolerated. The distinctive mark of the Faithful is the long beard. They appear superior beings by the side of the degenerate native Christians.

Next to the Christians, the Hindoos are the most numerous portion of the Community. They are held in the highest possible esteem and consideration, and no office unconnected with religion is closed to them. This fact may account for the admirable ease and freedom of manner prevalent amongst them. The Gentoo will enter your room with his slippers on, sit down after shaking hands as if the action were a matter of course, chew his betel, and squirt the scarlet juice all over the floor; in a word, make himself as offensive as you can conceive. But at Goa all men are equal. Moreover, the heathens may be seen in Christian churches, with covered feet, pointing at, putting questions concerning, and criticising the images with the same quite-at-home nonchalance with which they would wander through the porticoes of Dwarka or the pagodas of Aboo. And these men's fathers, in the good old times of Goa, were not allowed ever to burn their dead in the land!

In appearance the Hindoos are of a fair, or rather a light yellow complexion. Some of the women are by no means deficient in personal charms, and the men generally surpass in size and strength the present descendants of the Portuguese heroes. They wear the mustachio, but not the beard, and dress in the long cotton coat, with the cloth wound round the waist, very much the same as in Bombay. The head, however, is usually covered with a small red velvet skullcap, instead of a turban. The female attire is the saree, with the long-armed bodice beneath it; their ornaments are numerous; and their caste is denoted by a round spot of kunkun, or vermilion, upon the forehead between the eyebrows.

As usual among Hindoos, the pagans at Goa are divided into a number of sub-castes. In the Brahmans we find two great subdivisions: the Sashteekar, or inhabitants of Salsette, and the Bardeskar, or people of Bardes. The former is confessedly superior to the latter. Both families will eat together, but they do not intermarry. Besides these two, there are a few of the Chitpawan, Sinart, Kararee and Waishnau castes of the pontifical order.

The Brahmans always wear the tika, or sectarian mark, perpendicularly, to distinguish them from the Sonars, or Goldsmiths, who place it horizontally on the forehead. They are but superficially educated, as few of them know Sanscrit, and these few not well. All read and write Mahratta fluently, but they speak the inharmonious Concanee dialect.

Next to the Brahmans, and resembling them in personal appearance, are the Banyans, or traders. They seem to be a very thriving portion of the population, and live in great comfort, if not luxury.

The Shudra, or servile class of Hindus, is, of course, by far the most numerous; it contains many varieties, such as Bhandan (toddy-makers), Koonbee (potters), Hajjam (barbers), etc.

Of mixed castes we find the goldsmith, who is descended from a Brahman father and servile mother, and the Kunchanee, or Etuign, whose maternal parent is always a Maharatta woman, whatever the other progenitor may chance to be. The outcastes are principally Chamars, or tanners, and Parwars (Pariahs).

These Hindoos very rarely become Christians, now that fire and steel, the dungeon and the rack, the rice-pot and the rupee, are not allowed to play the persuasive part in the good work formerly assigned to them. Indeed, we think that conversion of the heathen is almost more common in British than in Portuguese India, the natural result of being able to pay the proselytes more liberally. When such an event does occur at Goa, it is celebrated at a church in the north side of the creek, opposite Panjim, with all the pomp and ceremony due to the importance of spoiling a good Gentoo by making a bad Christian of him.

We were amused to witness on one occasion a proof of the high importance attached to Hindoo opinion in this part of the world. Outside the church of St. Agnes, in a little chapel, stood one of the lowest orders of black priests, lecturing a host of naked, squatting, smoking and chattering auditors. Curiosity induced us to venture nearer, and we then discovered that the theme was a rather imaginative account of the birth and life of the Redeemer. Presently a group of loitering Gentoos, who had been strolling about the church, came up and stood by our side.

The effect of their appearance upon his Reverence's discourse was remarkable, as may be judged from the peroration, which was very much in these words:

> You must remember, sons, that the avatár, or incarnation of your blessed Lord, was in the form of a rajah, who ruled millions of men. He was truly great and powerful; he rode the largest elephant ever trapped; he smoked a hookah of gold, and when he went to war he led an army the like of which for courage, numbers, and weapons was never seen before. He would have conquered the whole world, from Portugal to China, had he not been restrained by humility. But, on the last day, when he shall appear even in greater state than before, he will lead us his people to most glorious and universal victory.

When the sermon concluded, and the listeners had wandered away in different directions, we walked up to his Reverence and asked him if he had ever read the Gospel.

'Of course.'

'Then where did you find the historical picture you so graphically drew just now about the rajah-ship?'

'Where?' said the fellow, grinning and pointing to his forehead, 'here, to be sure. Didn't you see those Gentoos standing by and listening to every word I was saying? A pretty thing it would have been to see the pagans laughing and sneering at us Christians because the Founder of our Blesed Faith was the son of a Burhaee (carpenter).'

Such reasoning was conclusive.

If our memory serve us aright, there is a story somewhat like the preceding in the pages of the Abbé Dubois. Such things we presume must constantly be taking place in different parts of India. On one occasion we saw an unmistakable Lakhshmi borne in procession amongst Christian images, and, if history be trusted, formerly it was common to carry as many Hindoo deities as European saints in the palanquins. On the other hand, many a Gentoo has worn a crucifix for years, with firm faith in the religious efficacy of the act, yet utterly ignorant of the nature of the symbol he was bearing and we have ourselves written many and many a charm for ladies desirous of becoming prolific, or matrons fearful of the evil eye being cast upon their offspring.

'A flourishing city...gradually swept away'

Jose Nicolau da Fonseca

Chapter IV

In the early 17th century, the population was composed of men of different races and creeds. There were, according to Linschoten, merchants from Arabia, Armenia, Persia, Cambay, Bengal, Pegu, Siam, Malacca, Java, the Moluccas, China, and various other Eastern countries. There were Venetians, Italians, Germans, Flemings, Castilians, and Englishmen, but scarcely any Frenchmen. There was at this time a considerable number of Musalmans, though in the first few years of the Portuguese rule thay had been almost banished from the city. There were also Jews, who had their own synagogues and their own mode of worship, but the Hindus were not allowed the public exercise of their religion. The population of the suburbs must have been considerable, but we have no data from which to calculate the exact number.

The aspect of the city at this time is described by travellers in such glowing terms as to justify the appellation of 'Goa Dourada' ('Golden Goa') which was given to it, and the proverb '*Quem vio Goa excusa de vér Lisboa,*' i.e., 'Whoever has seen Goa need not see Lisboa.' Pyrard writes about it as follows:

> It is about a hundred and ten years since the Portuguese made themselves masters of this island of Goa, and I have often wondered at the rapidity with which the Portuguese have been able to rear stately edifices, so many churches, convents, palaces, fortresses, and other buildings, after the European fashion; at the internal order,

regulations, and government which they have established, and at the power to which they have attained, everything being managed as in Lisbon itself. This city is the metropolis of the whole of the Portuguese dominions in India, and as such it commands considerable power, wealth, and celebrity. The Viceroy has his residence there, and keeps his court in the style of the King himself. Next in rank to the Viceroy is the Archbishop; we have then the functionaries of the High Court and those of the Inquisition; besides the Archbishop there is also a Bishop, so that the city is the chief seat of religion and justice in India, and every religious order has its superior there. All ships, both of war and commerce, belonging to the King of Spain (to whom Portugal was at that time subject) set sail from that port... As for the multitude of people, it is a marvel to see the number which go and come every day by sea and land on business of every kind. The princes of India who are on terms of peace and friendship with the Portuguese have almost all of them their ordinary ambassadors there, and often send extraordinary embassies to treat for peace; and the Portuguese also send theirs on their part. And as to the merchants continually going and coming from different parts of the East, one would say that a fair was being held every day for the sale of all sorts of merchandise, and even those princes who are not at peace with the Portuguese do not fail to send their goods and merchandise to Goa through the merchants who are on friendly terms with them...Thus, whoever has been in Goa may say that he has seen the choicest rarities of India, for it is the most famous and celebrated city, on account of its commercial intercourse with people of all nationalities of the East, who bring there the products of their respective countries, articles of merchandize, necessaries of life, and other commodities in great abundance, because every year more than a thousand ships touch there laden with cargo.

The city was intersected with numerous streets, many of which were paved with stones; in the rainy season some of them became impassable; no carriages were seen; in their stead palanquins were used, borne on the shoulders of Boyes. Besides the Rua Direita, the road frequented by merchants, there were many other roads, which were called after the names of the classes of people who resided in them, sometimes also after the nature of the traffic carried on there, so that a traveller says, 'It is a great convenience that when anything is needed it is possible to know where to find it.' Linschoten describes some of the streets in which pagan merchants lived, many of whom were very rich, having eighty or a hundred thousand escus (about £ 20,000). There was one street, says he, full of shops which were crowded not only with cotton and silk dresses and China porcelain, but also with velvet and other piece-goods of Portugal; on the opposite side were other shops where clothes of all sorts and ready-made shirts were sold, for the use not only of the Portuguese, but also of slaves and poor people. In another street lived those who sold wearing apparel and ornaments worn by ladies. The Banniyas were found in another street with goods of Cambay and precious stones, and were, according to the Dutch traveller, very clever in perforating pearls and corals. There was another street for those who made beds, chairs, and other articles of joinery, which were covered with *laca*, or hard wax, of various colours, presenting a goodly appearance. The goldsmiths and other artizans had their separate streets; and those who collected rents and taxes and acted as brokers had their own square, as had also the pharmaceutics, druggists and petty shopkeepers. There were streets and open squares or bazaars where fowls, fruits and other eatables imported from the neighbouring continent were sold in such abundance that, according to one of the travellers, provisions were there cheaper than in any other part of the world, and 'what in France cost fifty *sols* cost less than five in Goa'; in fact 'a man could maintain himself with one *tanga* or five *sols* (2d.) a month'. These and other comforts probably induced Ralph Fitch to say, notwithstanding his sufferings at Goa, that even if he returned home, he would come back to Goa again.

The buildings along the principal thoroughfare were in general spacious and good-looking; whilst in the interior of the city, far from the noise and bustle of the streets, were to be seen splendid mansions, surrounded by gardens tastefully laid out. Both the houses and mansions were not more than two stories high. There were built of stone and mortar, and covered with tiles. The stone required for ordinary buildings was procured from quarries in the island itself, but for constructing columns and other delicate work it was ordered from Bassein. The houses were painted red or white both outside and inside; they had large staircases and beautiful windows furnished with jetties (*sacadas*). Instead of glass panes the windows had thin polished oyster-shells fitted into wooden frame-work, as is still the fashion in Goa, and were provided with lattice-work, to enable the Portuguese ladies to enjoy the view outside without being exposed to the public gaze. The inner apartments were sufficiently large to admit of free ventilation, and were moreover richly furnished; and there was an attempt at neatness and elegance which lent quite a pleasing aspect to the interior of a dwelling. The principal nobility and gentry had not only their mansions in the city, but also their villas in the suburbs, where they resided occasionally with their families, amidst orchards and groves, bowers and grottos, walks beautifully laid out, and fountains fantastically playing. Here they gave themselves up to mirth and pleasure, whiling away the time in gossiping, sporting, or playing, reclining on sofas or lolling in chairs, attended by slaves who ministered to their comfort and convenience, some fanning them, others entertaining them with the dulcet sounds of music.

There were no hotels or inns in the city; but there were boarding-houses open to the public, and frequented principally by the lower classes. There were also gaming houses with saloons and chambers most sumptuously furnished, and elegantly decorated. These houses were subject to a licence tax, and were crowded with people of all classes, who repaired thither to enjoy their leisure hours. Those who were inordinately fond of gambling stayed there sometimes for days together, and were provided with board and lodging. They played generally at cards, dice, chess and ball; and whilst they were playing, there were fair damsels ready to entertain them with music and dancing, jugglers to astonish them with their tricks, and buffoons to amuse them with low jests and ridiculous pranks.

It is impossible in a cursory sketch of this kind to give a very minute or detailed description of the city in its palmy days. Suffice it to say that it displayed all the activity and bustle of a great commercial city. Alluding to this circumstance, Talboys Wheeler says:

Every morning the sun rose at Goa upon scenes which may be easily realized. The sailors and coolies loading or unloading in the river; the busy shopkeepers displaying their wares; the slaves bringing in the supplies of water and provisions for the day. There was the palace of the Viceroy, surrounded by majestic Fidalgos giving and exchanging the profoundest courtesies. Many were perhaps making their way to the great hall of council, which was hung with pictures of every Viceroy and Governor from Vasco da Gama downwards. There was also the palace of the Archbishop, with a crowd of black-robed priests, missionaries, and clergy of every description, native as well as European. Besides these were the courts and offices of the king's council and chancery, with busy clerks labouring at their desks, but all in grave and stately fashion after the proud manner of the noble Portuguese. Meantime, above the noise of offices and bazaars, the bells were ever ringing from the numerous churches and monasteries, and filling the whole city with an ecclesiastical clangour.

Chapter V

To complete the sketch of the city in the days of its prosperity, a short review of the manners and customs of the Portuguese seems necessary. They called themselves fidalgos or noblemen, and never cared to follow any trade or calling. They derived the greater part of their income from the manual labour of their slaves, whose earnings were entirely at their disposal. They had abundant leisure, which they employed in various kinds of diversions, among which may be mentioned equestrian exercises, games with canes and oranges, and boat excursions. The females did not participate in these amusements, but were left at home by their husbands, whose jealousy imposed on them such restraints, that they were seldom allowed to stir out of their private apartments, and, when they did, their movements were closely watched. Such treatment brought about its natural consequences. Excluded from society, and confined within their dwelling-houses, they were not open to any of those influences which are generally at work in civilized countries in elevating the moral character.

They passed their time in idle and frivolous pursuits, in singing and playing on musical instruments, gossiping with slaves of either sex, and especially devising means to elude the vigilance of their husbands. For this purpose they generally took into their confidence those very servants who had been kept to watch their conduct, and made them willing instruments for the gratification of their evil propensities. To such an extent did they abandon themselves to these pleasures, that we are told by almost every traveller who visited Goa at this period, that they did not scruple even to stupefy their husbands with narcotic drugs, and admit their paramours into their very bedchambers; and we are further told by Linschoten, that to give zest to those pleasures they made free use of stimulants. Profligacy had become in fact the reigning vice among the higher classes, and their morals were hopelessly corrupt and depraved.

The rich fidalgos always kept a luxurious table, to which they had the generosity to admit their less fortunate countrymen. They treated their guests to a sumptuous repast, consisting of the richest wines and choicest delicacies served on glittering plate: the table literally groaned under the weight of numerous viands, which were prepared by experts in the culinary art to satisfy their fastidious taste. As they feasted, there were slaves in attendance, ready to fan them or entertain them with music. What most distinguished this luxurious mode of living was the fact, that even in the height of their merriment the Portuguese never forgot to use wine sparingly: feasting never bordered on rioting with them, a circumstance to which universal testimony is borne by almost all travellers who visited Goa at this time.

Mandelslo gives the following description of a dinner at which he and the English President of Surat were entertained by a Portuguese gentleman who was appointed Governor of Mozambique:

> One of the noblest entertainments we had, was that which was made us the 15th of January (1639) by a Portuguese lord, who had been Governor of Bacim and was then newly come to the government of Mozambique. Every course consisted only of four dishes of meat, but they were so often changed, and the meat so excellently well dressed, that I may truly say I never was at the like. For with the

meat there was brought such variety of excellent fruits, that by the continual change and intermixture of both, the appetite was sharpened and renewed. But what was most remarkable was that though the Portuguese ladies are as seldom seen as those of the Muscovite and Persians, yet this lord, knowing he could not any way more oblige the English than by allowing them the sight of women, we were served at table by four handsome young maids of Malacca, while he himself was attended by two pages and an eunuch. These maids brought in the meat and filled our wine, and though he himself drunk not any, yet would he have the English treated after their own way, and drink to what height they pleased. Being risen from table, he brought us into a spacious chamber, where he again pressed us to drink, and when the President was to take leave of him he presented him with a noble coverlet of Watte, a quilted covering for a horse, a fair table and a rich cabinet of lacque.

At home, the Portuguese were seen in a plain loose dress. They wore a shirt and fine white breeches, with a light velvet or taffeta cap for their head-dress. The women wore a sort of loose smock called *baju*, which was so thin as to prove a very insufficient covering for their persons. From the waist downwards they wore a fine cloth of cotton or silk. Both men and women bore round their necks, or carried in their hands, large rosaries, telling the beads continually in apparent devotion.

The rich made an ostentatious display of their wealth when they stirred abroad. They were borne in palanquins, or rode on horseback, attended by a large number of lackeys in gay and fanciful liveries, some holding large umbrellas over them, others bearing arms, and some carrying their cloaks, gilt chairs and soft cushions, when they went to church. The same pomp and display attended them when they happened to pass through the streets on foot. The most attractive portion of this pageantry were the gold and silver trappings of the steeds on which the fidalgos were mounted. The saddle was covered with a rich embroidered cloth, the reins were studded with precious stones with jingling silver bells attached to them, and the stirrups were of gilt silver.

The example of the rich was but too readily followed by persons of moderate and even slender means. They too tried, as far as they could, to make an imposing appearance in public; but were obliged to resort to several make-shifts and devices to maintain an air of grandeur and dignity about them. Those who lived together had a few suits of silk clothes in common. These they used by turns when they went out, and hired the services of a man to hold an umbrella over them as they strutted through the streets. In fact they walked with such a proud gait, and with such an affected air of importance, that, as a traveller remarked, one might be led to take them for gentlemen with ten thousand pounds a year.

The ladies, as stated before, rarely stirred out of their dwellings, except on festive and solemn occasions. When they went to church, they appeared in all the glory of rich and gaudy attire, with a profusion of pearls and diamonds about their persons. Pyrard gives the following interesting description of their manner of attending church:

> Rich and noble women go seldom to church, except on the principal festivals, and when they do, they appear richly dressed after the fashion of Portugal, the dress mostly of gold and silver brocade adorned with pearls, precious stones, and with jewels on the head, arms, hands, and round the waist, and they put on a veil of the finest crape in the world, which extends from head to foot. Young maidens wear veils of different colours; whilst grown-up ladies invariably use black ones. They never use stockings. Their flowing gowns sweep along the ground. The slippers or *chapins* are open on the upper part, and cover only the extremity of the foot: the lower part is embroidered with gold and silver spangles, and the upper one is studded with pearls and precious stones. They have a sole of cork nearly half a foot in height. When they go to church they are carried in palanquins adorned as richly as possible; they take with them a valuable carpet of Persia, which they call *alcatifa*, which here (in France) would be worth five hundred *escus*; they have also two or three cushions of velvet or brocade, one to recline the head against, the other to rest the legs upon. And all these are taken with them into the church by their servants, who are either Portuguese or Eurasian. They take their children too with them in the palanquin. A number of servants and slaves follow them on foot, richly attired

in silks of different colours, with large fine crape over all, which they call *mantos*. But they do not dress after the Portuguese fashion, but clothe themselves with a large piece of silk which serves them as petticoats, and have also smocks of the finest silk which they call *bájús*. Among these slaves are seen very beautiful girls of all the races inhabiting India. And it is to be remarked that the ladies are also accompanied by pages and by one or two Portuguese or Eurasian gentlemen to assist them in alighting from the palanquins: frequently, however, they are taken into the church in their palanquins, so much are they afraid of being exposed to the public view. They do not wear any mask, but paint their cheeks to a shameful degree. It is not that the ladies fear being seen, but they are forbidden by their husbands, who are too jealous of them. One of the servants or slaves brings a rich carpet; another two costly cushions; a third a China gilt chair; a fourth a velvet case containing a book, a handkerchief, and other necessary things; a fifth a very thin beautiful mattress to be spread over the carpet; and a sixth a fan and other things for the use of the mistress.

As already stated, these ladies, when they enter the church, are taken by the hand by one or two men, since they cannot walk by themselves on account of the height of the slippers, which are generally half a foot high and have the upper part open. One of these presents holy water to the lady, and she goes afterwards to take her seat some forty or fifty paces off, taking at least a good quarter of an hour to walk that distance, so slowly and majestically does she move, carrying in her hand a rosary of gold, pearls and precious stones. This they all do according to their means, and not according to their quality. When they take their children along with them, they make them walk before them. The female servants and slaves are very glad if their mistresses do not go to Mass, for then they go alone, and can pay court to their lovers; they neither expose nor accuse one another.

A still more ostentious display was made by both gentlemen and ladies at marriages and christenings. These were solemnized in after years on such a grand scale that the Government of Portugal was at length obliged to put certain restrictions on the lavish expenditure incurred on these occasions.

The marriage ceremony was generally performed in the evening. The bride and bridegroom were accompanied to church by their respective godfathers and by a large number of friends and relatives richly dressed, the gentlemen riding on horseback, and the ladies in palanquins, followed by a crowd of pages and slaves, all moving with a slow and majestic pace. The ceremony was gone through with great solemnity at church, and when it was over, the bridal party retraced their steps homewards, amidst the sound of trumpets and cornets and other musical instruments. As they passed in procession through the streets, their friends and neighbours showered on them from their windows fragrant flowers and perfumes and fancifully wrought comfits. On reaching home, the bridal pair respectfully bowed to the whole company, thanking them for their attendance, and proceeded with the ladies to the gallery, thence to enjoy the sight of sports in which their friends and relatives took part. These sports consisted principally of horse races and the common games of canes and oranges... At the same time the company were entertained with the sweetest strains of music; and when the sports were over, they were led into a hall where fruits, sweetmeats, and refreshments of every kind were served—except wine, instead of which the pure and wholesome water of Banguenim was offered, the sobriety of the Portuguese in this respect being truly admirable. The company then departed, except the nearest relations, who were afterwards treated to a sumptuous banquet.

With almost equal solemnity was the ceremony of christening performed. The new-born child was taken to the church in a palanquin by the person who was to stand as sponsor, accompanied by two servants on foot, one of whom carried a gilt salver containing a few cakes and flowers, and a wax taper curiously adorned, and having fixed on it a gold or silver coin, which was to be presented to the parish priest. The other servant carried a plate with salt, a silver ewer, and a clean napkin to be used to the occasion. A large number of the friends and kinsmen of the child's parents followed in palanquins to witness the ceremony. After the child was baptized, it was brought back home, where the same games and sports were exhibited as on the occasion of a marriage.

Chapter VI

Dr John Francis Gemelli Careri, who visited the city in 1695, writes that Goa, once the centre of all the Portuguese conquests, a place of wealth and renown, and the chief mart of the East, was now reduced to a miserable condition. It had not more than 20,000 inhabitants. The Portuguese were few, but their descendants numerous, and the mulattoes constituted almost one-fourth of the population. Many of the natives were priests, advocates, solicitors, etc. The greater part of the merchants were pagans and Muhammadans, and lived apart from the Christians. The Portuguese, although fallen from their pristine grandeur, were still vain enough to parade themselves through the lonely streets in palanquins with slaves in their train holding umbrellas over them. Such slaves were found in numbers in the city, and could be had for fifteen to twenty crowns per head.

At the period of which we are speaking, the city presented an aspect which it was truly piteous to behold. Desolation, ruin, and misery met the eye on every side. Here were whole streets deserted and abandoned. There were houses already lying in heaps of ruins or gradually crumbling to dust; whilst three-fourths of the population was fast sinking down under the pressure of want and privation; only convents and churches with a few public buildings stood out amidst this general wreck as noble and enduring monuments of the past. The Jesuit Father Francisco de Souza, in his *Oriente Conquistado*, published in 1710, exactly two centuries after the conquest of Goa by Albuquerque, calls it 'the wretched capital of a poor and miserable State, so ruined and deserted that its ancient grandeur can be guessed only from the magnificence of the convents and churches, which are yet preserved with great splendour and veneration'.

These convents and churches were no doubt the only ornaments of the city at this time. The Viceroy, the Count of Ericeira, tried, by his *alavara* of 22nd August 1719, to preserve the few houses still standing in the immediate neighbourhood of the religious buildings, and to clear the roads of the ruins that obstructed them, but to no purpose. The fate of the city was already sealed. Captain Alexander Hamilton, who was in

Goa at this time, says that the city contained beautiful churches and convents, but that, its climate being considered unhealthy, it was poorly inhabited, whilst in its suburbs, and specially on the banks of the river, magnificent mansions and houses were seen. He counted from a neighbouring hill nearly eighty churches and convents, and these were such as he could see from his elevated position, but there were others, as he says, both in the city and the whole territory of Goa, where thirty thousand priests lived. Each of these churches had a set of bells, one or other of which was continually ringing, and being christened, as he says, and dedicated to some saint, they had a peculiar power to drive away all manner of evil spirits, 'except poverty in the laity and pride in the clergy'. Some shops were still seen along the *Rua Direita* in which articles of different countries were exhibited for sale, but the native merchants were exposed to the insults and oppression of the Portuguese, who ordinarily purchased articles on credit without intending to pay for them, and when the merchants demanded payment they ran the risk of being bastinadoed. He gives a sad description of the European soldiers of the time, who committed great excesses.

In 1759 the former Governor changed his residence from Panelim to Pangim; his example was followed by several persons of rank and influence. The suburbs were consequently gradually deserted. In the same year, by a Government Resolution, the Jesuits were expelled from Goa. The magnificent structures which they had reared in the city were declared the property of the State, but they were for the most part neglected and abandoned. The little commerce of the city, which had latterly been kept up, chiefly through the energy and enterprise of the Jesuits, received a fatal blow at this time. The city thus suffered materially from the expulsion of the Jesuits. In 1775 the population was reduced to about 1,600 souls, of whom there were 1,198 Christians.

In the following year the British Consul, Mr Abraham Parson, along with Commodore Moor, visited the city. They were struck with the magnificence of several public edifices, but they found the religious houses of the Jesuits shut up. Many beautiful mansions which were built in the suburbs in the European style, they saw vacant and unoccupied: 'while the Portuguese made but little figure in these parts, for, except Goa and the isle of Diu, they had no place of consequence on this side of the Cape of Good Hope'.

It was in this state of the city, when its commerce was totally destroyed, its population reduced to a considerable extent, and its houses razed to the ground, that the Marquis of Pombal conceived the project of rebuilding it. His views on this subject appear clearly from the instructions he gave to Dom Jose Pedro da Camara, when he was sent out as Governor or Captain General of Goa. He remarks: 'Divine Providence having placed the city of Goa in a situation by far the most advantageous and admirably fitted to make her the capital and mistress of the whole of Asia, and the incomparable Affonso de Albuquerque having raised her to that position, which she maintained with unrivalled power and glory till the intrusions of the so-called Jesuits, she has been overtaken by such calamities that she is reduced to a heap of ruins; so that she is now a mere wreck of what she was in happier times; for those wicked men wished the city to be deserted that she might be left entirely in their hands, with none to oppose the gigantic schemes of their insatiable and restless ambition.' It will be observed that the illustrious statesman who expressed himself thus was evidently led away by his prejudice against the Jesuits, who, whatever might have been their faults in other respects, were certainly by no means responsible for the fall of the city. For, as we have seen, the misfortunes of the city were due to the insalubrity of its climate and the collapse of the Portuguese power and commerce in the East, no less than to the indiscreet conduct of the Government in attempting to rear a new capital. It was impossible, in the face of these adverse circumstances, for the city to retain its pristine grandeur. The age of Albuquerque was separated from that of the Marquis by a wide gulf, representing as each did a distinct epoch in the annals of the Portuguese Empire in the East—the one identified with the greatness, the other with the fall of the city.

In the beginning of the 19th century the city of Goa attracted the attention of strangers chiefly by its religious buildings, many of which were still preserved in great splendour. Dr Claudius Buchanan wrote in 1808 that the magnificence of the churches in Goa far exceeded the idea he had formed of them from the descriptions given by travellers. Goa, says he, is properly speaking, the city of churches, and the wealth of all its provinces appears to have been spent in their erection. These specimens of ancient architecture are unrivalled in taste as well as in grandeur by any that can be witnessed in these days in any part of the East. They present a striking contrast to the gloom and misery that surround them. In fact, with the exception of these convents, the decay of the city in other respects was by this time complete. Texeira Pinto writes in 1823 that though no decree had been passed for the destruction of the city, like that of the senate of Rome, *de delenda Carthagine*; though no irruption of barbarians had threatened her with ruin; though no fury of conquerors, like Alexander, had been directed against her as against Persepolis; though no deluge, no earthquake, no natural calamity had overtaken her, still little or nothing remained of the city of Albuquerque except the soil on which she stood. The population in her suburbs was hardly a twentieth part of what it had been. The parishes which had from twelve to thirty thousand inhabitants were almost deserted. The city presented a scene of desolation and ruin; there were only convents and churches with their ecclesiastics and their dependants. The superior of the Augustinian convent said four years after (1827) to the Abbé Cottineau de Kloguen, who was in Goa at this time, 'Il ne reste plus de cette ville que le sacré, le profane en est entierement banni.' Nothing remains of this city but the sacred, the profane is entirely banished.

The Abbé himself has left us by far the best description of the city in the last days of its existence. He says:

> In the midst of its ruins the old limits of the city could be distinctly traced. The public squares and thoroughfares were still distinguishable, and most of them were still bordered on both sides with low and mouldering stone walls. But there was not a single decent-looking house in the city; a few wretched huts were scattered

here and there at a considerable distance from each other. It was a vast solitude. The greater part of the city was covered with cocoanut trees, which were a source of revenue to the church and convents and to private individuals. The suburb of Lower Daugim or of Santa Luiza on the east was also very much in decay; it contained only about fifty common houses on both sides of the streets; inhabited by Muhammadans and Hindus, but the suburb of Panelim or of Sao Pedro on the west was in a better condition, having a row of elegantly constructed houses facing the river and extending to Ribandar. The total population of the city and its suburbs was about 3,200, two-thirds of which belonged to Panelim. The city was found much in the same state by the Rev. Joseph Wolff in 1833, and by Dr. John Wilson in 1834.

In the following year the Home Government adopted a measure which proved a deathblow to the city. A resolution was passed for the suppression of all religious orders throughout the Portuguese dominions. Accordingly the friars, who were at this time the only inhabitants of the city, were obliged to abandon their convents, and settle elsewhere. The majestic buildings which they had raised with exquisite skill and preserved with unceasing care, and which had excited the admiration of all travellers and strangers who visited Goa, were now destined to share the fate which had overtaken so many other edifices in the city, both public and private. They became State property, but were either neglected and suffered to decay, or purposely demolished to furnish materials for the construction of new buildings at Pangim, which had already become the seat of government. At the same time the valuable property, both moveable and immoveable, which belonged to these convents was sold, and the proceeds were made over to the public treasury.

With the suppression of the religious orders, and the fall of the convents, the last spark of life in the city became almost extinct. The proud capital of the Portuguese Eastern Empire was humbled to the dust. It was reduced to a heap of ruins, and turned into a wilderness, infested by venomous snakes and reptiles. The spot hallowed by the fame of Albuquerque and St. Francis Xavier, which had witnessed so many triumphs of the sword and the Gospel, which had absorbed the wealth and commerce of the East, and had attained an almost classic name, now presented a piteous spectacle of wide-spread desolation and decay. The spacious squares and piers along the river-side, so full of life and activity, the crowded bazaars stocked with the varied products of different climes and regions, the public thoroughfares thronged with men of every race and creed, the noble edifices both public and private, religious and secular, rivalling in grandeur and beauty some of the best structures in Europe, the palaces and churches and convents with their lofty spires and turrets, these and other distinguishing features of a great and flourishing city were gradually swept away, till at length they have been almost completely obliterated. It is difficult to trace them with any accuracy amidst scattered ruins, overgrown with thick shrubs and bushes, and half-buried in cocoanut groves. A few religious buildings, happily preserved from the general wreck, stand in the midst of this awful solitude to attest the departed glory of the old capital. A few priests break the sepulchral silence which reigns all around by the melodious hymns they chant; a few individuals occasionally break in on the lonely scene to contemplate the noble remains of a fallen city.

In surveying its ruins, the tourist cannot help being struck with the decay and desolation which meets his sight in all directions. Dr. Russell, who lately accompanied the Prince of Wales on his visit to the city, speaks of the ruins thus: 'The river washes the remains of a great city—an arsenal in ruins; palaces in ruins; quay walls in ruins; churches in ruins—all in ruins. We looked and saw the site of the Inquisition, the Bishop's prison, a grand Cathedral, great churches, chapels, convents, religious houses, on knolls surrounded by jungle and trees scattered all over the country. We saw the crumbling masonry which once marked the lines of streets and enclosures of palaces, dockyards filled with weeds and obsolete cranes.'

The
Inquisition
in Goa

'I was seized with an universal and violent trembling'

Gabriel Dellon

About a quarter of a mile north of the Jesuits' Professed House, in the principal square, the Terreiro de Sabaio, was an institution of a very different kind. Occupying the whole southern side of the square stood a palace which all travellers of the period have described as superb. This was the palace of the Holy Inquisition. Its baroque facade, built of black stone, 'a fit emblem of the cruel and bloody transactions that passed within its walls', as Captain Franklin, a later traveller, puts it, had three doors, the two side ones leading to the private apartments of the Inquisitors, the central door opening upon a great hall, the Mesa do Santo Officio. Here suspected heretics were examined at a table, fifteen feet long and four feet broad, which stood on a dais in the middle of the apartment. The walls were hung with green silk and against one of them was an immense crucifix, the figure more than life-size and so elevated that the face was almost under the ceiling. Accused persons were required to gaze up at it, and so horrific was its appearance and terrible the occasion that many, it is said, fainted from fright. Behind were the cells, two hundred in number and ten feet square. These were whitewashed and clean, lighted by a grated window high up, and had double doors, food being passed through an aperture in the inner door, which always remained shut. The food and sanitary arrangements were good, but the imprisonment was solitary, no exercise being provided for, nor any books, writing materials, or work allowed.

The Inquisition was established in Goa in 1560. It is an interesting fact that St. Francis Xavier urged that this should be done. Humane, loving, and devoted though he was, he was also a disciplinarian. In a letter dated the 16th of May 1546 to John III, King of Portugal, he describes the Portuguese at Goa and the forts with their Indian or half-caste wives and concubines, and points out the evil influence of these women, many of whom were Catholics in name only, for they worshipped simultaneously the Hindu deities. An ecclesiastical court to prevent those baptized from lapsing into heresy was essential, if the pure Europeans were to retain their faith and not be swallowed up in heathendom. 'For these reasons your Highness should send out the Holy Inquisition,' he concludes.

The New or Spanish Inquisition had been established sixty-eight years previously in Castile and Aragon at the instance of the Dominican, Torquemada. It was directed particularly against the Conversos, Jews who had been baptized under pressure of penal laws, but were suspected of practising their old rites in secret. These Jews were the richest and most industrious people in Spain. Their plunder was one of the objects of the Inquisition, an object which appealed strongly to Ferdinand and Isabella, who were in need of money. The reader will be acquainted with the history of the Inquisition in Spain and Portugal; he will know that it was not identical with the medieval Inquisition, an ecclesiastical tribunal created to check the heresies and superstitions, the witchcraft and sorcery, which threatened to muddle and brutalize Catholicism. He will recall that, less a reforming body than the earlier institution, it represented from one point of view an alliance between the Crown and the Church for secular objects. Besides serving to rob the Jewish Conversos, it was used to terrify the nobility and the people. A lord too independent or a peasant agitator would be tapped on the shoulder one day by its Familiars and informed he was arrested on a charge of heresy. The events of these latter days have made us acquainted with secret police, with espionage in the home, with the breaking of morale by torture and solitary confinement. These were the methods of the Inquisition, and though they have been excused on the ground that they had their counterpart in the criminal procedure of the law and so must have appeared less unjust than they do nowadays, they were more efficient and so more cruel than the methods of the judiciary. A lay judge took action on public complaint or after a factual breaking of the law, but the Holy Office often selected its victims and hunted them down, concocting a process against them afterwards.

The lovable Francis Xavier may, in his saintly simplicity, have pictured the Inquisition as an honest disciplinary tribunal reforming the licence of colonial life. By Pyrard's time, forty-eight years after its introduction into Goa, it bore a dreadful reputation. Pyrard, a good Catholic, has left this in no doubt. After stating that its procedure was even more severe than in Portugal, and that it continued its old policy of hunting converted Jews, in this case oriental Jews who to obtain the advantage of a trade residence in Goa had declared themselves Christians, he goes on: 'The first time such Jews are taken before the Holy Inquisition, all their goods are seized; they are seldom arrested unless they are rich.' Speaking generally, he then declares: 'Nothing in the world is more cruel and pitiless than the procedure. The least suspicion, the slightest word, whether of a child or of a slave who wishes to do his master a bad turn, is enough…they give credence to a child however young, so only he can speak. When a man is arrested there is no friend will dare say a word for him. If a chance word should escape a man, having the smallest reference to the Inquisition itself, he must forthwith go and denounce himself, if he suspect that any has heard him. It is a terrible and fearful thing to be there even once, for you have no advocate, while they are prosecution and judges at once.' Speaking of its attitude to the native inhabitants, he states that though not subject to its jurisdiction unless they turned Christian, they might be arrested should they be accused of hindering one of their fellows from professing Catholicism. 'It would be impossible,' he concludes, 'to calculate the numbers of all those put to death.' To ascertain this, the records were examined in the middle of the nineteenth century by Jose da Fonseca, author of *An Historical and Archaeological Sketch of the City of Goa*, but he was unable to make a complete computation. He found, however, that seventy-one auto-da-fes were held between 1600 and 1775, and that the number of persons burnt averaged twelve on each occasion, which gives an estimated total of eight hundred and fifty-two.

There exists an inside account of an auto-da-fe at Goa written by a

Dr Dellon. It is contained in his book *Relation de l'Inquisition de Goa*, published in Paris in 1688, and translated into English the same year. The events it describes took place between 1675 and 1676, some sixty years after Pyrard had left Goa, but the tribunal had not changed in the interval, and the *Relation* provides with approximate accuracy a picture of an auto-da-fe in the first quarter of the century.

Dr Dellon, who was a French traveller of twenty-four, was staying at Daman, one of the forts north of Goa, when he was arrested on 24 August 1675. He had offended the Governor, Dom Manuel Furtado de Mendoza, by visiting his mistress. And he had imprudently made critical remarks about the Inquisition, and about matters of faith, such as baptism and the adoration of images, which those who heard them considered heretical, though he, also a Catholic, believed them justified by the theological books it was his hobby to read. These lapses gave Dom Manuel his chance of revenge. The Commissary representing the Inquisition at Daman was informed and a Familiar was sent to take him into custody.

His book provides a very full account of the dreadful misadventures which then befell him. To relate them in detail here is tempting, but would overbalance our narrative, and only his description of the auto-da-fe itself can be given. After two years in a cell of the Inquisition at Goa to which he had been removed from Daman, he became convinced in December 1675 that an auto-da-fe was about to take place. By this time his nerve was broken by solitude, by the raising of hopes which his tormentors dashed with cruel deliberation, by dark threats, silence as to the precise nature of the charges against him, or the time when he would receive his sentence, and by frightful forebodings about his possible fate. Acts of faith were ordinarily held on the first Sunday in Advent, now very close. The previous Advent had been without one. The dread celebration was never omitted in two successive years. Though the Inquisitors in the course of one of their many interviews with him had said he was liable to be burned, he felt a mixture of longing and fear. If he were not burnt, perhaps he would be released. He was most eager to take the chance. The prospect of another year in solitary confinement was horrible.

But the first Sunday in Advent came and went. Strange, when the prison was so full. Surely a gaol delivery must come soon. Another sign was that a new Archbishop, Dom Francisco da Assumpcio e Brito, had arrived, the Cathedral bells having been rung for nine days together. What more fitting than that this prelate's installation should be made the occasion of an Act of Faith?

But the second Sunday went by; Dellon began to despair. When the third and fourth were gone, his hopes went with them. He resigned himself to suffer for another year. But, 'on Saturday the 11th of January 1676', he writes, 'being about to give my linnen after Dinner to the Officers to be washed after the usual Custom, they would not receive it', but put him off till the next day. This departure from routine or may be something about the manner of the warders set him wondering.

Could it be that after all an auto-da-fe was at hand, that it would take place, perhaps, the very next day, Sunday, a day always used for that ceremony? In the evening he became certain that something was in the wind, for, as he explains, 'after I had heard it ring to Vespers at the Cathedral, it immediately rung to Matins, which was never before done while I was a Prisoner, except upon the eve of Corpus Christi day'. These two unusual events convinced him that an auto-da-fe was imminent. With the ordeal facing him so close he now became frightened. They had given him no intimation whatever regarding his fate. For all he knew, it might be the stake for him next day. 'They brought me my Supper, which I refused and which contrary to their ordinary custom they pressed me not very much to receive. As soon as the doors were shut upon me, I entirely abandoned myself to those melancholy thoughts which possessed me; and at last, after many tears and sighs, overwhelmed with sorrow and imaginations of death, I fell asleep a little after eleven o'clock at night.'

He had not been long asleep when he was awoken by warders entering his cell. They carried lights—he had never seen a light during all the nights of his imprisonment—and the chief gaoler, who accompanied them, 'gave me a habit which he ordered me to put on, and to be ready to go out when he should call me'. Leaving a lamp they withdrew without any explanation, but Dellon knew that at an auto-da-fe a special costume was worn by the victims. If he had been frightened before he went to sleep, he was now terrified. 'I was seized with an universal and so violent a trembling that for more than an hour it was not possible for me so much as to look upon the habit which they had brought me.'

At last he summoned courage to get up, and kneeling before a cross which he had painted on the wall, committed his soul to God's protection.Then he put on the dress. It was black stuff, striped with white, and consisted of a blouse and a pair of loose trousers.

At two o'clock in the morning the warders returned and conducted him to a long gallery. 'There I found a good number of my Companions in Misery, ranged round about against the Wall; I put my self into my place, and there came yet divers after me.'

When all the prisoners were assembled, there seemed to be some two hundred of them, of whom only twelve were Europeans, though in the faint light of the few lamps, and as all were dressed in the same dark clothes, it was hard to tell. Dead silence reigned. 'One might easily have taken all these persons for so many statues set against the Wall, if the motion of their eyes, the use of which alone was permitted to them, had not testified them to be living creatures.' Or it might have been they were come to attend some funeral, so sombre and melancholy was the company.

No women were amongst them, though there were some women prisoners, These were in an adjoining gallery, 'vested with the same stuff', and Dellon caught sight through a door of two more prisoners, beside whom stood monks in black habits and holding crucifixes. Having no knowledge of the Inquisition's procedure on such occasions he was unable to glean a hint of what his impending sentence was likely to be from the clothes in which he and the other prisoners were dressed, but as they and he all seemed as yet to be dressed the same, there being nothing about the blouse and trousers which had been allotted to him to distinguish his case from the others, he took a little courage, arguing it unlikely that so many people were for the stake.

But now the warders began to bring in more garments. These were like scapularies or large capes, of yellow stuff with a St. Andrew's cross painted on them before and behind. Dellon knew enough to recognize them to be *sanbenitos*, the penitential grab worn by prisoners of the Inquisition during their procession through the streets to the place of sentence. The *sanbenitos*, of which there were twenty-two only, were distributed first to twenty Indians and negroes, the twenty-first to a Portuguese, and the last one to Dellon. 'My fears redoubled when I saw myself thus habited, because it seemed to me that, there being among so great a number of prisoners, no more than 22 persons to whom the shameful *sanbenitos* were given, it might very well happen that these should be the persons to whom no mercy was to be extended.' While he was in this state of dreadful apprehension, five 'bonnets of paper', like dunces' caps in shape, were brought. These were painted with devils amid flames and bore the legend 'Sorcerer' in bold letters. Instinctively he realized that such caps must denote a greater degree of guilt, and narrowly watched the warders as they began to fix them on the heads of shrinking prisoners. One of those to receive a cap was standing next to him, and when Dellon saw the warder approach with the cap in his hand, he felt certain it was for him that the emblematic horror was intended. When it was .put on the other a sigh of agonized relief escaped him. The face of him upon whose head it was set was drawn and haggard, as if he 'believed his destruction to be inevitable'.

No more garments or accoutrements being produced, word was passed that the prisoners might sit down. The parade had been so early—so unnecessarily early as by deliberate intention to cause the greatest possible suspense and fear—that dawn was still a long way off. So they sat there in utter silence, the light of the 'lamps so weak that they seemed no more than shadows in the vast gallery'. At four o'clock the warders came with baskets of bread and figs. 'But altho I had not supped the night before, I found in my self so small an appetite for eating, that I had taken nothing, if one of the Guards coming near me had not said: "Take your Bread, and if you cannot eat now, put it into your Pocket, for you will be certainly hungry before you return."' Dellon did not venture to ask the man to be more explicit, but the remark, if it were to be believed and was not another deception, gave a faint hope which, taken with the other, that a sorcerer's cap had not been set on his head, heartened him a little.

At last, after they had waited what seemed a dark age, the first greyness of dawn began to creep into the gallery. The light strengthened and looking round Dellon was able to observe 'upon the faces of everyone present the diverse motions of shame, of grief and of fear, wherewith they were then tormented'. Yet he thought too that he could also detect relief, as if they were glad, though they might be going to their deaths, that their horrible captivity was at an end.

As the sun rose they heard the deep note of the cathedral's big bell, a bell which was only tolled on such occasions and was a signal for the inhabitants, Portuguese, Eurasian, and Indian, to line the streets through which the procession was about to pass.

The prisoners were then ordered to file out into the great hall, and when Dellon entered it he saw the Grand Inquisitor seated by the door with his secretary standing beside him, a list in his hand. To one side was a crowd of residents from the city, and as each prisoner stepped in a name would be called, when one of the residents came forward and the prisoner was allotted to him. These were known as Fathers in God and it was their duty to accompany their penitent throughout the procession, stay beside him during the ceremony of the Act of Faith, and produce him at the end of it. Dellon's Father in God was no less a personage than the Admiral of the Armada, a Portuguese nobleman, for it seems that the duty of attending upon penitents was regarded as an honour, not only by ordinary citizens but by the aristocracy.

When the business of appointing each his keeper was done, the whole concourse left the palace of the Inquisition and descended the wide flight of steps into the great square in front of the cathedral.

With the January sun gaining height about him, Dellon stood and sniffed the air of morning, which seemed to blow from paradise, so fresh and sweet it smelt after his long captivity.

'Now the procession began to form. At the head of it were the Dominicans, who had this privilege by the right that St. Dominic had been the founder of the first Inquisition. Before them was borne the banner of the Holy Office whereon was embroidered a picture of St. Dominic, holding in one hand a sword and in the other an olive branch, to which a legend was attached, 'Justitia et Misericordia'.

The Dominicans moved off, behind them following in a long line the penitents, each with his godfather beside him and a taper in his hand. About a hundred had entered the procession before the officers of the Inquisition commanded Dellon to do so. His head was bare as were his feet. The procession was so long that he had passed out of the square before the end of it was complete and so was unable to tell who formed the tail.

There was a very large crowd; the inhabitants, European and Indian, not only of Goa, but of the districts in the neighbourhood, lining the route, business being abandoned for that day. As he walked Dellon's bare feet were so cut by loose flints that they were bleeding profusely by the time the procession reached its destination, the Church of St. Francis, actually quite close because it was behind the cathedral, but which was approached after parading all round the town. The staring crowd he had found an ordeal; unaccustomed for so long to exercise he was exhausted; and his godfather, the Admiral, would answer no questions, remaining cold and distant throughout the progress.

On entering the church, which was the most gorgeous in Goa—the Italian traveller, Gemelli Careri, who visited it twenty years later, says: 'It has a roof curiously adorned with fretwork and is like one entire mass of gold, there being so much of this metal on its altars'—Dellon perceived that it had been made ready for the ceremony, for the great altar was spread with black 'and there were upon it six Silver Candlesticks with so many tapers of white Wax burning'. On each side of it was a dais, where, to the left, sat the Grand Inquisitor and his staff, and to the right Dom Furtado de Albuquerque, Count of Lavradio and Viceroy of the Indies. Dellon walked up the aisle, pews having been placed on both sides for the members of the procession, those entering first being placed nearest the altar.

When he had taken his allotted seat, with the Admiral beside him, he looked round to watch the rest of the penitents march in. Following had been many more in *sanbenitos* of the kind he was wearing, and behind them at last came the five with pointed caps, a lofty crucifix bringing up the rear. But this was not the end, for he now saw a man and a woman behind the crucifix, and as if by design the face of the Saviour had been turned away from them. They were both Indian Christians and along with them were carried four effigies and four boxes. The significance of this—who were the two penitents, what the boxes, and the effigies— Dellon was to learn later on. At the moment he noted that these two were differently dressed from all the others, their *sanbenitos* being of grey, not yellow, stuff, and painted not with a St. Andrew's Cross but with devils, flames, and burning firebrands, in the midst of which was a portrait of the wearer. The face was on the chest and repeated on the back, with the name below and the crime in large letters, the words in both cases being *crimen magicae*. They also wore the pointed caps, similar to those worn by the five who preceded them. Dellon had not seen these two persons in the gallery nor, therefore, had he witnessed the bestowal upon them of their costumes, and he surmised them to be those of whom he had caught a glimpse through a door, with black-stoled monks holding out to them crucifixes. These monks attended still, marching instead of the godfathers.

The symbolism of the whole pageant was becoming clearer to him. If he were not mistaken, these were the victims destined for the stake. He shuddered, believing, yet not daring to be sure, that he had escaped an awful death. As for the effigies and the boxes, he did not yet guess what they signified, but it was strange that the former, borne aloft on poles, wore, too, the flaming habits and the tall pointed caps. The divine service of the auto-da-fe began. Everyone was in his proper place, the last mentioned unhappy pair seated at the extreme back, and the crucifix which had faced away from them, now set on the altar between the candlesticks. The Provincial of the Augustinians, the head of that Order in the East, ascended the pulpit. Besides the two hundred penitents, and the like number of godfathers, there were present as many of the public as could push their way in, the Franciscan monks also having their set place, grey friars, with cords about their middles, sandalled and, on their backs, the broad-brimmed hats they wore over their cowls.

The Augustinian prelate opened his discourse.

In spite of Dellon's anxiety for if he now hoped to escape death there were many other severe punishments which might be inflicted on him— he listened carefully to the sermon, a short one for those times, for it lasted only an hour. Among the Provincial's points was a comparison of the Inquisition with Noah's Ark 'between which yet he found this difference that the Animals, which entered into the Ark, went out again after the Deluge, invested with the same Nature which they had when they entered it, but that the Inquisition had the admirable property to change in such sort those who are shut up in it, that in coming out we see those to be Lambs who when they entered it had the cruelty of Wolves'. This was hardly a correct description of his case, thought Dellon, who had been as mild, if as foolish, as a lamb from the beginning.

The sermon being finished, two clerks of the Holy Office entered the pulpit and began to read in turn the judgements passed upon the prisoners. During the reading, the head gaoler led each man into the centre of the aisle, to stand with alighted taper in his hand. In due course Dellon was called. He heard the clerk read a summary of the allegations, his remarks about baptism, images, and the Inquisition, all of which he had made argumentatively, carelessly, for he was an ingenuous, talkative fellow. But it was held he had spoken with deliberate malice. For these crimes he was declared excommunicated, his goods were confiscated, and himself condemned to five years in the galleys, the sentence to be served, not in Goa, but in Lisbon. How monstrous this sentence was he did not fully realize at the moment, so relieved was he to have escaped the stake or further imprisonment in the Santa Casa. To be a galley-slave seemed to him almost a happy prospect, for no matter what his treatment he would be out of the hands of the Church.

When the sentence had been pronounced he was taken to the altar, at the foot of which was a missal, whereon he was ordered to make a confession of faith after a clerk, who read it from a breviary. He then returned to his place and listened while the rest of the judgements were pronounced. As there were two hundred this took all day. After a while he noticed that the congregation was eating and, remembering that he too had food in his pocket, made a meal with good appetite.

At last the reading of the judgements came to an end, that is of those relating to the penitents who had walked in front of the crucifix. Their punishments had been various, but none were sent to death, not even those with the flaming caps of sorcerers. Judgement upon the two who had been behind the crucifix was reserved for the moment. The Grand Inquisitor left his dais and put on alb and stole. Then accompanied by twenty priests, each carrying a wand, he took up a position in the middle of the church, where after praying for awhile he absolved the convicted penitents from the excommunication which had been passed upon them, his attendant priests striking them one by one a blow on their breasts. When Dellon had been so absolved by the touch of a wand, he was surprised to see a sudden change in the manner of his godfather, the Admiral. This worthy's stiffness had been due wholly to fear and not to any coldness of heart. When he heard his godson's absolution pronounced and knew that he had been taken back into the bosom of the Church, he wept, called him his brother, though he was a galley slave, and embracing him warmly, offered him tobacco.

This part of the ceremony ended, the Grand Inquisitor returned to his place on the dais and directed that the man and the woman should be brought before him. Their judgements were then read out: they were indicted of the crime of magic: and they had both relapsed, this being their second offence. As Hindus by birth this may have meant no more than that they had practised such arts as astrology or divination or engaged in one of the many occult practices connected with Hinduism. But they had had the temerity to enter so strict an association as the Catholic Church of seventeenth-century Portugal, perhaps for reasons of temporal advantage, and now were paying the penalty of their rashness. Their judgements ended with the words always used when condemned persons were to be burnt, to wit that they be delivered to the secular authority, which was earnestly requested to show mercy, but that if, indeed, the penalty of death were imposed, it might at least be inflicted without effusion of blood. At the last words of the Inquisitor's a sergeant of the Secular Justice approached and took possession of those unfortunate persons, after they had received a light blow on the breast from the hand of the Alcaide of the Holy Office, in token that they were abandoned by him.'

Their burning was to take place at a selected spot on the river bank, and thither Dum Furtado de Albuquerque adjourned with his glittering Court, as did the Inquisitors, for, of course, everything had been arranged beforehand; there was no appeal nor conceivably would the civil authorities dare to show mercy, in spite of the apparent earnestness with which it had been demanded of them. Dellon did not see carried out this last cruelty, this abominable stupidity, for stupid it was if the Holy Office desired to commend to the enlightened attention of Asia the Catholic Church and the message of compassion, which it had received from its Founder. No Church of the Orient inflicted such punishments. If there were disgraceful practices in Hinduism, they were immoral rather than cruel, or if cruel, the cruelty was self-inflicted. To find a parallel one must leave Asia and go to the America of the Aztecs. Yet there is no parallel even there, for the victims of the Aztec priests were sacrificed not in punishment but oblation.

The Inquisition's dark fanaticism had also its ludicrous aspect. The four boxes above-mentioned contained bones, the remains, in three of them, of prisoners who had died in the Inquisition, and in the other those of a man who, never accused in his lifetime of heresy, had been found guilty of it after his death, when his corpse was 'plucked from his Grave after they had formed a Process against him, as he had left very considerable Riches'. The effigies carried on poles with the boxes represented these four deceased. The bones and the effigies were burnt at the place where the man and the woman suffered death.

Dellon records that the portraits of all those burnt at the stake were hung in the Dominican Church. Each face was painted surrounded by flames. 'These terrible representations are placed in the Nave of the Church as so many illustrious Trophies consecrated to the Glory of the Holy Office,' he adds with bitter sarcasm.

While the execution was being carried out, he was back in his cell. 'I was so weary and so sore at my return from the Act of Faith,' he writes, 'that I had almost no less desire to re-enter my Lodging to rest my self than I had before to go out of it.' Indeed, the head gaoler on taking charge of him again from the Admiral only led him as far as the gallery, leaving him to walk on alone and shut himself in. He lay down on his bed, hoping for supper. This came at last, but instead of being fish or curry, the usual evening meal, consisted only of bread and figs, for the cooks had taken a holiday and were still out watching the burning.

He slept better that night than he had for a long time. At six o'clock the next morning the head gaoler came to get the clothes he had worn at the auto-da-fe, not the *sanbenito*, for that he would have to put on when he left the prison, but the striped blouse and trousers which had been underneath it. At seven his breakfast appeared and he was told to pack, an order which he obeyed 'with all possible diligence'. At nine o' clock his door was opened for the last time and with his luggage on his shoulder he was taken to the hall with the green silk hangings and the huge crucifix. Most of the convicted prisoners were already assembled there. Some had received sentences of whipping, the hangman having already carried them out. The Inquisitor appeared and took his seat at the great table. 'We fell upon our knees to receive his blessing, after we had kissed the ground near his Feet,' says Dellon.

The prisoners then were disposed of according to their sentences. Numbers of them, it appears, were not Christians at all, but Hindus or Mohammedans who had incurred the displeasure of the Inquisition on one or other of the grounds we have previously noted. Of these some were ordered to leave Goa (a happy sentence one would think, though if they were shopkeepers and all their goods were confiscated, it may have meant ruin). Others were condemned to hard labour in the Arsenal, and a few to the local galleys. The Christians, both European and Asiatic, were to go to a house in the town, there to undergo certain preliminary instruction. Dellon, with his sentence of deportation to the galleys of Portugal, was sent along with them. An Indian shouldered his trunk for him, which was light enough, for though they had made a careful inventory of his possessions on arrival, anything of value had been confiscated.

It was January the 13th and he remained in the house for ten days in semi-imprisonment until the ship on which he was to embark for Portugal was ready to sail. It is interesting to note that the Prior of the Dominicans at Daman, a monk with whom he had actually been staying when he became involved with the persons who informed against him, came to see him now, embraced him tenderly, and wept at his disaster. This Prior apparently considered that he had been harshly treated, and had even interceded with the Procurator of the Inquisition on his behalf at some period during his imprisonment.But though a leading Dominican he had no influence whatever with the Inquisitors. The tribunal had absolute power to take action in defence of the Faith and not even senior members of the Order with which it was so closely connected could hope to move it in favour of prisoners. The only information vouchsafed to this kind monk when he went to see the Procurator, also a Dominican, was that Dellon still lived. Now he showed his good heart by procuring for him provisions for the voyage, without which he might never have reached Lisbon alive.

On 23 January he was summoned finally before the Grand Inquisitor and made to swear that 'he should keep exactly the secret of all which he had seen, heard or said or which had been acted concerning him either at the Table or at any place of the Holy Office'. It was this oath, taken on the Gospel, which made him hesitate for ten years to publish his history.

That night, preparatory to embarking, he was lodged in the Archbishop's prison, the infamous Al Jabir, a dungeon similar to the Salle to which Pyrard was sent, dark, stifling, and filthy, crowded with galley slaves. But now he himself was a galley slave, and such a horror had he taken of the Inquisition and his solitary cell, clean though it was, that the Al Jabir seemed human, and, so, happy in comparison. After being there forty-eight hours, he says, 'An Officer of the Holy Office, clapping Irons upon my feet, carried me to a Ship which was in the Road'. They weighed anchor on 27 January and making a very fast passage reached Brazil in May, remaining until September, awaiting a good wind. Dellon was shut up at night in the local prison, but allowed in the daytime to stroll about the town.

On the passage from Brazil to Lisbon he had a narrow escape, not from drowning or other mishap of shipboard, but of being declared a relapsed heretic. A certain friar was celebrating Mass. When Dellon approached the Holy Table to receive the Sacrament he shut his eyes out of devotion. The friar, who had a prejudice against him because he had been convicted by the Inquisition, sent for him afterwards and declared that his conduct smelt of heresy, 'since I vouchsafed not so much as to look upon our Lord, when he was presented to me in the Communion'. Dellon was much alarmed at this accusation. On arrival at Lisbon he would be in reach of the Inquisition again. If this friar chose to lay a complaint against him he might find himself charged with relapsing, when nothing could save him from the stake. He hastened to apologize in the most contrite manner, assuring the friar that his motive in closing his eyes had been wholly that 'of humbling myself in the presence of God'. It was with difficulty that he succeeded in soothing the fanatic, who accepted the explanation with very bad grace.

Galleys, in the proper sense of that term, had been abolished in Portugal some time before this date, and when Dellon was handed over to the authorities at Lisbon he was not, as he would have been some years earlier, chained to an oar and sent to sea to row a man-of-war in some expedition against pirates, but was consigned to a prison near the docks called the Galley, in which all criminals, who had received from either a lay or ecclesiastical court the old-fashioned sentence of so many years in the galleys, were incarcerated and sent to hard labour. On arrival there, he was chained by the foot to another victim of the Inquisition, a Portuguese who, he learnt, had escaped the fire by confessing the evening before he was to be burnt. Most of the other prisoners, he found, were either fugitive and incorrigible slaves or Turks who had been taken prisoner on the pirate ships of Barbary. He was later to meet a few educated men of his own class.

The work was hard and the overseers brutal. Every morning early, except on a very few festival days, the slaves were marched from the

Galley to the docks and there set to unloading ships, stowing cargoes and collecting ballast. All the prisoners, no matter what their rank in life, were employed on such labours, 'unless they have money to give the Officers who conduct them and who exercise an unheard-of cruelty upon those who cannot mollify them somewhat from time to time'.

The hours of work were from dawn till eleven, and from one o'clock till the sun set, when they returned to the Galley, chained in couples, and slept chained in dormitories. Their rations were a pound and a half of ship's biscuit a day, and six pounds of salt fish a month with vegetables, though they could supplement them from charitable persons outside. Priests would call to give spiritual comfort. In short, the Galley was less rigid than a modern prison, and, if it was managed with more brutality, there were compensations that prisoners do not find today. You were not cut off from outside succour; private benevolence could have its way; and if you wanted to visit the town, a warder would take you there if you paid him. 'The liberty of seeing and speaking to the whole world rendered it much less troublesome to me than the horrible Solitude of the Inquisition,' says Dellon. The day after his arrival he was shaved, given prison clothes, and set to work with the other galley slaves. Five years of penal servitude had to pass before he could hope to see his country again. 'There was no great appearance that any favour would be showed to a man who had spoken against the Integrity and Infallibility of the Holy Office.' Yet he began at once to cast about how he might obtain the ear of influential persons.

Inquiring whether any fellow countrymen lived in Lisbon, he was delighted to learn that the Queen of Portugal's physician was French and, moreover, that he was popular with the grandees of the Court. He appealed to him at once, begging his protection, which he gave 'in the most obliging manner in the World, offering not only his interest in all things which lay in his power, but also his Purse and his Table, where he did me the honour to give me a place, enchained as I was, whensoever Liberty of going to him was granted me'. Here again we have the human element mitigating the barbarity of the law, which had lagged behind the best public opinion.

All this was pleasant enough, but it did not produce immediately any practical result. The Queen was approached but apparently nothing could be done at the moment. Dellon also wrote to his relations in France, acquainting them for the first time with his situation and beseeching them to use what interest they possessed.

Later, on the advice of his friend, the Court Physician, he presented a petition to the Inquisition of Lisbon, setting out his case and asking for a reduction of sentence. But no answer was given, though he sent several reminders. Eventually he learned that a new Grand Inquisitor had only recently been appointed and had not yet taken up his residence.

Three months passed. Then towards Holy Week, 1677, the Grand Inquisitor arrived. But during the Easter celebrations no official business was done, and it was not until after Quasimodo Sunday that the Tribunal opened. Whereupon Dellon immediately presented a fresh petition, which reached Dom Verissimo de Lancastre, such being the Grand Inquisitor's name, and to which he gave answer that he could not believe what was stated in it, 'there being no appearance that they would have condemned a man to serve 5 years in the Gallies for matters of so little consequence'.

Dellon then wrote entreating him to read his process, for it seems that a copy of the proceedings relating to his condemnation in Goa had been forwarded with him. On this application the secretariat of the Inquisition noted that, as no appeal lay from a decision by the Grand Inquisitor of Goa, his status being equal to that of the Grand Inquisitor at Lisbon, it would be improper, indeed illegal, to review the process.

That would normally have been the end of the matter had Dom Verissimo been a bureaucrat. Though at first he declared it impossible for him to do more, his niece, the Countess of Figveirol, 'who had a very particular esteem for the first Physician of the Queen', talked him round till he assented, with the charming smile for which he was noted, to have the process read aloud to him. Finding that no further charges than those stated in Dellon's original petition were contained in it, he repeated his view that the sentence was excessive. As he was not an appellate authority, he carefully refrained from passing any order on the process, but calling for the last of Dellon's petitions wrote at the bottom: 'Let him be set at Liberty as he desireth and let him return to France.'

This good news was conveyed to Dellon by a Familiar of the Holy Office on 1 June 1677. Nearly four years had elapsed since his arrest in Daman, He felt 'a joy which persons who have not suffered Captivity will scarce be able to conceive'.

But he was not yet completely out of the clutches of the Inquisition. For another whole month he was to remain in chains. As often happens in an office, the secretarial staff were not too pleased at their chief having taken the law into his own hands, contrary to the legal opinion which they had submitted. Accordingly, they decided to put an interpretation on his hastily scribbled order which it was not intended to, but might, bear. Instead of the words 'let him return to France' being allowed to stand for an additional favour, they were declared to be mandatory and, moreover, to mean that Dellon was not to be set at liberty until he had actually embarked for France. When, therefore, he asked the Familiar to inform the Governor of the Galley prison that he was free and desire him accordingly to strike off his irons, the fellow expressed surprise, drew his attention to the proviso, and admonished him to seek a ship with all expedition.

At the moment Dellon did not fully appreciate the malice of the trick which had been played on him. It was not until he had obtained leave of absence and gone to the wharves from which ships sailed to France that he discovered how difficult it was, dressed in prison garb, dragging his chain and with a limited time at his disposal, to get the shipping clerks to listen to his request for a passage or, indeed, to find out when a ship was sailing. The gaolers refused to let him hang about the pier and he soon perceived that unless he were first liberated he could not arrange the matter of his departure, He therefore memorialized the Inquisition to that effect.

Days, weeks passed and no answer was received. Finally, on 28 June he was informed that if he entered into recognizances with one surety in four hundred crowns for his early departure, he would be released.

Knowing at last exactly how he stood, he went to his good friend the

Court Physician (he does not give his name out of discretion) and asked him to finish what he had so kindly begun. 'Some urgent affairs hindered him from going the same day to the Inquisition, but going thither the 30th of the same month in the morning gave caution for me.'

That afternoon they sent a Familiar to the Galley and Dellon's irons were at last struck off. He was then taken to the Inquisition and formally declared at liberty. 'I answered only with a profound reverence,' he says, 'and as soon as I had set foot out of this terrible House, I went into the next Church to render thanks to God and the Holy Virgin.'

His second action was to call and thank the French doctor, who wept and embraced him with tears of joy. Thence he returned to the Galley to collect what little luggage remained to him and to say good-bye to these poor afflicted Persons, who had been the companions of my Misfortune, with some of whom he had become warm friends. Dressed in his own clothes again, he went to the pier, and it was not long before he found a ship willing to take him and, he writes, concluding his narrative, 'I had the happiness to arrive in my Country in perfect Health.'

The reader of Dr Dellon's story will have been struck by the difference between the Inquisition and the Society of Jesus. The second with its modern hospital, its up-to-date college, its attitude towards the Hindus exemplified in the careers of Xavier and de Nobili, has a pleasing freshness compared with the haunted atmosphere of the Santa Casa. Yet, perhaps, the first was more characteristic of the Goa we have been describing, That city of fidalgos and slaves, with its murders, its adulteries, its poisons, its ignorance, was of a piece with :the spectral hall where under the crucifix reared to the ceiling the Grand Inquisitor sat at the giant table.

The
Contemporary
Traveller

'Hunting Satyagrahis'

Homer A. Jack

I had the tragic experience to cover one of the strangest wars in history: the march of 4,000 unarmed satyagrahis into Goa on August 15, 1955. Satyagraha, the marvellous tool used by Mahatma Gandhi, first in South Africa and developed here in India against the British, was never before used on an international scale. But on August 15, for the first time in history, satyagraha was directed by the nationals of one nation against the governor of another.

Before beginning my story of my experiences inside Goa, let me explain that I went to Goa as a freelance journalist for several American and European periodicals. While some foreign journalists had their way paid from Karachi to Goa by the Portuguese government and were their guests while there, I paid my own transportation from Bombay to Goa and return. However, I accepted their offers of free transportation inside Goa, but otherwise paid all my bills myself. While transportation facilities were thus put at my disposal—and also guide-translators—in fairness, I must state that I was free to move about in Goa with or without transportation, with or without a guide-translator.

However, the limitations of nature (jungle and roads) and of time made my tours fairly circumscribed. Also, since it is obvious—inside as outside—that it is a police state, I chose not to place Goans in jeopardy by visiting them and thus I could not at all times use the freedom of the country which technically I and the other members of the press were given, at least on August 14-16.

Did you ever 'hunt satyagrahis'? Well, I did. On Monday, August 15, we were called at 3 a.m. in our hotel room in Panjim, capital of Goa.

Two hours and two ferry rides later, we arrived at the army post at Pernem in Northern Goa, just a mile south of the Rio de Tiracoi, the river separating Goa from India. Our taxi developed tyre trouble, but the commander said my French companion and I could ride in the back seat of a jeep. He said there were already some reports that the satyagrahis had crossed the river.

We left the post at six o'clock, just as it was getting light. A Portuguese lieutenant was driving the American-made jeep, and his companion was a young Portuguese soldier with military helmet and carbine rifle with bayonet. (The many African soldiers from Portuguese territories were kept away from the borders.) We roared down the dirty roads, along the exceptionally green rice fields and under the tall coconut trees along the river. Constantly, the driver was on the lookout for the 'invaders'. He was hunting satyagrahis. For the soldiers—as for us—it was really a safe kind of hunt, for at least I felt no danger whatsoever from possible snipers.

We bumped up a hill and passed some Goan farmers oblivious of the day—August 15. Then we met an old man on the road and he pointed in the direction we were going. The driver gave the jeep a burst of speed, but then he stopped suddenly. On the bamboo fences on both sides of the road were red and white lithographed posters. The subcontinent of India was printed in red and superimposed on it was a picture in white of a satyagrahi, in Gandhi cap and holding the Indian flag. In Hindi there was this legend: Quit Goa, August National Congress, Goa.

The lieutenant hurriedly got out of the jeep and he and his associate grabbed all the posters in sight—about 15—and put them into the back seat of the jeep. Just as they were jumping back into the jeep, they spotted an Indian flag on the top of the roof of a nearby building. With difficulty, they hoisted themselves up and recovered the flag, breaking the pole in two and thrusting the flag into the auto. And then we sped on, knowing that the satyagrahis were not far ahead.

In the next village, the satyagrahis appeared—all in one group by the side of what appeared to be a wall of an old church or temple. They began to yell their slogans: India and Goa are one, Long live Goan

Independence, Goa zindabad, Azad Goa, etc. The lieutenant and the soldier, both with guns drawn, rounded the men up, going into the group to take away their large Indian flag. There was a minor scuffle, but I saw no obvious violence. The presence of myself and my associate may have prevented violence, perhaps even death.

I took some photographs and the lieutenant gave orders for the soldier to search the men for literature—and great rolls of the red-and-white posters were thrown on the ground, along with piles of a ten-page magazine printed in Marathi with a picture of Mr Nehru on the cover. The soldiers made the Indians throw away their white identification badges which were held to their shirts by safety-pins. Suddenly, the lieutenant ordered the men to sit down—which they did quietly—and then he sent the jeep back for reinforcements.

As the men silently squatted on the ground, I interviewed the leader, N. L. Salaskar. He said there were 46 persons in the party and that they came from all Indian political groups, most of the men coming from Madhya Pradesh. According to their instructions, he refused to tell me exactly how they entered Goa, but obviously the men came across the river at night, either by boat or swimming.

They told me that they distributed about 200 posters and about 200 leaflets until they were discovered by our jeep. They felt that the reaction of the villagers they met was quite good. They did not know what would happen to them now that they were apprehended.

By now a Goan priest and one or two other villagers were watching. Soon two jeeps arrived with soldiers as an early-morning monsoon rain began to fall. Then with enthusiasm, as much as duty, the lieutenant said to me in very broken Portuguese-English: 'You want to find more satyagrahis? Come along.' This we did and drove perhaps three miles west to another village.

There we found a jeep and another group of satyagrahis already rounded up and seated on the ground. A Goan youth of 19 was guarding them, an umbrella in one hand and a rifle in the other. Our lieutenant gave him a pat on the back and attached a bayonet to his gun. The boy told me that he was a school teacher. He found the Indian flag near the

Marathi school. He broke the flagstaff and took the flag to the vicar. He said he was a Christian.

When I asked him why he was carrying this gun in front of unarmed Indians and if he would use the gun on these satyagrahis, he replied: 'No, I am carrying it just because the Europeans (Portuguese) told me to do so. Anyway, I like to carry a gun.' Soon the bell sounded for Mass, and the young school teacher eagerly gave up the gun. Along with many other villagers, he went off to Mass—August 15 is a feast day in the Catholic Church—although the Hindus in the village continued to watch the satyagrahis with curiosity.

This group of 52 satyagrahis came mostly from Hyderabad and many were members of the Kisan Party. As I talked to them, another jeep came and the policemen who took charge (the police apparently took over from the military once the 'invaders' were apprehended) made the half-a-dozen men wearing Gandhi caps throw them on the ground. Then he lined them up to march in rows of four. Just then a car-load of six correspondents drove up, but our lieutenant was impatient to hunt more satyagrahis, and so we jumped into the jeep and were soon off.

After several miles, we came to a small village and a moss-covered Hindu temple. There were two soldiers in the early-morning shadow. I stayed in the jeep waiting for more activity. My companion, a photographer, jumped out, hoping to get some good photos of Hindu architecture in Goa. But suddenly he beckoned me to come and I knew it was urgent.

There, in the centre of the temple, 50 men were silently sitting around one of their comrades who lay on the stone floor, dead. There was a bunch of dried mango leaves, and in front were three lithographed prints, one of Krishna.

The dead satyagrahi was Panna Lal Yadav, a 32-year-old Harijan from Rajasthan. He had a wife and four children. He was a member of the Praja Socialist Party and also a member of the Municipal Council of Ramgangmandi. He was secretary of the Stone Quarry Workers' Union. The leader of the group was Swami Madhodas, also from Rajasthan. He was holding a wounded hand.

Slowly, precisely, the spokesman told me the tragic story. They crossed the border early in the morning, again the exact method they would not reveal. Around five o'clock—when it was still dark—they entered this village in a formation of three abreast. They put the Indian flag on top of the Hindu temple. Then they began to shout slogans for the villagers to hear.

Shortly, four military men appeared. At least one had a sten-gun. They began to fire in the air and asked the satyagrahis to stop shouting slogans. The Swami said they continued to raise slogans in a peaceful manner, adding: 'We did not move.'

Then one of the soldiers struck one of the satyagrahis with the butt of his gun and then moved back and fired, one blank into the ground and then one at Panna Lal Yadav, from the back. Previously, the Swami was injured in the hand by a bullet when he raised his arms during the slogan-shouting. When Yadav fell, they asked for medical aid, but none was forthcoming. They were told to take him into the temple. He was dead and now they were guarding his body.

As we were talking, one satyagrahi said: 'They fired like a hunter hunts animals.'

Another told me: 'This is our motherland and the Portuguese want to keep it by our blood and by treating us like animals.'

I asked them if they remained non-violent throughout.

One replied: 'We believe in non-violence and that is why we came 1,000 miles to participate and that is why we walked twenty miles.'

Another said: 'This method is given in the Bible and in the Buddhist books, but people are losing faith in it and we want to show the world that there is a force greater than these bullets.'

In the meantime, the white-clad administrator of the district arrived. He questioned the soldiers in front of us to get their side of the story. But the soldier who had actually done the shooting had left long before. His colleagues insisted, however, that nine warning shots were fired into the air and only then did the soldier 'nervously fire toward the ground'. During all this conversation there was never a hint that the satyagrahis were armed. Again, the lieutenant was eager to continue his patrol.

Again we hunted satyagrahis, going to a little village at the farthest north-western part of Goa, along the Arabian Sea. We went through narrow, muddy roads and nowhere were more satyagrahis to be seen—or Indian flags or Goan National Congress posters. We returned to headquarters at 10.30 a.m., only to be told of two more batches of satyagrahis in another direction.

This time we took our taxi and soon encountered the fourth batch of satyagrahis, peacefully being guarded by one soldier, sitting under a cashew tree. There were 49 men there. They had penetrated eight miles into Goa. Most had still the white identification tags. It was noon and they had had no food since the previous evening. They had left Belgaum two days earlier and, since the government had banned the use to them of private carriers, they paid their fares in state transportation buses. I asked if they had any trouble crossing the border—with the Indian police. They said that they eluded the Indian police.

Just then the Portuguese officer, who knew English, volunteered this information: 'You mean the Indian police closed their eyes.'

Since he started talking, I asked him to give his opinion of the satyagrahis.

He cut me off by asserting: 'I'm the police,' but then he added: 'don't have to ask your opinion; I can read it,' which probably was very true!

We saw the last batch of volunteers in the town of Morgem, just above where the Rio de Chapora reaches the sea. Here a group of 41 rested in the shade, led by Y. N. Jadhav of Bombay state. They walked for six hours and the police did not catch up with them until 10 o'clock. They hoisted the flag on a Hindu temple. The people showed co-operation and even gave them cigarettes until the police came.

The satyagrahis told the villagers. 'We freed India from Britain by use of non-violence and now we will help free Goa.' They also had nothing to eat for 18 hours.

They had asked for tea, but the one soldier guarding them said it was not available. I tried to help them get food, pointing to the coconut trees overhead, but none was forthcoming from the villagers who were under the gaze of the soldier. The ages of the satyagrahis ranged from 21 to 39. Three wore the blood-red khadi caps of the PSP (Praja Socialist Party).

A leader from Poona who was in the group told me that he had taken part in the Gandhian campaigns from 1930 to 1942. He felt that the satyagraha today was run properly on Gandhian lines. He felt that had Gandhi been alive today, he would have been the first to offer satyagraha in Goa for this purpose. To a man, they waited their fate at the hands of the Portuguese authorities patiently, and without hate.

As I left one told me: 'We are, after all, human beings and we expect good treatment.'

We returned to the Pernem headquarters where I found Swami Madhodas sitting against the wall, his hand by now properly bandaged, and then somebody asked me if I had seen the two wounded satyagrahis. Earlier, two Indians had been wounded at Pernem when they allegedly tried to wrest a machine-gun away from a soldier. The gun went off and these two men fell.

I talked to the blue-clad man who did the shooting, but he insisted that it was both provoked and accidental. The Portuguese physician, white-robed, told me that the two Indians were badly hurt and he doubted if they would recover. I went to the military truck and saw them deep in pain, but conscious. I made the folded-hand sign to them and told them to have courage—which was gratuitous for or from an American. I did not even ask them their names, for they were obviously too much in pain.

Soon after three o'clock—after 12 hours on the battle-front—we headed back in our taxi for Panjim. On the way to Mapuca we were held up by the ferry crossing and it was right that the military van with the two wounded men went ahead first. Several persons peeped through the canvas—later I learned that the men who were indeed badly wounded died.

A curious turn of responsibility came when, while waiting for the ferry, I was told that the physician attending these men said that if they die it will be the fault of India and not of Portugal, since India is refusing to let an X-ray machine expert come into Goa from Bombay to fix one of their machines! Always those morally in the wrong try to shift the onus to another.

I had many other thoughts about morality and violence as we went through the little Goan village en route to Panjim. And on the back window of our taxi, when we took our last ferry ride into Panjim, I was horrified to find a sticker reading: Foa os Invasores, Foa os Traidors, Viva Portugal (Throw Out the Invaders, Throw Out the Traitors, Long Live Portugal). They threw out Panna Lal Vadav—out into all eternity.

After 'successfully defending' their colony on August 15, the foreign rulers of Goa held a press conference for the visiting journalists. At 10 p.m., some 40 journalists gathered in a second-floor chamber of the Governor-General's office building in Panjim. Life-sized oil paintings of ex-governors looked down on the handful of khaki-clad Portuguese army officers as they tried to preserve their four-century-old empire from crumbling.

Major Hormes Oliveira, Chief of Staff of the Commander-in-Chief, presided on a high dais, attended by a blue-clad interpreter. His opening statement was of the nature of a battle commuiqué given in Portuguese and then translated, sentence by sentence, into English. Dramatically, he began by asserting that 'We have witnessed today events which implied methods hitherto unused, with a country carrying these out against another independent and sovereign country.'

While he said that all of the journalists had seen events during the day, they were not able to get 'the whole picture' and so the Commander-in-Chief had invited them to this press conference in order that they may have 'a complete view'.

This consisted of the initial statement that about 3,600 Indian nationals entered Goa during the day at various points. He broke down these figures, saying that 'the greatest' was at Caronzol near the eastern border of Goa—where 'only eight on our side' withstood an invasion of 2,070 Indians, 2,000 at one instance. (These great numbers were never confirmed by the Indians, although Caronzol later turned out to be the scene of perhaps the greatest violence.)

The Chief of Staff then stated that 'inside the territory (ie, away from the borders), the action of the adversary was absolutely nil and caused not the slightest alteration in the lives of the people' (we had our doubts, as recounted below). Indeed, he said that 'in frontier regions, you saw a part of the population come forward voluntarily to face invaders and expel them from the territory' (at least I did not see such an occurrence at the northwestern border of Goa).

Confidently, the Major said: 'You saw for yourself the peace, calm and indifference of our people in the face of events on the frontier and this is proof positive that the liberation movement is not the work of the people of Goa.' Then he asserted: 'We have concealed nothing because there is nothing to conceal; we work with loyalty, sincerity and love for truth. And thus no restrictions were imposed on the movements of any journalist. Anywhere, at any time, you could see whatever you like!'

He concluded by saying: 'I have nothing more to tell on my own initiative.'

A perplexed hush fell over the assembled journalists and one articulated what all of us were thinking: 'One small detail you have apparently forgotten; what were the casualty figures for today?'

And indeed, in this first battle communiqué against the forces of a non-violent army, the Chief of Staff had omitted all deaths and injuries. Would it be true non-violence on both sides? This was too much to expect and some of us knew of at least one death and three injuries in the small sector of the border which we had watched.

The government spokesman appeared somewhat surprised at the question, but looked at his figures and said that two Indians were dead and two were wounded.

The Chief of Police of Goa had earlier that evening told some of the journalists filing daily dispatches that 13 were killed. Here was a discrepancy which had to be reconciled. The reporters, who had already sent stories to New York, London and elsewhere were irate and confused. There were bitter questions and answers for almost half an hour as the careful public relations-minded build-up of the Portuguese toward the visiting journalists suddenly went down the drain and into the Rio Mandovi.

Exasperated, the Major finally said: 'I find that on the part of the journalists here there is a certain preoccupation with the number of persons dead.' This, more than any other statement, symbolises the distance the Portuguese authorities are from the normal feelings of humanity. He found it hard to understand our preoccupation—which suddenly turned from casualties to the fascist mentality. Refusing to accept the higher casualty figures, the Major finally conceded that his figures represented 'bodies actually in our hands' and not those which may have been taken to India.

As this 'preoccupation' still led all questions, the Major finally confessed that 'We are the first to regret that blood has been shed'; then to show how careful they were 'to avoid this (bloodshed), we have taken measures'. And then he revealed 'the secret instructions' to the military and the police for August 15. The preamble even admitted that the satyagrahis would be unarmed: 'In face of an invasion of national territory by unarmed adversaries, the police force should regulate their conduct according to the following rules.'

First, warn invaders 'by all means at hand' that they are committing an act of invasion and if they continue they will be punished.

Second, if 'elements' (ie, invaders) continue in their movement, the garrison should concentrate themselves and renew the warning 'making them realise the unshakable resolve to put an end to the situation'.

Third, in case the warning is not heeded, the chief of the garrison 'shall fire three shots in the air, thus trying to frighten the invaders'.

Fourth, 'in case this result is not obtained, the commandant of the garrison will fire some shots on the ground close to the invaders, but always taking care not to hit them'.

Fifth, 'if in spite of this the adversary persists in his movements, threatening the safety of the garrison, the latter will try to defend itself by resorting to fire in the last extremity'.

These were the Portuguese battle orders to the police and soldiers on August 15. The Commander summed up his orders in these words: 'All these attitudes will have to be characterised by an unshakable firmness, although tempered by good sense and calm.' Good sense and calm apparently induced the Commander to send another last-minute battle instruction to his men on the very eve of combat: 'At all costs should be avoided the use of violent means against unarmed persons who violate our frontiers in groups: only in extreme cases are firearms to be used against such unarmed persons.'

These were, of course, ambiguous orders and gave scope to every trigger-happy soldier in Goa who could always excuse any gunfire by asserting that the satyagrahis 'threatened their safety' and the shooting was thus the outcome of an 'extreme' situation.

At this point in the press conference, I tried to change the subject slightly by asking how many people—Goans—inside Goa were arrested on August 14 and 15. (I had information from nationalists inside Panjim that arrests were made.) The Major tried to toss aside my questions by implying that, of course, there are the normal number of arrests in any city and country, but what kind of arrests did I have in mind? I shouted back: 'Political arrests, of course.'

This seemed to surprise the Major, but he recovered his composure and said carefully and gesticulating freely: 'When events such as those announced here today were expected, there usually is a small number of persons, who can be counted on the fingers, who could be regarded as persons who might become sources of disturbances, and natural precautionary measures are taken and they are brought into custody as in England or America or anywhere else in the world.'

He forgot that England, America and many other places are not yet police states with protective custody a normal procedure.

Then another reporter asked him pointblank: 'Do you mean then that ten persons have been arrested—the fingers of both hands?'

The major replied that we should not take him literally, and that only a 'very negligible number were arrested who did not get the confidence of the police' (as a matter of fact, the next day the government officially announced that 30 were arrested in Marmagao, but did not mention any further arrests, which I understand did take place on August 14 and 15).

With the Chief of Staff dodging questions right and left, and showing utter ignorance of the give-and-take of a press conference in a democracy, the reporters just past midnight took the initiative to adjourn the press conference, realising that they were wasting their time, if not the Major's.

A freelancer, sitting next to me, who was definitely pro-Portuguese and earlier in the day boasted to me how colonialism was a good thing in Asia and Africa, mumbled that the Major was that evening 'a bit stupid'.

We walked the two blocks back to our hotel in the silent streets of Panjim that midnight, knowing first-hand the inhuman, callous mentality of the rulers of this police state. The slogans along the buildings protesting loyalty to Portugal took new meaning in the starlight. The protestations of the Chief of Staff of loyalty, sincerity and love for truth were shown to be empty words, and no impartial friend of truth could be unmoved by that press conference, quite apart from the real events of the day.

As I walked along the river and into the hotel, I wondered what all this talk, this double—and triple—talk meant to Panna Lal Yadav, who for all I knew, still lay stiffly on the floor of the Hindu temple. He truly sacrificed for loyalty, sincerity and love for truth, and I knew his life and the life of 12 of his comrades all around the border would not be given in vain inside prison

What is life really like inside Goa? Is Goa really different from the rest of India? Do the Goan people want continued Portuguese colonialism, independence, or integration with India?

In the few days that I was inside Goa, I could not possibly answer these questions. And yet, I tried to make the best use of my time, and what I saw and heard may be revealing.

At 7 am on Tuesday, (August 16, 1955), I visited the lock-up in the Central Police Station at Panjim. The man in charge took me to visit Mrs Sudhabai Joshi, President of the National Congress (Goa). She was arrested in April for delivering her presidential speech at the ninth annual session of the Congress inside Goa.

Mrs Joshi is a brave woman, with a husband and two sons, aged eight and 15, still in Poona. In the cell with her was a young Goan girl who had apparently been arrested on August 14 or 15—along with two other girls—for 'political activity'. In the presence of the Portuguese prison authorities I did not want to put Mrs Joshi into further jeopardy—she is still awaiting trial—and so my visit took on the aspect merely of a friendly call, before the gates close again and prison life without visits of friends becomes cruel and monotonous.

I continued my 'free' morning in Panjim by seeing the Patriarch. The Goan 'helpers' at the press room of the hotel sent a guide-translator with me, but the Patriarch spoke good English and so I dispensed with the translator. But what the Patriarch told me need not have been said behind closed doors! Born in the Azores, the Patriarch has a full-sounding title: Patriaca das Indias Orientais Priniaz do Oriente, Arcebispo Metropolitan de Goa e Domao, Arcebispo de Cranganor. Besides the title, he is a very human, warm man and talked with me eagerly.

The Patriarch is head of the Roman Catholic Church in Goa. The diocese was established in 1533 and history oozes from the residence, from a picture of an old patriarch on the wall to the gorgeously carved wooden furniture with red velvet in the visiting room. Today, he told me, there were 2,40,000 Goans who were communicants on the Church books—3,50,000 of Catholics residing outside Goa were included.

Contrary to what I heard elsewhere, the Patriarch insisted that Catholicism in Goa took on no special Hindu aspect. He admitted that Goan Christians still strongly believed in caste, but he felt that this was not a religious matter, but a social one. More than the Protestants in Asia, the Catholic Church in Goa was using Asians and not Europeans in its work. Almost all the clergy—save five and himself—were Goans. More than 200 Goan priests ministered to Catholics outside Goa.

The Patriarch would not unequivocally say that the present tension between India and Portugal over Goa was, as the Pope told Mr Nehru, completely political. In fact he had brought me a copy of the official Vatican newspaper to show me its statement. He did admit that if Goa went to India, 'the Church will carry on'. He said the Church carried on under all political conditions, under communism or capitalism. He told me that, before 1951, he was a bishop in South India and that the Union of India was 'very kind and respectful to me'.

I turned the conversation more toward the satyagraha, and I must say that the Patriarch volunteered no profuse regrets for the butchery of the day before. He did not know that any Indians were killed. I asked him if satyagraha was not really a religious method of opposing evil, a kind of religious war without violence. I asked him if satyagraha was not really the method of Christ.

He replied: 'No, for remember what Christ said, "Render unto Caesar the things that are Caesar's."'

He felt that there were many ways of doing violence and that satyagraha was, basically, disobedience, and obviously to a Roman Catholic bishop disobedience of any sort was a cardinal sin.

Asked if shooting was not a denial of Christianity, the Patriarch replied: 'The satyagrahis make them forget their Christian qualities.'

From the Patriarch I went just a mile behind his palace to the prison in a made-over mental hospital. The officer accompanying me on this trip admitted that, since the beginning of the satyagraha movement against Goa, the jails had been full and more prison space had to be obtained (shades of India in the 1930s and 1940s!). And so the army took over the whole mental asylum, partly for a prison and partly to quarter the army (which from my observations, seems exceptionally large for a tiny colony). There was no trouble at all—in these brief days of relaxation of the rules for foreign correspondents—to visit at least some of the prisoners.

I had brief talks with N. G. Goray and S. P. Limaye of Poona, and Tridib Kumar Chaudhary, MP, of Calcutta. Goray led the first batch of satyagrahis into Goa on May 18. The others entered later. All are still awaiting trial. Since an officer who knew English was half-overhearing our talks, I felt it prudent again not to press these men for their opinion of prison conditions or other matters. It was again in the nature of a friendly and unpolitical visit.

However, they seemed to be in good spirits and seemed not to be too badly treated. (I am not, however, generalising on the treatment of Indian or Goan prisoners at the hands of the Portuguese.)

All the three gave me the addresses of their families. Since mail from Goa was not apparently reaching India, I promised to write to each of their families and report that they are well and hopeful.

Back in the press room at the hotel, the white-clad chief of the Cabinet of the Governor-General was there with two bottles of liquor, and waiters were passing drinks around freely to the newspaper men who, in the main, were just preparing to leave Goa. The chief admitted that the press conference of the previous evening was 'most unfortunate' and that now the government could confirm that probably as many as 13 satyagrahis were dead, although not all the 13 bodies were inside Goa. He suggested that, because of communication difficulties, information was tardy in reaching Panjim; (for example, just previously at the central police headquarters news was received for the first time that 515 satyagrahis entered Sukla the previous day).

The chief of the Cabinet handed me, since I raised the question at the press conference the night before, an official communiqué in which he admitted that 30 individuals tried to demonstrate in Margoa, in groups of four, five, nine and eleven. Two of these demonstrations were in the morning and two in the afternoon. And even then he tried to minimise this dispatch by suggesting that those arrested were of 'low social position' and hired by a man 'already under arrest'. He added that the 30 were, therefore, acquitted, although one Indian national with them was sent across the border.

Through circumstances just as well not detailed here, I did meet one Goan who talked to me freely and honestly. We met in a neutral place— myself and this 42-year-old physician, born in Panjim. He told me that the police were watching his activities, but not yet his home. He said he belonged to an informal group inside Goa asking for autonomy, although he personally was for an autonomy leading to integration with India. He believed integration was inevitable, just from the economic point of view. He showed me charts to prove this. He said that since tenant farmers in parts of Goa now got only half of the produce they grew (the other half going to the landowners), they would be favourable to integration since they would then keep five-sixths of the produce.

He added that, like it or not, the scope and field of activity of Goans was in India, not in Europe or Portugal. It was to India they looked for better education, even for better jobs, not to far-off Portugal. Many Goans felt that, had they been born on the other side of the border—in India—they might have become a Gandhi or a Tagore. Here in Goa there was no opportunity except to be a puppet of the Portuguese.

The Goan doctor further said the agitation for autonomy intensified after 1946, and in 1947 the Portuguese asked some leading Goans what they wanted. Twenty-three sent back a memorandum demanding full autonomy. The Portuguese sat on this request until 1953, when they changed the name from colony to province, although, he said, this change fooled nobody.

He added that Portugal really had no material or economic interest in Goa. It exported some wine and sardines to Goa and had a bank monopoly. It was, he felt, principally a prestige problem for Dr Salazar, who boasted of having built the modern Portuguese empire. This Portugal was only incurring expenditure without receiving anything in return— except prestige.

I felt I was talking to a Goan who would one day become a leader of Goa.

There were some other experiences inside Goa, some other impressions of Goa—a country not unlike adjoining India, in landscape, in agricultural produce, in at least the superficial habits and even dress of the people. I cannot vouch for the adults, but at least naked children in Goa looked remarkably like naked children in India—and, for that matter, naked children the world over!

And so this myth that Goa is somehow vastly different culturally does not hold examination. Granted there are some cultural differences, as there are among the various sections of the Indian Union—Assam and Punjab, to name only two. Surely Assam is no less different from 'India' than Goa.

While most of my important experiences were inside Goa, I must recount some en route to Goa from Bombay and return. I left Bombay on August 12, and had a quiet enough time on the train to Poona. At the station I saw large groups of satyagrahis marching, after having reported to their headquarters. And just before train time, there was an air of patriotic excitement as batches of satyagrahis marched through the station to take the same train to Belgaum as I was taking. They waved the Indian flag, raised slogans and gave the station a sense of rare excitement.

In my compartment was a physician from near Raipur who was going down to attend on the injured. He said all the political parties had united on this single objective of non-violent satyagraha. And representatives from the various parties were making together the kind of day-to-day decisions which Gandhi alone used to make. They were giving each batch an Indian flag and telling them that they had a moral right to plant it inside Goa. They should hold on to the flag to their last breath but not retaliate. And the mass of satyagrahis till then (up to August 13) had not retaliated.

Then I talked to V.D. Chitale, the communist who was designated to lead the total group of satyagrahis on August 15. He said communists had no hesitation in using satyagraha. In the given circumstances, this method alone was possible since negotiations with a colonial regime were impossible. He felt that Mr Nehru faced a dilemma and ultimately force would have to be used. He said the communists demanded police action, but because the government refused, non-violence was being used.

Just before the train reached Belgaum, a batch of youths came into my compartment and I interviewed them. I asked them why they were participating in the satyagraha.

One young man of 19 replied: 'To liberate Goa by non-violent means.'

Another youth of 17 said: 'Goa is part of India and I do not like any part of India to be ruled by foreigners.'

A third boy, only 16, said he 'wants to liberate Goa'. His father was a mason and willingly consented to his participation. He said he was 'ready to die for the sake of my country'. He told me that he would not fight back.

I asked him where he learned the discipline of non-violence, and he replied: 'The teachings of Mahatma Gandhi which I learned from the Congress Youth Organisation.'

The leader of the group, Hemant Soman of Poona, was formerly a teacher in Goa and last year hoisted the Indian flag over the palace. He was severely beaten and imprisoned.

The boys also told me that, at the headquarters of the satyagraha in Poona, they signed a pledge. Freely translated, it read: 'The people of Goa, to obtain their own independence, are fighting against the Portuguese government—a Goa which is considered to be a part of Portuguese sovereignty. I wish to enter into this non-violent satyagraha and I solemnly pledge that I will gladly accept whatever physical difficulties be committed on me. I realise all the responsibilities of entering this movement. I myself am personally responsible for whatever consequences there are, and will not, in any circumstance, adopt violence. Goa Liberation Committee.'

Each satyagrahi signed this pledge and, in turn, was given a white badge pinned on to his shirt.

I left the satyagrahis at Belgaum, they to report to their headquarters and I to take the eight-hour bus ride to Karwar, since that was the only entrance into Goa which, both Indian and Portuguese authorities agreed, journalists could use. On my return to Belgaum, on August 17, I called at the headquarters of the various organisations working on the satyagraha. If Panjim was the battle command headquarters for the Portuguese, Belgaum was for the satyagrahis.

I met once again Mr Joshi, and he kindly took me around the city. He showed me the mill where 'some of the satyagrahis were housed— once 1,200 in a single night'. He showed me the Hindu marriage celebration hall which had been turned into a dining room. It was a sight to see even two days after August 15, large groups of satyagrahis walking through Belgaum on their way to get food. There were great piles of *chapattis*—I was given a corner of one to taste—and a group of women were preparing vegetables.

Then I was taken to the civil hospital, and the attending physician told me that 69 wounded satyagrahis were there and still others were expected. Half of those in the hospital had bullet wounds. I saw at least one wounded man I had ridden with on the train down from Poona. All seemed in good spirits and accepted their fate with poise. I heard many stories of horrors, especially from the men who fell at Tunnel No 10 past Castle Rock.

And everywhere I went in Belgaum, Karwar, or Bombay, they asked me: 'How many people were really killed on the 15th?' We inside Goa saw no killings, although we did see dead men afterwards, and for sure we knew of 13 dead by the time we left Panjim. But if we did not see any killing for the benefit of our newspapers and magazines, at least we prevented some killings by our very presence. It is probably no coincidence that the most killings took place far away from where the reporters assembled in Panjim could possibly have motored or walked on that fateful Monday.

Satyagraha is an honest method and wonderful too. However, it is a kind of tool that does not necessarily show immediate results. Because Goa was not liberated on August 15, because many people were savagely slaughtered, satyagraha was by no means a failure. For satyagraha works in several directions. It puts courage and determination into the heart of the satyagrahi. It gives concern and a kind of commitment to the wider public. And, ultimately, it changes the heart, through love, of the opponent. I must admit that I saw little love shown by the satyagrahis toward the Portuguese, nor did I see little outright hatred.

Since satyagraha is a new tool on the international scene, August 15, 1955, will go down in the annals of history as the beginning of a new era. Who knows, perhaps the peace-making started in our time by Mr Nehru and given an impetus by the 'summit' conference in Geneva, will result in the replacement of atomic weapons on the international arena by satyagraha!

Some say the butchery shows that satyagraha could be used internally or with the British, a human race, but not with the fascists, not with Hitler, Mussolini or Salazar. Gandhi always insisted that (1) the British were not as humane as often claimed, and (2) in any case, the method could be used against the most ruthless dictator using the most modern weapons. Gandhi felt that the Jews could have resisted Hitler non-violently and he told the world, toward the end of his life, how even atomic warfare could be resisted non-violently.

That 20 or even 30 satyagrahis got killed is a terrible tragedy, but it is no commentary on the efficacy of satyagraha. Suffering and death itself are part of the price of being a satyagrahi. Satyagraha is not a method of going across the border and then coming quickly home to be acclaimed a hero. It means suffering. It means death. And Mr Nehru is perfectly right in insisting that the Indian government cannot protect these people—they must expect the worst.

That the Portuguese have shown themselves to be violent and trigger-happy is beyond doubt. And as far as I know, the killers were pretty much the Portuguese soldiers themselves and not their armed lackeys of Goan or African background. Indeed it is reported that the Portuguese were afraid to give the Africans guns—at least near the border—for fear that they would desert or, perhaps, turn their guns against their masters. Also, there is not much evidence that Goan members of the police and army did any of the shooting. This was a specialisation left, for several good reasons, to the Portuguese soldiers themselves.

The orders issued to the soldiers give them every latitude to shoot. How could, therefore, anybody expect the military not to shoot, with the ambiguous orders they were given. It is a wonder more Indians were not slaughtered!

Do the Goans want their freedom? How to evaluate what a people want—especially a people under the iron grip of totalitarianism? I think it correct to assume that people everywhere are more preoccupied with problems of food and family than with politics. That large numbers of Goans were ploughing and otherwise going about their business on August 15—it was a Church holiday—was obviously not a show staged by the Portuguese. The majority of the people in Goa, as probably in Portugal itself, just do not care enough to be politically courageous.

Of those in Goa who identified themselves one way or another, it is necessary to break them into several groups, eliminating, of course, the Portuguese living there. Of the Goans who are in the government administration or in business many want to hold on to what they have. This is understandable. And yet there are a number of professional people and perhaps even business people who, from principle or expediency, see the writing on the wall and are covertly against the Portuguese. Then there are the courageous ones in prison, perhaps 400 or more.

But it would be a denial of truth to say that the streets and villages of Goa are overrun with people eagerly and openly welcoming a political change. I saw no such evidence and—in a police state—I really did not expect to see any, however much I perhaps hoped that I might.

An American cannot comment on Goa without feeling very uncomfortable about American policy toward the whole Goan question. I must admit that I do not know what this policy is, but the very fact that I do not know means that we Americans have no policy or, worse yet, it is one of being so tied to our sister NATO nation Portugal, that we dare not criticise what she is doing, colonial wise, in Africa or Asia. I know the revolting events of August 15 are bound to make the American people more sympathetic to the Indian claim to Goa. I think in time—and I hope in a short time—this sympathy will change official American policy.

This one American cannot also refrain from stating that he feels that Mr Nehru's position on Goa is right, if difficult. Yet public feeling in India has risen so high that any other statesman but Mr Nehru would long have been driven out from office by such an unpopular policy. Mr Nehru apparently can afford, politically, to be more right than popular in his own country as, in recent years, he has had to assume this same attitude towards the whole world.

His repeated assurance that India will never use force against the Portuguese strengthens his hands internationally, for it shows that he practices what he preaches—which is a rare thing anywhere in the world. And he practices what he preaches despite the methods used by Portugal to goad him into stronger action. Had Mr Nehru succumbed to the popular outcry and used police action—a polite euphemism for war—he may have had the overwhelming support of the Indian people, but his huge world influence as a man of peace would have suffered grievously.

And many of his enemies around the world are eagerly waiting for such an opportunity. Mr Nehru is right from principle and from long-run politics.

As for the future of Goa, I always tend to be an optimist in matters of justice. Three years ago I had the privilege of watching the non-violent defiance campaign of the Africans and Indians in South Africa against apartheid. At that time I publicly said that White domination of South

Africa could not last ten years. I still feel so today, but I have not won any prizes yet as a prophet.

Nevertheless, I feel substantially the same way about the future of Goa. It is impossible for Portugal to hang on much longer—indeed, it is only fascist colonial pride which had made Portugal hold on as long as she has. At my hotel in Bombay, since I returned, Goans have come up to me and asked me what I think of the future.

I feel that within three years Goa will be free from Portugal. You can ask me why, but please don't ask me how. And yet I hope responsible leaders of the recent satyagraha, representing all Indian parties, will get together and keep together and base their future plans on a careful estimate of their present results.

After saying and writing what I have, I know I will not be allowed back into Goa by the Portuguese. And yet I am sure I will be back in Goa the next time I come to India. And I shall never forget the supreme sacrifice of Panna Lal Yadav and how, so silently, so determinedly, so wonderfully calm his comrades sat around his body on the stone floor of the ancient Hindu temple. *Azad Goa! Jai Hind!*

'Meagre presence of the Portuguese language'

Orlando Ribeiro

Orlando Ribeiro, a renowned Portuguese geographer-historian, who published *Goa em 1956: Relatório ao Governo* (Lisboa, CNCDP, 2000) refers to 'mestiçagem espiritual' in Goa, implying thereby what Gilberto Freyre, a Brazilian sociologist of Portuguese origin, on a Salazar-sponsored visit to Goa five years earlier, in 1951, to propagate 'Luso-tropicalismo', defined as 'unidade de sentimento e cultura', meaning a common heritage of feelings and culture (an expression appropriated by Orlando Ribeiro on pp. 82, 119 of his Report). Orlando Ribeiro's academic credibility and relatively high degree of impartiality and critical perspective make his Report valuable for all interested in evaluating how much of the impact of the Portuguese in Goa was really Lusotopic, Lusophonic and Lusophilic. Obviously, Salazar did not like the report and it remained unknown till it was published recently by the Portuguese historian Fernando Rosas, with an introduction by Orlando Ribeiro's wife Suzanne Daveau. Here follow some extracts translated from the Report:

> My inner feelings and what I have discovered compel me to be very frank and not to hide those aspects which are less pleasant or to avoid those aspects which hurt our national feelings. I think that it is good to face the hard reality, however painful it may be to us. It is only in this way that we can avoid ambiguities, illusions and hesitations, and can know for sure on whom we can depend and what should be the ground for our decisions.
>
> Unlike elsewhere where the Portuguese, attracted by the coloured females had produced very quickly a mestiço population (população

mestiçada), the rigidity of the caste system in Goa forced the Portuguese to produce only a new caste of descendentes. Albuquerque's dream of creating a Luso-Indian population, as insistently recommended by D. Manuel, vanished very early. Only a few women, whose caste condemned them to low social status, sought to marry these foreigners to gain upward social mobility.

Unlike in Brazil, where so many illustrious and humble families proudly acknowledge their Portuguese origin and mixed descent; unlike in Cabo Verde whose Creole population feels very close to us because of their old African slave-ancestors who shared the blood of their white masters, the Goans have preserved the purity of their caste, but yet reveal a surprising degree of assimilation of our habits and living style. Here we have only a spiritual miscegenation (mestiçagem espiritual). It is hard to believe though that no Portuguese blood runs in the veins of the rural aristocracy of Salcete or the old Christian families of Margão.

It is also surprising to note the meagre presence of the Portuguese language among the Goan Christian population. Only the educated inhabitants speak the Portuguese language correctly and fluently, and not rarely with remarkable eloquence. Many families in Margão use Portuguese to converse among themselves. But they invariably use Konkani with their servants, just as it happens with the general village population. However, during feast celebrations, in roadside conversations, in dramatic performances, it is not difficult to pick up Portuguese words like pai, mãe, família, casamento, sacramento, which reveal the deep influence of the Portuguese language on the day-to-day lives of the people.

I have known reasonably well the adjacent Islands and have a small book written on Madeira. I have visited all the Portuguese territories in Africa, starting from Mozambique, and have studied better Guinea and the islands of Cape Verde. I have spent four months in Brazil and observed its deep recesses and have known something about the Muslim world since my days as a student and after my visits to Morroco, Egypt and West Africa. I had thus acquired some good preparation to initiate my research in Goa. Goa appeared to me as the least Portuguese of all the Portuguese territories I had seen so far, even less than Guinea, which came into our possession in 1912! I witnessed a near total ignorance of our language, the persistence of a society not only strange and indifferent, but even hostile to our presence, our limited influence encrusted as a schist in the body of renascent Hinduism; all this has left me very disillusioned about Goa.

Unlike in Portuguese Africa, where the expressions Metrópole and Metropolitano are used with some discretion, in Goa it is common to hear the binary use of Province/ Portugal and Goan Christian/Portuguese. That is how Portugal and the Portuguese are mentioned by Goans who share our language and customs, but not our feeling of patriotism. Pátria for a Goan is his Goa, not Portugal, and it is in Goa that they want to experience their freedom and their privileges. The Hindus in general and many Goan Christians as well, entertain ideas of closer relations with Índia and autonomy for their land.

Twenty-three years ago I had gone on a boat-cruise to our Atlantic islands, and I remember the affection and warm welcome that was accorded to the Portuguese by the African populations. My longer visits to Guinea, Cabo Verde and São Tomé confirmed that experience. In Goa it is different. The predominant relationship is of distance and suspicion, when it is not outright or camouflaged antipathy.

'A certain bitterness remains after "liberation"'

Graham Greene

At night, lying on the verandah of a village house in Anjuna, watching the constellations wheel out of view across the great arc of sky with what seemed the speed of satellites, I found it possible to forget the poverty of Bombay, 400 miles away, the mutilated beggars, the lepers squatting near the Pro-Cathedral.

The silver stubble of the paddy fields, squared off by the trees and hills, lay in a strong wash of moonlight; at five in the morning a church bell woke me, sounding twice with a short interval between—the first notes urging men to pray against the evil spirits abroad at night (perhaps in the form of a sow followed by her litter trotting through the dark), the second to summon men to work.

At the close of the night, just before the colours of the sunrise, a pack of jackals would course back across the stubble to the hills, raising a cry like that of a crowd at a ball game—'Rah, rah, rah'. Ox-carts began to creak invisibly, a few figures passed across the paddy carrying torches of coconut fronds, the red and yellow trickled like coloured water along the horizon behind the banyans, the mango trees, the cashews. Someone watching from an aeroplane would have seen in every direction white churches appear like splinters of moonlight on the landscape: the uniqueness of Goa.

Outside Goa one is aware all the time of the interminable repetition of the ramshackle, the enormous pressure of poverty, flowing, branching, extending like floodwater. This is not a question of religion. The Goan Hindu village can be distinguished as easily from the Hindu village of

India as the Christian, and there is little need to drive the point home at the boundary with placards. The houses in the Goan village were built with piety to last.

There are a few extremes of poverty and affluence: most houses, however small, are constructed of laterite blocks with brown tiles of great beauty. They were built by Goans, not by Portuguese (for the Portuguese lived only in the towns), often by Goans in exile, in Aden or in Africa, who hoped to return one day, for the far-ranging Goan has loyalty to his village you seldom find elsewhere. It seemed the first thing one Goan asked another, not in what city he worked but from what village he came, and in distant Bombay every Goan village has its club of exiles— 350 clubs.

In the first Indian village outside Goa on the road to Bombay you are back to the mud huts and broken thatch which are almost a sign of affluence compared with the horrible little cabins made out of palm fronds and bits of canvas and any piece of old metal on the outskirts of Bombay. These are dwellings to escape from; how can their inhabitants feel loyalty to Maharashtra—the huge amorphous member State of the Indian Union neighbouring Goa, into which Goa must almost certainly be sooner or later submerged?

No wonder that in villages like Anjuna you find sad old men sitting in almost empty rooms and carved Goan chairs, regretting the past—the green and red wines of Portugal, the Scotch whiskey at thirteen rupees a bottle which will cost now, if you are lucky to find a bottle, fifty or sixty.

There is prohibition in Maharashtra State—in Goa there is only prohibition by price, which leaves the raw Indian gins and whiskies relatively cheap, with what effect on the health of the drinker cannot be known. A certain bitterness too remains after 'liberation', a word which began to alter its meaning in 1944 and is now as soiled as 'democracy'. There were military casualties, not many for these days, but there were also cases of rape and looting in Panjim, the Capital of Goa, for in the last 'colonial' years Goa had known a mining boom and the luxury goods which came in with every boat from Lisbon fetched good profits across the border. A postman in those days received higher wages than a professor does now in India.

The last Portuguese Governor has left friendly memories (he is said to be in disgrace for having disobeyed Salazar's orders to destroy Panjim— it would have been no great architectural loss perhaps, though one would regret the dramatic statue of the Abbe Faria pouncing like a great black eagle on his mesmerised female patient). Nor do you hear anywhere a word against the Portuguese as individuals.

And yet in December the majority of votes by a small margin went to the party which favoured merging with Maharashtra. It was a communal vote—nearly all Catholics voted for a separate State and nearly all Hindus for a merger, but watching the face of my Hindu driver, as he saw for the first time ragged out-of-heels Poona and then the squalid outskirts of Bombay, I wondered whether his opinions were changing already after leaving the tidy streets and the great clean river of Panjim.

As for the Congress Party—it was nowhere. It fought as the party of 'the liberation', which did not count in its favour, and perhaps credibility, but suicidally, the party tried to keep the question of merger out of the election, as something which would be solved in the course of time. The Congress view now seems likely to prevail and Goa to remain a territory administered by India for at least another five years.

Perhaps in some minds there is a hope left that at the end of that period, after industrialization, with the growth of tourism, Goa may prove financially capable of becoming a separate State in the Union, while Congress has an equal hope that in the course of time Goan Catholics may see the advantages of government from Bombay, Maharashtra's capital.

I doubt whether it is the closed Catholicism of Goa (the Patriarch in exile and little communication held with the Catholics of Bombay) which will decide the issue. Panjim, the capital, was celebrating Christmas, when I arrived, in Capriote rather than Indian style. Cars drove in procession around the streets on the way to Midnight Mass decorated with greenery, the passengers playing snatches of music and flinging firecrackers into the street. A little tidy provincial town with white-washed 18th-century buildings, Panjim is by no means the 'God-forgotten place' that Lady Burton described a hundred years ago.

Indeed there is more than a hint of the worldly Babylon which shocked Camoens. Serenaders played their guitars at night to a young woman who had arrived in town for Christmas; at a party I found myself handed as a matter of course a Benzedrine tablet at four in the morning; naked bathing parties take place at a secluded beach; and who sleeps with whom is known to all Panjim.

Up in Old Goa all is silence and desolation. The huge square, 250 yards across, once lined with palace, prison, churches, is overgrown and only a small stone like that on a child's grave marks the site of the dreaded Inquisition. On Christmas Eve a pig running before the footlights seemed at first the only living thing up there besides ourselves. But in the Cathedral there was a congregation of perhaps a dozen people sitting in a gloom the candles could not penetrate, while a choir of old Canons sang the Mass—elongated, emaciated, El Greco figures in dingy scarlet dickies, half starved on thirty rupees a month, and up near the invisible roof bats twittered as loudly as their voices. At the High Altar the sacrament was not reserved, for fear of robbers, and after Mass Communion was given by the light of one candle at a little side-chapel reluctantly unlocked for the purpose.

I had a sense that I was attending one of the last ceremonies of Christianity. This might well be St. Peter's 300 years hence if the door on to the world is not kept open, and I was reminded later of the old tattered monseigneurs by the relics of another Raj in my shabby hotel at Poona, where the waiter was dressed in what remained of the semi-military uniform which his English employer had given him thirty years ago. 'No bacon,' he said sadly when I tried to order an English breakfast. 'No one asks for bacon now.'

It seemed a grim, apocalyptic place, Old Goa, with the shrinking body of St. Francis Xavier in the great church of Bom Jesus, built in 1594, the bit that a lady tore off preserved in a reliquary, and the silver crucifix on his tomb twisted awry by a Catholic thief a week before; in a cupboard of the same church were the skulls of martyrs, and other dubious portions preserved in bottles of spirits which reminded me of those you see in the windows of Chinese specialists in Kuala Lumpur advertising cures for piles.

In the convent of Santa Monica, where Burton tried to abduct an orphan and picked up the Lady Abbess by mistake, there is a weeping crucifix, and in Bom Jesus stuck obscurely away is the cross found on a hillside which miraculously grew, so that it had to be shortened to enter the church. The headpiece was strengthened by metal to prevent it shooting up farther—a sagacious measure which, needless to say, had complete success.

Catholic Goa is divided into two halves by the great Mandovi river— on the right bank lies Franciscan Goa, on the left Jesuit Goa, and as you might expect Catholicism is richer and superficially stronger on the left bank. Here are the iron ore mines, Margao with its elegant square lined with great houses, and on the outskirts the monstrosities of the new rich built like plastic soap dishes.

In the villages of this region, Goan families still maintain their state. In the façade of one house I counted sixteen great windows in a row, and the salon was thirty-six paces long. In another house I saw in the granary a great wooden storage chest larger than the biggest barrels of Oporto, far larger than the cabins in which whole families live on the outskirts of Bombay. (Here there was even a flush lavatory in place of the usual hole in a laterite block above a trough where a pig stands honking to receive your droppings.)

In the big houses too are private altars of carved Goan wood, with tier on tier of little figures surrounded by artificial flowers, and in every spare space examples of china from Macao. The cellar will still contain a few last bottles of green and red wine, port, some liqueurs, even a little Scotch. They will be assembled for your choice: Goan hospitality will not cease till the cellar is empty.

Here emotional stories may be told you of the last Portuguese days. 'There are still three seats on the plane, the Governor said to me. Come with us. You will be recompensed for all you lose here. I tell you there were tears in the Governor's eyes when he embraced me.'

This Jesuit Goa will find it harder to accept merger in Maharashtra, though it shares with India one evil characteristic against which Gandhi successfully fought—the hierarchy of caste. The early Jesuit missionaries worked closely with the Brahmins, and the Brahmins remain all-important around Margao. Caste has even been extended by Christianity, for Catholics consider themselves superior to Hindus, and Hindu Brahmins accept the superiority of Catholic Brahmins.

But in the village of Anjuna I was in Franciscan Goa, a poorer but surely a happier region, where the merger with Hinduism has already begun. Horoscopes are consulted, and even a Goan finds it hard to say which superstition is of Hindu, which of Catholic origin. A silver crucifix is buried under the lintel of every new house—that is Catholic, but what of the navel cords of children born there which are tucked under the floor or into the walls or even into a pillow?

Both Catholics and Hindus practise the same ceremony for removing the evil eye with the help of a wise woman: the sprinkling of salt, four or five chillies cast into a fire—if an explosion occurs all is well. Until recently at midnight the ghost of a woman who had drowned herself would walk across the paddy fields in front of my friend's house. She was not seen: she was only heard—jingling the bangles on her arm that all brides must wear (a Hindu or a Catholic custom?). A man in the village across the fields laughed at the sound—'She does not frighten me,' so she came and rattled the bangles by his head and he never spoke again. A year later he was dead.

My friend's aunt had many such stories to tell one night, speaking in Konkani, the Goan language. There was a solitary tree standing above the paddy where no other tree grew—an old tree: one could not say what was its highest common factor, for many kinds of trees had grafted themselves on to the main trunk. It was an unhealthy spot to pass at night. You might be 'carried away'——this seemed a speciality of the spirits of Bardez where Anjuna lies. When you wake you find yourself up a coconut palm. 'It happened to your aunt. She had heard mangoes falling in the night, and she went out at the first strokes of the clock to gather them when she should have been praying for the evil spirits to pass. She was carried right away all over the rocks by the seashore, and put up a coconut palm. She was sitting there when the fishermen came down in the morning.'

This is what I will remember chiefly of Goa—the voice in Konkani telling of strange events, the cry of the jackals coming down from the hills, the golden evening light across the paddy, the sense of deep country peace.

Industrialization is bound to come, a tourist department has opened in Panjim, and there are great beaches waiting for great hotels, while just over the hills lies the enormous poverty of the sub-continent, ready to spread along the seaboard as soon as the fragile barriers are raised.

Portugal helped to form the special character of Goa and Goa's character may survive Portugal for a year or two. But you cannot hang a skull at the entrance of Goa as you can on a mango tree to avert the envious eye. No wonder that even in the great houses of Jesuit Goa you have a sense of impermanence. Dust lies on the furniture, in the best bedroom suitcases are piled on the floor with an overnight bag on top. It is as though the family has not had time to unpack properly, and yet already it is nearly the hour to leave.

'Psychedelic conquistados'

David Tomory

My first time in Goa was October 1976. I had arrived on a series of trains from north India, and was tired of trains and heat and distances. On the platform in Margao—or Madgaon, it had two names—were some French people. They lived nearby, in Colva, and wanted to know where I was going. I said north, to Anjuna. There followed a long pause in which that lovely name hung in the air like a confession; then one of them said, 'Ah, but that is definitely somewhere else.'

The bus going north was blue, and it was called *Mahalaxmi*. The name of the Hindu goddess was painted along the side in green italics, the down strokes picked out in white. I walked around the back, by the taillights red with dust, to ask the driver if he was going as far as Mapusa, and saw that along the other side of the bus was painted another name: *Mother Mary.*

Inside this bus blessed by two religions a tape boomed out odd music, a yearning soprano ballad, Indian quarter-tones over Iberian horns. As it ended, we left town for the landscape of monsoon electric—green paddy fields and terracotta earth. We passed a little wayside chapel freshly painted white and barred with iron, the tall roadside palms high above it leaning into an empty sky. I was sure that somewhere near would be the deeper blue of the sea, but then we turned inland. *Mahalaxmi/Mother Mary* traipsed around Goa for a while, stopping apparently at random, and eventually came to rest in Mapusa. I stayed the night, and the next day took another bus to the coast, getting down by a red-and-blue blockhouse of a bar called Starco's, the first bar I had seen since Park Street in Calcutta that didn't look ashamed of itself. 'Kingfisher', the beer billboard announced 'Most Thrilling Chilled'.

I walked on through the village—a vast and unwalled village of old houses widely set apart—and halfway to the beach I found a place to rent. It was a little room with a porch, quite new, tacked on to the massive flank of a much older and quite decrepit mansion.

Staying in Anjuna a few years after the Portuguese departure, Graham Greene wrote Goa would be transformed by India within a few years. But it took much longer. Salazar's retrograde regime had ruled Goa by gloom for nearly half a century, and in the mid-seventies, gloom lingered on. There were plenty of rooms for rent in big old houses (amongst the palms, within earshot of the sea and the exuberant birdlife) that shut out the sun and exuded tropical *tristesse*. Crepuscular, with creaking four-poster beds that leaked ant dust, with bottomless cane chairs and sepia prints of interments—so many places were like this. The reliquary boxes and framed martyrs cast long shadows. My landlady's family were rentiers and small landowners reduced to genteel poverty. Several days a week they went to church or attended litanies at the wayside icons of patron saints. Their two men, one just back from Africa, the other a pensive unemployed uncle, wore Sunday suits. The boys were thoroughly starched; the girls and women wore flounced, frilled, multilayered, satiny dresses suggestive of Mexico. The widows went along in widows' weeds.

On the big saint's days I was invited to elaborate feasts, though the dull decades had made even these rather prim. I sensed standards being kept up in obligation to old protocol and the remonstrating pulpit. My neighbour Ratko had a grim landlord: outside on his balcao on St. Sebastian's Day I once saw him sitting at table, sweating through his old black suit, gazing through the roast boar's ribcage like a prisoner. Long popular in Goa, Sebastian was a legendary martyr of the Romans, a centurion condemned for his faith. From the sixteenth century he was heavily promoted all over the empire as the exemplary suffering Christian soldier, with his eyes on heaven and his abdomen full of arrows, which he is said to have miraculously survived—whereupon the emperor had him clubbed to death.

My landlady's family occupied a house opposite and had interests in properties round about, but I never did find out if anybody actually lived in the decrepit mansion which abutted my little room.

'Hello,' my landlady would say, pocketing the rent money. 'Goodnight.' Then she would vanish round the comer into the dusk. There was no public lighting at all, but no villager ever needed the hand-candle in the half-shell of coconut without which I was helpless on moonless nights. I understood why we foreigners loved the moon so much.

Where the back wall of my room met the side wall of the mansion, plaster had come off the laterite. Through several gaps between the weathered blocks could be seen a huge and derelict dining room-cum-kitchen, the tiled worktop, its decayed earthenware pots, and at the end of it, wood-barred windows—opening into what seemed to be another room with the same sagging wormy rafters and ant-ridden walls, cracking furniture and festoons of webs. Desiccation was universal, and bandicoots had tunnelled the floors. The walls of the nearest room had at some time been whitewashed as high as the painting-pole would reach, but above them hung a smoke-blackened ceiling of impossible altitude.

In my own room there was nothing at all but a bowed bed and a disembowelled suitcase and a graffito on the wall reading 'Spaceship Lenny Has Not Yet Landed'. I remember going outside to sit on the tiny white porch, and seeing the moon come up to silver the palms. The silence was absolute, until a dog barked, and then another, and then every dog in north Anjuna. All together they suddenly stopped, and through the silence came the generator thud.

In the Rose Garden I heard a man eating crab and talking about the Anjuna of five years earlier. This must have been the period Ratko called Early Hip. 'It didn't last long. The equality was a youth thing, and shared poverty kept it going. It vanished as soon as people started making money.' At which point the broke and the egalitarian had fled for Vagator and Arambol. This left Anjuna with the movers and shakers and a certain mystique. Its fame spread. Famous counterculture folk were said to go there. The movers and shakers began to appear all over the planet in silk, silver, brocades and exotic jewellery, telling tales so beguiling that by the mid-seventies Anjuna was being overwhelmed by its admirers.

Once upon a time there had been naked hermaphrodites to astound the fully dressed men. The mobile Californian commune called the Hog Farm had visited. There was at least one Family of unrelated adults; there were the Green People, each bearded patriarch marshalling his wives and babies. I saw Early Hip as the American discovery of Goa. America radiating from world conquering California her visionaries, deft New World navigators of the modern flux, psychedelic conquistados. In Anjuna in 1994 I met a man searching for the very spot where he had been spontaneously seduced by a 'nymphet' in 1972, on his way home from a party. He told me that spontaneity had been everything, openness had been everything, freedom had been everything, and now he was on Wall Street.

'Then there were the Italian Beautifuls,' Eve Green recalls, 'all walking on the beach naked except for the silver belt, the silver necklace. Super-poseurs, very elegant and in control, though I didn't know they were junkies until over the years they began to die off, and I asked what had become of them. When they wore anything it was white. Always white.'

There was nowhere like it; it was too rare to last. Anjuna in 1976 had an aggrieved air, like an artists' colony suddenly chosen to host a beer festival. There was the public Anjuna, the parties, the flea market, and within it another Anjuna that was not somewhere you went but something you joined.

Ratko had been there quite a while, but he was not a joiner. He was a gruff old wanderer from somewhere in Yugoslavia. His hair and beard were not long but disordered, he was obsessively bookish, a sort of Gurdjieffian beatnik, and about forty years old; to me, ancient. To him, hippies were romantics yearning for a golden future or the golden past or both. Where he came from, the romantics had finished up endorsing communism, because communism itself yearned for those things.

And he worked. You didn't work in Goa, you *were*. Every evening he would retire early, and all night the big petromax lamps shone through the cracks in his door. He spent all night with his books and slept by day, except for every second Friday, when he would leave blearily in the morning for the Mapusa post office with a heavy parcel. When he had finished reading his books, he said, he sent them back. That night he would sleep. Late on Saturday morning, genial, he would invite me over for tea and a lecture, all the time fondling his latest tome, invariably a weighty hardback on something like Sanskrit prosody, or bio-chemistry.

He said he was too grim for parties. He didn't even read the Anjuna magazine, *The Stoned Pig*. Nevertheless, he got wind of everything. Anjuna came to him in emanations.

I would drink tea and he would talk. 'It's not that there are too many people. It's because they're the wrong kind of people.' Ratko's bony finger would shoot out and lock on to some guileless youth tripping across the clearing. 'Begone, Bilbo Baggins! You will not last a week here! This jungle is too dark for you, it tolerates no small vices.

'In godless times,' he would continue, 'where does the poor Westerner go to find God? India. But he shouldn't go to Goa. Goa is not for truth-seeking, but for vision-seeking. Now the dull colonial time is over, this place has been reinvented as—of all things—a location for improbable dreams, an Eldorado. The new kings of the mild frontier—well, just look at them. Of course the moralists are enraged. They have never seen that kind of jungle craziness before.

'Raleigh died for Eldorado. Aguirre went mad in the jungle. Utopias were founded, and all of them failed. No perfect place has ever been found in the West, so in our time the vision-seekers came east. Here in Goa they found freedom. You know Grass?'

'From Thailand.'

'From West Germany. Gunter Grass talks about "the freedom of the playground". That is the freedom you see here, against a backdrop of exotic scenery. Here there are no rulers, no police, no pressure.

'So you get awesome displays of hubris, jungle craziness, an impressive casualty rate. Freedom means just that: you're free to live and free to die. It's accepted. A young girl swims out to sea—this happened a month ago—keeps on going and never comes back, and there's nothing to be said about it, apart from "She wanted to go beyond," or something metaphysical like that. What *does* get the vision-seekers in a rage, on the other hand, are the halfway hippies, the camp-followers, the bongo-players and god-botherers, the people with peace signs on their headbands. The mules. The legions of the uncool. You've heard it: "Loosen up, you uptight bitch, you're in Goa!"

'But these are democratic times. The legions of the uncool have the victory, and the old elites are in full retreat. These days, everyone has a right to everything, and access is universal. That rarest of experiences, visionary experience, is freely, democratically available in pill form. The legions of the uncool have broken into this sacred grove, and are feasting on its bohemian delights—though one day, of course, they too will be outnumbered by new generations, the hordes to come.'

Then he would descend from the prophetic to the ordinary plane. It was Ratko who advised me never to ask anyone what they did for a living, and never to suggest the group photo. I never knew what was coming in my Saturday lecture. But one morning as I approached his balcao I saw a brand-new tin trunk on it; and coming out with the tea, he announced that he had decided to leave.

Because I didn't really know anyone else in north Anjuna. I decided to leave as well. He was off to Belgrade, and I thought I'd move to Vagator, where I had friends. After his customary week of sleepless nights he left one morning for the Bombay boat, labouring under the trunk. It was all books. 'Ratko,' I said, 'I hope you're going to be okay with that lot.'

'Lord, yes!' he exclaimed, in a sudden access of emotion. 'So do I.'

I start off up the long winding path that runs up and around the Vagator promontory. It begins at the Paraiso, the alfresco dance club owned by the grandson of the founder of Pakistan, overlooking the north Anjuna beach. I walk over the unspoiled hill, down to the twin coves of Vagator and their fine, silvery sand—and here are the remembered rocks, the terraces, the tall palms whose tops are twisted by the wind.

Both Utopia and Arcadia were states of perfection, Ratko had said, but there was a difference between them. Utopia was an ideal of the future, and Arcadia was an idyll of the past. The Lord of the Rings to Anjuna's Lord of the Flies, Vagator had been kept nicely idyllic by an extreme simplicity of life. The terraces climbed steeply up the cliff and there was no village to begin a civilization in. It was palm-leaf huts, beach fires and bongos or nothing.

Of course Ratko had warned me that Arcadia was an illusion too. It hankered for the golden age—but we had all been evicted from the Garden too long ago, and there was no going back. The earthly paradise was not to be regained, especially not by befriending serpents. A well-known Vagator story underlines this: and here is a version of it.

'The guy had something on a leash. A turtle, was it? We came down on the boat from Bombay, you know how you used to group upon the boat, about ten or twelve of us, and this guy, he was Belgian, I think, young, one of those people you knew straightaway was an oddball, not the full shilling.

'He'd got into an animal trip, he was communicating with the animals, that's what it seemed to be all about. Later we heard what happened to him.

'In Vagator there was a spring in the back of the jungle there, and a cobra used to come to this spring every morning at four o'clock—an hour before sunrise. Someone told the Belgian about this snake, so he goes to catch it. And he does catch it. He's caught this cobra, and it's bitten him. He decides he'd better go to the hospital, and he takes the snake with him: he's communicating with the animals. So he gets on the bus with the snake in a bag, but it gets him again a few times.

'In the hospital the snake escapes, and they have to clear the ward out. Then the guy dies. Do things like that happen now?'

Ratko had been right about Vagator. It was peopled by Arcadians. The tropical weather, the light breeze, the rhythmic sea, the primeval rocks, the pristine sand—all of these in concert put the inhabitants in mind of heaven. Heaven is a place, the song goes, where nothing ever happens. Events, even alarming ones, come and go against the backdrop of an apparently unchanging world. This enables those events to be seen as unimportant, and encourages an interest in metaphysics.

And in the tropics even an ascetic may live well. The Renouncer lived on a small terrace, high up the cliff. He was a small bearded man who wore the religious seeker's saffron lungi every day and strenuously practised yoga on the beach. By night, however, he abandoned self-denial and went about practising all the usual countercultural vices: and this had earned him his nickname, which he bore with an affronted dignity. After all, he had been careful to renounce only the things he would never do, like eating people or being judgmental.

Walking along, I look up towards my own small terrace, where once I lived with two friends in a palm-leaf hut called the Smack Hut, from its function of the season before. Now someone has built a toilet there; even Vagator has eventually tired of timelessness. Along the beach I count a small catamaran, a trampoline, a score of beach umbrellas and six or eight big restaurant shacks. The two shacks nearest the cliff have decorated it with little glaciers of garbage, which in the old days would have been cow food. But now a patrolling cow in search of paper bags (for the glucose, it is said) is disappointed, and goes down to the beach to stand ruminating by the sea, next to a juggler and a bikinied girl doing headstands.

'So not much changes,' the juggler says to me in conversation. 'Anjuna's still kind of precious, Candolim's the suburbs, and Chapora's where you go to see your dead friends.' He has no designation for Vagator. No one lives there: it's just a beach.

It isn't far to Chapora village, but I want to stay on the sand to the end of the beach and then climb up to the fort. My first day's walk will end there, high up on the curtain wall of laterite blocks warmed by the sun. You have to watch out for dozing snakes up there.

When Sambhaji's Maratha cavalry came down from the north and took the fort in 1683, they captured forty cannon and as many Portuguese, who were led away naked in chains. Thirty years later the fort was renovated and provided with escape tunnels to the river and the sea; but was promptly lost again, this time to clan raiders from Satari. After that the fort saw no more combat for 245 years—until a big techno party in the 1980s. The organizers had forgotten to square the police, so they stormed the fort at midnight, flailing at the fleeing partygoers with their bamboo staves. After that there were no more parties at the fort. Nor does the Archaeological Survey of India want its historic stones done up in Day-Glo.

In a cool breeze I walk along the beach, talking into my recording Walkman and deciding that if someone sees me and wonders what on earth I'm doing, I will hold it up to my eye and pretend it's a camera. In the mid-seventies a camera would have been an object of suspicion, but to be seen walking along the beach talking to it, or to nothing in particular, would not. The beach was the promenade of the mad. In 1976 a woman meticulously made up as the goddess Kali—black body, black tongue arid necklace of skulls and all—imperiously paraded along here, tearing up her travellers' cheques and throwing them into the sea. I watched this theatre of renunciation in the company of a man on vacation from his sex commune in California, and another from, as I recall, Brazil, who was wearing a costume composed entirely of feathers. Someone once said that Surrealism was not a movement but a prediction.

'Like no other place on earth'

Helene Derkin Menezes

The soft knock on the boardroom door distracts me just for a second as I place the story board on the narrow ledge—custom made so that all can see the latest efforts of the creative department.

It's Lisa, the Managing Director's secretary. 'Urgent phone call, H.' I nod at her and excuse myself from the client meeting; Fi's on the line. Fi is my tallest female friend; she must be five ten, easily six feet tall in stilettos, which she wears often. This is the nineties after all and in Soho, W1, London it's all about power dressing and labels. Fi and I are planning our holiday. St. Lucia. Le Sport. Seven days of pampering and overindulgence, and boy do I need it. Working for the country's leading financial marketing and advertising agency means simply—work hard, party harder. The hours are long and often closed by a cocktail or three before the journey home, ready to do it all over again the next day.

'What do you think of Goa?'

'Where? What are you talking about, Fi?' I cast a wary glance back at the boardroom door.

'Goa. Nick says he can get us a really good deal there, a week for quarter of the price we are paying for St. Lucia.'

'Nick? Who the hell is Nick? I don't want to go to India, I don't even own a rucksack, and I hate the smell of patchouli. I want pampering!'

Turns out Nick is the travel agent and he has convinced Fi that after the recent plague scares in India, Goa is going really cheap. For me India is a hippy destination, somewhere you go to find yourself—hot, smelly and dusty with no credit card provision or whiff of Harvey Nics. Not only that, you need time to explore somewhere as vast as India, don't you? A week just doesn't cut it.

I call my well travelled parents while Fi holds on the other line. Mum convinces me, 'You'll love it, it's like the Caribbean but the people are nicer, and the food is fantastic! Go—you won't regret it.' Turns out Mum and Dad have been twice!

'Go on then, book it,' I tell Fi, not knowing the impact those words would have on the rest of my life. I replace the phone and go back to my clients. By the time my meeting is finished there's another message from Fi—not only has the holiday price gone down again, but Nick's giving us two weeks for the price of one, B&B, allocation on arrival, and we're leaving in four days! This is to be my first (and last) charter holiday.

It's a chilly grey day in October 1994. The temperature is a shivery nine degrees when we leave Gatwick Airport for the subcontinent. I am well travelled but this is my first charter flight. I can't believe how tiny the seats are, so many loud people squashed in, and this journey is going to take us twelve hours!

We stop over in the Gulf to stretch our legs and get our malaria medicine from Duty Free. Fi's granddad was stationed in the tropics and swears that a paracetamol and a shot of brandy are all you need every night to keep the mosquitoes at bay. Neither of us really likes brandy and there's a special offer on vodka, so we settle on a bottle to ward off fatal diseases.

We land at Dabolim Airport, stand in endless queues, have our passports and visas checked about twenty times, every twenty paces, by what looks like the same man dressed in khaki. We finally collect our bags and step out into what feels like a sauna.

The sights, sounds and smells of India are like no other place on earth. We feel totally alien in our dark winter clothes. We find a rep and give her our names; she looks at both of us quizzically and tells us to wait over at the side, away from the other guests. I am paranoid, there's something about the way she keeps looking down her list and glancing at us. Anyway, we wait. And we wait. Finally, when all the other tourists are packed onto coaches and on their way, another flustered rep bundles us into a taxi saying, 'Bob Malley, right?' The door slams and we are on our way.

'That bloody Nick! *Bob Marley*! Crikey, it's a reggae commune or something! We are probably being abducted and sold! I bet you anything we are being taken to an ashram or worse a campsite,' I whine. I don't have the chance to whimper for long. The taxi ride soon brings me back to earth.

There seem to be absolutely no rules of the road here. A truck hurtles towards us on our side of the road. Rather than brake or pull over, our driver heads straight for it and actually floors the pedal to increase speed. 'We're gonna die!' we both scream. A miracle—the truck weaves to its side of the road and our driver carries on as if nothing has happened. We take a right turn down a potholed road, adjacent to a railway track, navigating pigs, dogs and cows on the loose, down into a little fishing village. We slow down and suddenly the sparkle of the Arabian Sea hits me.

'Bob Malley' is a beautiful little cove called Bogmalo, and we are heading to a little white guest house right on the beach. We are both a little speechless. It's beautiful. There are some fishermen casting their nets, no one else around, not even from the four-star hotel at the other end of the cove, no sunbeds on the golden sand, no noisy tourists from the plane—we are in paradise!

Our room is freshly painted white, with a colourful bedspread, spotlessly clean. We dump our bags, tear off the London layers of dark clothing as if possessed, pull on our swimsuits, run to the sandy beach like two little kids and dive into the warm surf.

We didn't realise then that we were the first ever residents in this little guesthouse which was formerly a family-run restaurant. We ask about the name of the property and find it's called after the owner, Nelo's dad Jose and his mum Etelvina—a marriage of names resulting in 'Joets'.

The bar and restaurant overlook the bay and the rooms are attached to the rear. There are a few nervous young men about the place who don't know where to look when we try to talk to them. At first we aren't quite sure who works there and who doesn't. They are shy and not used to talking to foreign girls, least of all when they are scantily clad in swimwear. But we are carefree; we've escaped from gloomy, cold Blighty where it's all central heating, tights, hats, gloves and scarves to thirty-two degrees of heaven where to wear anything more than the bare minimum is simply sacrilege against the sunshine.

There are no tables in the restaurant and we can't get a cold drink as there's no fridge either. From the noise there's obviously building and painting going on in the other rooms. A couple of days pass and though we are in paradise, there are a couple of mishaps in our room. Nothing major. A light fitting comes out of the wall and when we flush the loo it seems to flush the floor at the same time. And there are men asleep outside our room with nothing but tea towels wrapped around their waists! We are two street savvy girls from London, so we aren't easily unnerved, but these guys sleeping in the corridor have us wondering what on earth is going on. We have no idea they are working every hour to finish off the pending work for Joets' first tourist season.

All is quiet in Bogmalo and we have barely seen another soul. Fi and I easily fall into holiday mode: she meditating and getting at one with the Goan vibe and me with a bag of books. I am up at the bar sampling something called 'palm feni' which is brewed in the village, when she dashes up the steps saying, 'I've just met an Indian from Hampstead and his name is Derrick!' To which I reply that it's impossible, no Indians are called Derrick. She gets a drink and we have a chat about what we are going to do during our stay. One thing is unanimous, both palm and cashew feni will take many samplings to get used to…

We like our little guesthouse and the guys around seem to be really nice and trying to get things ready. The missing elements are slowly appearing, but it's still just not quite what it says in the brochure. We both agree that Joets is not yet ready for business. One of the tea towel chaps is painting a wall a brilliant white at the bar. We have our eye on the four-star down the other end of the bay. Armed with the holiday brochure, we set out to meet the area manager of the charter company we booked with.

The taxi takes ages to get to Panjim, the road full of dogs, cows and goats that all need slow and careful navigation, though our driver obviously doesn't think so. We go at breakneck speed overtaking on blind corners, indicating left and turning right! Fi and I hold hands and say a prayer to as many Gods as are listening. We have never been on a journey like this—the ride from the airport was tame compared to the NH17.

It takes a while to locate the office in the capital, Panjim; we eventually find it above a Punjabi restaurant and meet the manager, a Scottish girl called Lynn who has beautiful long, thick, strawberry blonde hair. We relate our tale, telling her it is not the boys' fault, they are trying their best, but the owners are just not ready for guests. I put on my advertising hat and say the guesthouse is just not what it claims in the brochure, so they are breaking ASA regulations. Fi chips in with we like the beach there, so could she just move us along to the four-star please? We of course have no idea that she knows we booked this holiday last minute and got it at a knockdown price. The brochure rate is four times what we paid. Lynn says she is really sorry, she knows the boys at Joets, she will have a word and in the meantime she offers us a complimentary overnight trip to Palolem to experience sleeping in huts on the beach to help pacify us. If things aren't better when we get back, she'll see what she can do. But no way she's going to move us into the four-star; it will be another guest house in the north. We want to go to Palolem anyway, so this seems like a fair deal.

We take a look around Panjim trying to absorb the culture and not look too amazed at how different from home everything is. Feeling rather like outsiders from the attention we are getting, we then realise we are staring as much as the locals are. We try to blend in. Not easy, we are used to dogs on leads, cows fenced in fields and pigs in sties. And perfect fruit and vegetables immaculately cleaned on shelves in supermarkets along with row upon row of items we buy but never really need. This market scene is so alien to us. The ladies with their laden baskets on their heads walk with as much poise and grace as girls in finishing school. In the fish market the ladies with their legs spread around their wares heckle for customers. The smell everywhere is overwhelming.

We walk past the flower sellers, enjoying the greetings of bright blooms and perfumes. We stare astonished at the barber conducting magic on his customer with a cut-throat razor, then gently massaging his head. We squeak when the barber is suddenly thumping him all over, the customer unfazed by what looks like an attack rather than a treatment. We take it all in. We have lunch at a local joint; this is nothing like the Indian food we have back home. The fish curry we order has our taste buds popping on our tongues like fat in water. We guzzle lime sodas to pacify our tongues and quench our thirst. We can't get over the cost of the meal, comparing it to the crazy London prices we are used to paying.

We head back to the south. The cab often brakes and we're thrown forward off our seats. The driver seems to keep his thumb continually on the horn and it soon becomes apparent the only use he has for the rear view mirror is to check his reflection. We are incredulous when we have to stop and pay a toll when the road is in such an appalling state. When we are not shrieking in terror at this totally new approach to traffic sense we are laughing nonstop at the difference of it all.

When we arrive back, there isn't a workman in sight and the restaurant area has tables and chairs set up! We order drinks and sit and soak in the glorious sunset while gassing about the adventure of our day and what we would need for our trip further south the following day.

Suddenly Fi shrieks: 'There he is! That's the Indian from Hampstead!' I turn round and the world stands still. I feel myself blush and turn back to Fi. I gulp on my drink—the next thing we hear is 'Hello, girls' and are greeted by a huge grin of nutmeg skin and gleaming white teeth. Turns out his name really is Derrick and he's just back from spending the summer at his aunt's house in Hampstead. He buys us both another drink and chats amiably with us. I don't think I have ever met a man who smiles so much. During the conversation he asks us if we would like to go to a church dance at Colva with him the day after tomorrow. Fi and I look at each other…church dance? Neither of us has ever been to a church dance, but what the hell…Fi says yes before I have time to think about it. He goes off to the bar and chats for a while with some guys dressed in football jerseys. He waves to us as he hops into a black jeep and drives off along the track that edges the beach.

The next day after a fantastic lunch of fresh prawn curry and rice washed down with more feni (that would have blown our socks off if we were wearing any) we are picked up for our trip to Palolem. By now we are slightly hardened to the 'road rules', and manage to take in the view without thinking it's the last thing we will ever see.

Palolem is idyllic. The little camp is well geared up to take care of our needs. Our hut has little hammock-style beds and is set just yards from the breaking ocean. We laze around, read our books and go out on a local canoe to fish but we are far more interested in the dolphins that follow us, breaking the water gently as they rise to say hello. In the evening there's a barbeque and camp fire. We move away from the few other tourists and sit under the stars, drinking in their delicate light, watching the phosphorescent waves breaking a short distance away. We feel a million miles away from the stress and strain of the West end of London. This is nirvana. How can something so simple be so indulgent?

We are brought down to the reality of India when we arrive back at Joets to find a small white-and-brown dog with a broken leg hopping about the place—apparently one of the drunken fishermen had thrown a stone at it. We are horrified but no one seems very bothered. There is no RSPCA to call and the guys at the bar don't seem to think the poor thing warrants a vet. We are both very upset. We know there are plenty of stray animals here and this is a country that is more concerned with feeding its growing population than the welfare of a stray but we can't help but feel sad and helpless. As we wonder what to do, we see someone out on the water, windsurfing. Fi and I both sail, so we decide to ask Derrick about hiring a sailing boat when we meet him later at the dance. There doesn't seem much we can do for the little dog so it is with slightly heavy hearts we set out that night.

Derrick picks us up in his jeep with a friend in tow and we set off for dinner before the dance. Fi and I still have no idea what to expect. We stop at Colva and have dinner at the Longuinhos hotel. We listen to mandos sung in the local language—Konkani. The conversation flows, like the drinks, with an ease that we are growing rapidly used to and wonder if we will actually bother to make it to this church dance. Not that it matters, we are all enjoying ourselves. We tell the story of the little dog and Derrick says we can take it to the vet in his Gypsy tomorrow, while he is at work.

Then out of the blue I hear Western music blaring out nearby and frown in annoyance—don't want to be reminded of home. I recognize the song, it's in the top ten back in the UK. Derrick says the dance must have started and Fi and I exchange glances—we are sure we're in for some very staid and dreary music as we drive up to the venue, but by the sheer volume of what's being played that is obviously not the case. The dance is called 'Noite de Fama', traditionally held on the day of the Colva church feast. I walk inside the cloth barrier vowing not to be too judgemental. What I thought was recorded music is actually a live band called Lynx. We are astonished—how can a bunch of Goan guys sound exactly like Take That one minute and Big Mountain the next!

The crowd is throbbing, these Goans are certainly not shy about dancing and not the foot-shuffling-arms-flinging stuff we know—this is the real deal. Around us in the most diverse fashion statements, in a rainbow of hues from saris to puff sleeve ensembles (not the designer labels and street fashion we were used to seeing), people dance. Partners dance ballroom style, and dance well—neither of us has ever witnessed anything like this before. All this is happening under a blanket of a million stars. Back home you feel like a lottery winner if you can go out in the summer without a coat on and here we are in the middle of the night revelling in the balmy weather in our sun dresses. It's a beautiful night, great music, good food, fine company—great conversation and lots of laughter. We all dance under the stars.

The sun is just waking up as we get back to Joets. We go back to our room though I am too much on a high to sleep. My mind is on the tall dark handsome man who has swept me off my feet...'Oo Baby I Love Your Way' reverberates in my head as I relive our slow dance together.

Later that day, Derrick drops off his Gypsy for us to take the little dog to the vet. I can't believe I'm going to negotiate that traffic and those roads but that pitiful little pup has broken our hearts with his limping about, his eyes give me the courage to do it. We somehow find the vet, and come away three thousand rupees poorer—he saw us coming a mile away. But it doesn't matter. 'Puppy' is now on the mend.

The rest of the holiday flies by with Derrick making daily appearances, showing us around the little state he is obviously very proud of and we feel so at home in. Everywhere we go someone seems to know the smiling Derrick. We learn he's a windsurfer, it's him we see out in the bay every day, practising for the forthcoming Nationals. We ask him about a boat and he says he can arrange it. Fi feels sick on the day arranged to go sailing, so Derrick and I set out on the surf alone.

We sail out towards Grande and Bat Islands. He knows how to handle a boat alright and we scud along catching the wind, we tack and gybe like we have sailed together for years. The salt spray cools our smiling faces and time disappears like the seahorses on the crest of the waves. Eventually we rest in the petite secluded bay locally known as Santare and while the water gently kisses the sides of the boat, we steal our first kiss under the warmth of the Goan sunshine.

When our fortnight in the sun is over and Derrick takes us to the airport. I don't want to go home. I tell Fi, 'I'm not coming, I love it here and I really, really like this guy, I am going to stay.' Derrick is the voice of reason (and panic, he has another girlfriend arriving on my landing flight!) telling me he isn't going anywhere…'Go home, make sure it's not the sun and the palm trees you've fallen for.'

Poor Fi has to put up with me sobbing on the flight, I just can't believe I'm leaving the man or the place. Five weeks later I have rented out my house, handed in my notice at work, said goodbye to my family and friends in the UK and am flying back to Goa!

It's my first Christmas in India. On Christmas Eve, Derrick phones my dad in England and asks his permission to marry me. On February the 14th we are civilly married followed by a surprise party in the tiny cove of Santare where we first kissed. In April we get married in the beautiful Mae de Deus church in Saligao. We have a fairytale reception at the Taj hotel and Lynx plays 'Oo Baby I Love Your Way' as our first dance. Lynn—the area manager with the strawberry blonde hair—and her fiancé Nelo are among our guests. Turns out that Lynn had phoned

Nelo from the office and read him the riot act for not having everything ready at Joets, their first joint venture. Nelo had consequently phoned his friend Derrick to help him by getting Fi and me out of the way so he could finish up the work and get back into the good books of Lynn!

The plan worked. Joets is still one of the best kept and well run guesthouses in Goa. These days Lynn and I are great friends. Our daughters are in the same class at school. Fi travels often to Goa and, thanks to the Internet, we are in touch on a daily basis. I don't think anyone, least of all me, dreamed that by trying to get an upgrade meant I would fall in love, leave my past life behind and never ever want to leave.

'Sex on the beach'

Katharina Kakar

A place that becomes less of a journey and more of a destination for most foreign tourists, however, is the beach and they rarely move beyond its sun-n-sand-n-surf pleasures. They escape the miserable winter months in Europe, Russia and other cold parts of the world, and see little of Goa beyond their chosen beach for their entire holiday. They come to relax and soak up the sun, to get away from the stressful pace of their lives at home and take in a little bit of Goan *susegad*. Nothing wrong with that. Most of them, however, do not take part in the drugs-and-sex scene for which Goa's beaches have gained a notorious reputation.

Most Goans are outraged by the state's reputation as a haven for junkies and sex-trippers. Whether it is the sensational case of fifteen-year-old Scarlett Keeling, a British teenager, who was allegedly drugged, raped and murdered on Anjuna beach in February 2008, or other headlines relating to sun, sex and surf that make national and international news, Goans are very prickly about anything that highlights sexual permissiveness or questionable morals in Goa. In 2011, for example, the Hindi movie *Dum Maaro Dum* that depicted the Goan drug mafia made headlines in local newspapers even before it was released, because its trailer carried a line referring to Goan women as being 'cheap' ('Over here...liquor is cheap, and the women are cheaper...'). Eventually the producers agreed to cut parts of the dialogue that offended so many Goans. Another recent example is the response to *Tehelka* editor Tarun Tejpal, who in November 2011, jokingly remarked during the opening of the Think Fest in Bambolim, 'Now you are in Goa, drink as much as you want, eat...sleep with whoever you think of...' The response from the local media and 'concerned citizens' ranged from disgust to boiling anger, and his remark was quoted so often that I stopped counting.

Why do Goans react so violently to such perceptions? The real Goa, as Goans perceive it, is a place of 'deep social conservatism, of folk religiosity in its village temples and churches, of simplicity of lifestyle…and of immense pride in its plural, multi-cultural heritage.'* I have lived long enough in Benaulim to have seen for myself the importance people in my village give to caring for the extended family and protecting their children, especially their daughters. In that respect they are no different from families in the rest of India. Most visitors are not aware of the day-to-day life of the common man in Goa, their customs and rituals, the things that engage and interest them or the beauty of the state's hinterland, because they rarely move beyond the beach belt. For them the plurality of voices and diversity of lifestyles will remain a blank spot.

Nevertheless, sex, drugs and raves on the beach are also a slice of Goan reality, a facet of *Goa Dourada*, the Golden Goa, that cannot be denied. Along with foreign backpackers and young Indians visiting from other states, Goan youth too are a part of this Goa. And casual sex is not confined to tourists alone—it is also widespread among locals and visiting youngsters from other Indian states. Take, for example, the many young waiters who work in the beach shacks during the season, local youngsters as well as migrants from Nepal, Darjeeling, Rajasthan and other places. For them, the attraction of the job is not the hard work and bad pay, but the many opportunities they get to hit on European girls. Ever since we moved to Benaulim, Sudhir (Kakar) and I have been frequenting three beach shacks for a sunset drink or dinner. Over the years, watching the beach boys grow and listening to their stories, we have become good friends with many of them. They told me that in one particular beach shack in north Goa, the waiters have put up a world map on the kitchen wall, and each time a waiter successfully seduces a girl (or claims to have done so), he pins a needle to the respective country of his conquest.

---

*Jason Keith Fernandes, 'Of Rapes, Murder, Drugs and the "Real Goa"', in *Gomantak Times*, 26 March 2008, p. A8.

When I started writing this book, I asked some of the waiters we have known for years if they would agree to be interviewed and if they would speak frankly. All of them agreed: the condition was that they had to be shamelessly honest about their views and experiences. But I won't reveal the most interesting stories, as those would give away their identities. At one of the shacks where we are regulars, the boys have a system of competing among themselves for the girls. There is an unwritten rule that the waiter who first gets into a conversation with a girl who shows the slightest interest in him, such as listening to what he has to say, will be the one who will serve her again if she comes back the next day. This way there is a hope of 'deepening' the relationship. Surprisingly, the charms and methods of the beach boys prove to be quite effective. Needless to say, their targets are only women without male companions, though the age of the woman is no bar. The range of conquests among lonely women looking for sex varies from (preferably) young and beautiful girls to sixty-plus, (preferably) generous and well-to-do women. Once the new waiters gain confidence, often with the help of an older woman in their first or second season, they try their luck with younger women. They soon find out that it is easiest to hit on young girls, because, explains one waiter, 'after 25 they are too experienced and ask too many questions'.

The transformation of a first-season beach boy into a confident Casanova is a long journey full of hurdles. 'You have to learn to read the signals,' said one good-looking veteran. He added—and this was confirmed by others—'Almost all of us have our first "experience" with an older woman.' He told me about foreign women twice or thrice the age of the young waiter, often staying for weeks or months at the beach, initiating him and his colleagues into the art of sex. One of these women is a divorced, educated, sixty-plus lady. I have met her, since she comes back every year and always stays at the same beach shack which has become a second home to her. I would never have guessed that she had a sizzling secret life! Indeed, sexual encounters between women aged forty to sixty with waiters who are still virgins is pretty common. But unlike other tourist hotspots such as Thailand or Tunisia, where prostitution of young males is common, waiters in Goa do not prostitute themselves. For all my interviewees, having 'done it' with an older woman is simply an entry point into their own sexual life, a necessary initiation to gain enough confidence to interact with attractive young women.

However, before the newcomer ventures into his 'first experience' with a mother-lover, he usually suffers through a range of innocent passions, like the young man who fell madly in love with a thirteen-year-old Russian girl staying with her parents at the beach shack. He recounted to me that he hardly ate for days and could not think about anything else but his Russian beauty, though he never spoke to her and their communication did not go beyond eye contact. 'Does she know?' I asked him when he revealed his dilemma. 'I think so, she gave me that look,' he answered, looking down at his feet in embarrassment. A couple of weeks later, when his beauty had long returned home, he gathered enough courage to write to the parents, asking politely for a family photo. Her parents must have had a sense of humour: they promptly replied and sent him a picture of themselves and the girl's grandparents—the object of his adoration herself was missing from the photograph!

Goa's reputation as a land of free sex and endless parties began in the late sixties 'when the first lot of hippies began to straggle into Anjuna and Arambol…They attracted only a cursory look from fishermen and toddy tappers. What were a few Whites zonked out on hallucinogens compared to the authoritarian Portuguese that ruled for 451 years?' writes journalist Devika Sequeira.* They were a bunch of self-absorbed, confused idealists, who were uninterested in local culture, customs or history. Although the villagers might have disapproved of their skimpy clothes and careless manners, they lodged them and took their money. It is the hippies who should get the credit for starting Goa's beach-tourism, because sensational stories in Indian newspapers about naked youngsters from Europe and America dancing through the night acted like a magnet to hundreds of 'hippy-watchers', who travelled to Goa to have a closer look. Fifty years later, only a few hippies are left and a lot has changed. Sex on the beach

---

*Devika Sequeira, 'Not a Sin City', *Deccan Herald*, online at <http:// www.deccanherald.com/content/47169/not-sin-city.html>

and sex in the minds, however, has remained. Indian men, generally from a conservative background, still come in busloads during the tourist season to watch naked, pale flesh turning pink on beach-beds. They also see Goan girls in bars and clubs, talking to men who are neither their brothers nor their uncles, reinforcing their image of the 'cheap Goan woman', not to speak of their ideas of Western women, who they believe would like nothing more than to sleep with strangers like them. Any white woman moving around in Goa on her own will be lecherously targeted, as I have been countless times, once even when I was driving our car on the highway at noon, the windows down. A motorcycle zoomed up next to me, and the driver shouted hysterically through the open window: 'Want to have sex? Want to have sex? Want to have sex?' I showed him the middle finger and he zoomed off. It was like a slapstick scene from a B-grade movie.

The beach boys, however, claim to be different from the sexually repressed, conservative Indian males who come to Goa's beaches in droves on weekends from the neighbouring states of Karnataka and Maharashtra, their eyes riveted on tourists in bikinis. Perhaps it would be more correct to say that the sexual attitudes of the beach boys change after the first couple of seasons, by when they have learned to read the cues and signals of foreign women, and have become adept at striking up relationships. As one of them, who prides himself in having around five affairs per season, told me, 'When I go out with friends and we meet some new girls and nothing much happens—no signals and signs—I leave.' He does not want to waste his time: 'It is less about feelings, it's really about sex,' he says. He admits that sometimes, if a girl stays on, he gets attached and develops tender feelings towards her. He does not like this, because the relationship then becomes complicated. In one such situation, the girl returned the next season and he had to handle her and his new affair at the same time. He slept with both, a situation which eventually put him in a lot of trouble with the two girls after they found out. He and the other beach boys emphasize that while they treat the girls with respect, these encounters are about having a good time with no strings attached. They claim that by and large, the girls and also the middle-aged or elderly women know the rules of the game with the beach boys—just a holiday fling, with no emotional involvement. 'But did you ever seriously fall in love with one of the girls?' I asked. Many of them said they had been through this experience, but learned their lesson when the girl went back to her own country and they were left heartbroken. When I asked them if they could imagine marrying a foreign girl, one of the young men came back with this memorable reply: 'Why buy the cow if you can milk it?'

Over the years, however, we have seen a few relationships between the beach boys and foreign women ending in marriage—usually with women around ten to fifteen years older and much better educated. The attraction here was simply the chance such a marriage gave to get out of the country, to make real money and secure their future and dreams abroad or back in India. Such women, say the beach boys I talked to, are regarded as a 'money tree' to be shaken. Often, though, it is beyond the young man's imagination to realize that moving to Europe will expose him to humiliating experiences and that his lack of education and exposure to harsh working conditions will also strain the relationship. And indeed, most marriages from such vastly different backgrounds do fail. As my conversations with the young men as well as the older women involved have revealed, when passion and sexual desire fade and the reality of day-to-day life sets in, the mismatched partners start to realize that they cannot overcome the barriers of their backgrounds and the culturally different expectations they have from each other. By the time this realization has dawned, the couple often has a child, making a break-up more difficult.

Clearly, one of the perks of a beach boy's job in Goa is an active and adventurous sex life. But where do they do it? I imagined it must be difficult to sneak in and out of rooms of the shack where they work without being noticed. 'Everywhere,' was the answer I got—'rooms, cars, showers, in the water.' They even do it at the back of the stalls where tourist items are sold during the day and which are just covered with a sheet of plastic at night, enough to give them some privacy. Then, there are the sand dunes slightly off the beach and at times, in the cover of night, on the beach itself. Often, if the girl is staying just for a few days or a week, the sex happens on the last day, before she is leaving for good. 'It takes time to talk and win her trust,' says one of them.

By and large they have affairs with Westerners. Indian girls, though they may appear outwardly Westernized, are mainly taboo—caste and class structures are still deeply ingrained in the Indian mind and these boundaries are hard to cross for both sides. The moment my questions were directed towards Indian girls, avoidance set in. The beach boys did not like to talk about them. Perhaps the thought of sex with an Indian girl brings their mothers and sisters back into their own conscience: what would they think if they only knew…thus leaving them uncomfortable about the boundaries they have crossed. The beach boys also find it much easier to be around and strike up a conversation with foreign girls and, as many of them pointed out, sex is not a big issue with them. Indian girls are for marriage, as one of them told me; Western girls are for fun.

The beach boys, even in their relationships with Western women, have their own code of conduct and pretty clear rules about dos and don'ts in public. Thus, while it's fine to display one's flab in the skimpiest bikini on the beach, they do not approve, for example, of Western tourists who go shopping or into restaurants in their swimwear, or who treat the beach restaurant like a dressing room. Often they are told to cover up, or to go into the bathroom to change. One of the waiters once went up to a woman sunbathing topless and told her to get dressed or leave (in south Goa, unlike north Goa and its old hippie hangouts, going topless on the beach is not common).

The beach boys I have known over the years in the different shacks Sudhir and I regularly go to are also very protective when they see foreign women being harassed or intrusively ogled by Indian men who travel to Goan beaches expressly for that purpose. 'Such men have a bikini problem,' observed one of the boys wearily. 'They only have TV experience with American girls and misunderstand,' he added.

One of the waiters, thin and very young when he came to Goa for the first time, told me how he dealt with his own physical arousal, never having seen half-naked, white, female bodies lying in the sun before. He was overwhelmed by this sight, but also shocked and confused by what this did to his own body. He did not know how to cope with his excitement. That first season, way too shy to approach one of the women on a beach-bed or in the restaurant, he often ran into the shack's toilet to jerk off, after which he continued serving his customers. Five years later, that same boy has a new avatar as he talks self-confidently about his erotic adventures and flaunts his body which he rigorously trains through body-building exercises.

Many waiters have intriguing life stories, having moved to Goa from other parts of India to seek their fortune, and finally managing to turn their lives around. One of them, hailing from Rajasthan, was only fifteen when he fell in love with a girl from his village, who belonged to a different caste. The girl's clan threatened to kill him for his effrontery and he was forced to flee his village at night, hiding in a truck. For years he did not dare return home, doing odd jobs for a pittance in a number of places, including Mumbai, until he fetched up in Goa. Now, after many years as a waiter, he has prospered. Together with a Goan partner, he runs his own beach shack in winter and a business in Ladakh in summer. Another one is a native of Goa, bright and good-looking, and an untiring Don Juan, if one believes the stories told about him. He took a risk to start his own business with the help of a foreigner a few years back. Today he spends a lot of his time in Mumbai, taking classes in scriptwriting for films, and I would not be surprised if he finds success in this venture too. Most beach boys have a common story to tell—of poverty, joblessness at home and then finding their way to Goa, usually through someone in their village who takes them along and helps them get a job in a shack and a place to stay. For the beach boys, being in Goa is an adventure that also allows them to send some money home to the family. Add to that, as one beach boy told me, 'Free sex, good food and good times—why should we not like it here?'

Those too inhibited or timid to indulge in sex on the beach could just order the drink of the same name—it is sweet, heady and exists in many different variations. Here's the classic recipe: 1.5 oz vodka, 0.5 oz peach schnapps, 2 oz cranberry juice and 2 oz orange juice. Shake well and serve in a highball glass. Bon appétit!

'The shady invasion of the beach umbrella'

Manohar Shetty

I first came to Goa in the early seventies, ostensibly a college student—ostensibly because like most other students in my college I didn't attend classes, and only sat for the final examinations after a month of intensive studying. I came on the steamer, the *Konkan Sevak*, along with two friends. That steamer—scrapped after a stint with the Indian Peace Keeping Force in Sri Lanka—has sailed into cult status. It was where a holiday to Goa actually began with its endless rounds of housie and loud, old-fashioned music. Old-timers, both Indian and foreign, still recall those trips wistfully. The ship chugged off from Ferry Wharf in Bombay in the early hours and arrived at Panjim jetty the next morning, welcomed by a luminous sunrise and the friendly waves of the Mandovi River.

We were not interested in housie or the old-fashioned music. We found a corner in the lower deck, and watched, with some respect, amidst the din of the diesel engine, long-haired foreigners sniffing cocaine and mainlining heroin, veins in their wrists and forearms bulging out like twisted high-voltage wires. Unlike some of my friends, I didn't do the hard stuff. And unlike the maestro Nissim Ezekiel, I didn't experiment with acid. I lacked the courage to lose my mind unconditionally to the clutches of a whimsical chemical. But we were armed with smooth Afghani hashish and grass from Kerala—not the inferior Bombay Black, which was laced with opium and looked like goat droppings, that we usually smoked.

We spent two weeks in Calangute, Baga and Anjuna and stayed at 'Souza Lobo' on Calangute beach. 'Souza Lobo' was then an L-shaped shack with a few cheap rooms, separated by bamboo screens—not the pucca structure and popular restaurant it is now. Besides us, there were a few square foreigners—'square' because they didn't smoke dope. We didn't interact with them, but did the usual rounds of the flea market at Anjuna where, the air thick with marijuana, emaciated foreigners sold or bartered old cameras, tape recorders, semi-precious stones from Nepal, home-made cheese and hash cookies, Swiss Army knives, books, musical instruments, sleeping bags and haversacks—the last two items much prized after a thorough wash in Dettol.

Much of our time we spent in a narcotic haze, contemplating the sea and watching feline-eyed freaks (as they were known in those politically incorrect days), utterly self-absorbed, slowly injecting themselves into a state of nirvana and an early exit from the temporal world. I didn't find much evidence of flower-power gentleness and there were areas in Anjuna, especially, where foreigners were openly hostile to the local community and gawking visitors. There were restaurants with an unwritten code that effectively debarred Indians.

I was then a scrawny, longhaired young man at odds with my family and the college curriculum, and as callow as they come. It was the era of Woodstock; all my friends swore allegiance to Bob Dylan, Joan Baez, the Rolling Stones, Jimi Hendrix, Janis Joplin, Jim Morrison and a host of other 'far out' anti-establishment musicians. I hummed along tunelessly, but I also buried myself in books. Unlike my friends, who were far more interested in music, I was a compulsive reader. In the boarding school I went to I read the westerns of J. T. Edson, Zane Grey and the 'Sudden' series by Oliver Strange. Other favourites included the Jennings series and some of the Biggles adventures. In college I read everything that came to hand: early favourites were J. D. Salinger and Colin Wilson's *The Outsider*. I read Camus (a tattered copy of *The Rebel* bought for three rupees at the flea market), Dostoyevsky, Gogol, Kafka, Andre Gidé, Bernard Malamud, Graham Greene, the then fashionable Herman Hesse, and the obnoxious philosophy of Ayn Rand. For a while I went through a science fiction phase and was captivated by the novels of Stanislaw Lem and J. G. Ballard. I also harboured a strange and illicit secret: I wrote poems—or what I thought were poems. They were savage outpourings heaping scorn on the establishment and reflections on my own raw uncertainties about my future. I hadn't read much poetry then and after the mandatory Tennyson and Longfellow in school, thought of it as something vaguely pompous.

Apart from what I felt was my focused, justified and uncompromising rebelliousness and the enervating battles with my family, I was studying such exotica as Mercantile Law and Statistics in a suburban Commerce college I loathed. For the first time in my life I failed an examination. All this was enough to drive me to those secret outpourings in a diary. In the early years I was writing in a complete vacuum, with only nebulous notions of rhyme and half-rhyme, drawn mainly from the rock lyrics of the time. I knew no other writers or poets, only another young man, intense and handsome, with light eyes and brownish hair, who wrote page after page of Hindi film lyrics. He was always broke and I was a willing cadgee to his hooch and omelette-pao needs. I was highly impressed when he told me that he spent his nights sleeping in the local crematorium. One night he invited me to his fiery digs, and amidst shots of reeking narangi—the local rotgut—and swirling ganja smoke, shadows of flames fanning the dingy walls, he showed me the obituary register, which he occasionally helped fill up. The names of the dead were scrawled one below the other with their ages. I was relieved to find that no young person figured in that list. I could not always understand the lyricist's high Hindi when he read his songs to me, but to me he was the ultimate ghostwriter.

Buffeted around by music directors and other better-connected songwriters in the harsh tinsel world of Bombay, I don't know what eventually happened to him. But I had made a discovery. In Rampart Row at Thacker's Book Shop I found a shelf containing the Penguin Modern Poets series. Each slim volume carried a selection from three poets. Over a period of time, I bought most of them and read them all slowly and raptly. Brownjohn-Hamburger-Tomlinson; Holbrook-Middleton-Wevill; Murphy-Silken-Tarn; Black-Redgrove-Thomas; Amis-Moraes-Porter. I had never read anything like it before. Sharp, terse, unequivocally modern and the language polished steel. This was poetry, palpable and profound, sometimes inaccessible and opaque, but always intriguing. For some reason the Faber poets were not included in the selections. But I soon discovered them too. Ted Hughes' *The Hawk in the Rain*, Seamus Heaney's *Death of a Naturalist* and Thom Gunn's *Fighting Terms* were the first full-length collections that I read, followed by Ian Hamilton's *The Visit*, borrowed indefinitely from the British Council library. The poems of these four poets struck me with their powerful immediacy and their poise. In later years, I would lose the uncritical enthusiasm in the first flush of discovery I had for some of the Penguin Modern poets, especially after I read more poets in translation from Russian and various European languages and the work of contemporary poets in India. Even in those surcharged Beat-fashionable years, I was not taken in by the Beat poets or the Liverpool 'Mersey Sound'. But at that time of ignorance and innocence, the discoveries were overwhelming and thrilling.

The poetry of Ted Hughes, Gunn and Heaney has always stayed with me. They are 'My Sad Captains' and in those difficult years, my lifeline. In Goa I was armed not just with dope, but with books by these poets. I remember reading Ted Hughes' 'Hawk Roosting', one of the great poems of the last century, late one night in that threadbare shack in Calangute, the waves crashing like drumbeats, my eyes dilated in wonder and intoxication, the room filled with the unmatched fragrance of hashish. The words seemed sentient, rising in eidetic loops and whorls. I remember, in a freakish attempt at connectivity, writing in long hand the last stanza of the poem and gazing at it incredulously:

> The sun is behind me.
> Nothing has changed since I began.
> My eye has permitted no change.
> I am going to keep things like this.

The banality of evil as seen through the cold soul of a hawk, the tone despotic and menacing. I see it even more clearly now: there are hawks all around us.

We spent most of our time lazing on the beaches of Bardez—we were known by our families as 'spare parts'. But one morning I took a rickshaw from Panjim to visit a friend in Dona Paula, about seven kilometres from the city. The driver took me through a landscape so rocky and desolate that I felt I was being escorted to a mugging. The sight of a huge monitor lizard soaking up the sun on the pre-Cambrian rock only enhanced the primaeval air of the place. However, nothing exciting befell me. But I was not to know then that twenty years later I would buy a home there. And, admiring the refulgent natural beauty of Goa in those drifting two weeks, I was not to know that seven years later I would meet another natural beauty who would one day lead me to Goa.

At that time, I was bonded to Bombay. Its vicious inequities apart, the city unleashed a pulsating and infectious energy. It was a combative place, though I was a poor runner in the rat race. It was a city which retched you out every evening from crammed trains and buses and regurgitated you the next morning. The queues at bus-stands were like the tails of reptiles which grew back tirelessly and the traffic an endless purring, choking chain. But the city still had a hold on me. At night it was a giant electronic circuit board, emitting siren-like signals. But its sleazy underbelly stank of sewers and a scatology uniquely its own. A few years after the trip to Goa, I wrote a poem called 'Bombay', in which the city is seen as a beast devouring itself and everything around it. A stanza read:

Marooned by the unkillable
Cycle of mutilations, it widens
Mutant serrated teeth
To rip and masticate the tightening
Tourniquet of the sea.

There is an obvious reference to land reclamation; however, it is not the kind of poem I usually write. I do not relate to places directly and with the same authenticity I do to personal relationships and to undefined, marauding inner anxieties. But a city will grow invidiously into you with its smells, its clangour and overpowering physical presence. Images of it will flicker in and out unconsciously. Soon after 'Bombay' I wrote a poem called 'Mannequin', which to me conveys a truer, more subtle view of the city. Here is a mannequin, in her own plain words:

> Bathed so long in this rich ring of light
> I can now discern a recurring face
> In those scudding hordes. I watch his
> Worried brow, the perpetual briefcase
> Weary with age, as he vanishes past
> Too pressed for time to appreciate
> My groomed slender frame, my glass blue eyes
> Gleaming all day from my elevated place.
>
> Sometimes, under the harsh neon light, a woman
> Stops before my transparent cage, transfigured till
> Closing time by my silks and earrings.
> I would like to erase that longing
> In her eyes—ornaments can be replaced;
> But a vacant darkness swarms
> Within me too, and I cannot go beyond
> This fixed fond smile.

Thom Gunn in 'In Praise of Cities' talks of the city as a feminine entity, both sweetly seductive and whorish:

> 'She presses you with her hard ornaments,
> Arcades, late movie shows, the piled lit windows
> Of surplus stores. Here she is loveliest;
> Extreme, material, and the work of man'.

The city, Gunn writes, 'is indifferent to the indifference that conceived her' and it 'compels a passion without understanding'. I was soon to discover passion of another kind and the indifference that would turn the city into a trap.

I first met V, an ineffably beautiful Goan Catholic, in the offices of *The Indian Express* at Nariman Point where we both worked as sub-editors.

Her very first glance had a seismic effect on me, an effect so irradiating it scorched my shyness and sense of reserve. She worked in the daily and I was with the Sunday magazine section. Unlike me, she worked on shifts and there were days I could not see her. After some adroit manoeuvring, I managed to get her transferred to the magazine section, thus ensuring greater proximity. I had by then met a few poets—the genie-eyed Adil Jussawalla who later became the literary editor and Dom Moraes— quaint English accent, whisky flask in the bottom drawer—who was, for a while, the editor of the magazine. When the magazine, then known as *The Sunday Standard*, shifted its office temporarily to a dreary, empty building at Sassoon Dock, the hub of the fisheries market of Bombay, my relationship with V flourished with its own felicitous fragrance. The warehouses below were full of frozen fish but the waste strewn everywhere turned the office into a putrid, piscine hell. The stench of rotting fish seeped into the newspapers, our clothes, the stationery, even the tea and the galleys. When the breeze swelled the smell rose to epic, ossuary levels. The roads were littered with comb-like bones and the translucent shells of prawns. In the rains, floating fins clung to our shoes and the ends of our trousers. Escapee crabs scuttled around and legions of cats hankered after our fin-filmed shoes outside the docks. One of the staff, a vegetarian, puked regularly at the end of the day. I tried to rise above the miasma and did what any smitten young man does: write a love poem. I called it 'Gifts':

> You unfold, like starfish
> On a beach, your touch
> Stills the rumpled sea,
> Hair plastered seaweed.
>
> I come from the labyrinths:
> Traffic lights park in my eyes
> Before I cross, highways fork
> And stream like veins in my hand.
>
> You hunger for a blade of grass
> In the welter of concrete,
> I step on softening sand
> Suspiciously. Together

We trace a bridge: you pick
A shell translucent as neon,
And I a tribal earring
Reflected in plate glass.

When this poem found its way into Arvind Krishna Mehrotra's *The Oxford India Anthology of Twelve Modern Indian Poets*, and from there into an Italian translation for a journal called *ClanDestino*, and then into a wonderful, multilingual anthology of love poetry, *Amore in Verse*, published in Rome I sensed that a spark, phosphorous-like, had bobbed up from the sea of dead mackerel, shark and bummalo.

But apart from the poems, the 'arcades, late movie shows, the piled lit windows', the city was building an ominous wall around our lives. The salaries of two subs could not sustain a decent household in the city. And there were changes at the senior level of the magazine that made us wary of our future there. There was also talk that the magazine section would be shifted to Delhi. I found no refuge in dope—I had long since given it up after a bummer of such terrifying intensity that I doubled my intake of nicotine. (That trip into paranoia was triggered off by my smoking almost an entire chillum of hash, undiluted by tobacco, in an adda at Churchgate. In that trip, the city stood starkly and grotesquely still, my pulse pounding with the terror that the terror itself would not end.) When the offer came of an arranged marriage, with a dowry masked in some huge property, I was almost as petrified as in that tailspin into palpitating stasis. I had also grown tired of commuting, of being thumped back and forth like a dirty volleyball. And V longed to return to Goa.

For me, leaving Bombay was still an awful wrench. I had published *A Guarded Space*, my first book of poems and had made friends in the small bardic fraternity as well as in the newspaper world. It was the place, where years before, I had discovered the work of Hughes, Heaney, Gunn, and the Americans Richard Wilbur and Robert Lowell, all on my own. I would miss the Fort area the most, not only its magnanimous bustle and helter-skelter efficiency, but as a place where I lived much of my life. My mother, an only daughter, had six brothers and some of them owned and ran restaurants and bars in the area: 'Ankur', 'Apexa',

'Alankar', the hugely popular 'Apoorva', the jauntily named 'Garden Jolly' and in recent years, 'Wall Street'. I ran 'Ankur' for two years in the hope of instant prosperity, but soon realised that there were obstacles far beyond my realm of control. There were unwritten laws I could not transgress. I left Bombay in 1983, with a cavernous bag of books, and little else.

Some months after I left Bombay, I wrote a poem called 'Departures', about a lonely and disorienting bus journey. The poem is a trifle long to be reproduced here. But a few years later, married to V on borrowed money and settled in Goa, I wrote a poem called 'Moving Out', whose immediate motivation was the shifting of our house in Panjim, but whose echoes I can track back to my departure from Bombay.

After the packing the leavetaking.
The rooms were hollow cartons.
The gecko listened stilly—
An old custom—for the heartbeat
Of the family clock.

After the springcleanings
Now the drawing of curtains.
I thought of the years between
These grey walls, these walls
Which are more than tympanic.

There remained much, dead and living,
Uncleared, unchecked: dust mottled
Into shreds under loaded bookshelves;
The fine twine of a cobweb
Shone in the veranda sunlight.

All this I brushed aside along
With the silverfish in flaking tomes,
The stains on marble and tile
Scoured with acid; but the ghosts
Loomed like windstruck drapes;

Like the rectangle left by
A picture frame: below a nail
Hooked into a questionmark,
A faint corona,
A contrasting shade.

∽

Old Goa was once a city, the 'Rome of the Orient', the most prized metropolis in the Portuguese dominions. The magnificent 16th- and 17th-century churches in modern Old Goa are testimonials to that past glory when travellers coined a proverb in Portuguese, 'Quem vio Goa excusa de ver Lisboa'—'If you have seen Goa, there's no need to visit Lisbon'. Contemporary Goa is, of course, not a city, but a state of 1.3 million people, the smallest in the country. But it is still a state, and for most Goans statehood in 1987 came as a benediction. It released them from the arbitrary whims of succeeding, all-powerful Governors and invested real power in democratically elected leaders. That Goa has seen an astounding thirteen changes in the chief minister's post in the last ten years is another story—and a prize claimant to doggerel verse. My assimilation into Goan society was made much easier by my marriage to V. Xenophobia existed in 1985 as it does now, as hordes of 'outsiders' find a place in the sun in this blindingly green state. Curiously, my Mangalore origins also paved the way for easier acceptance here. Perhaps it has to do with the early history of Goa when thousands of Hindus fled to neighbouring areas in the wake of Portuguese ecclesiastical zeal.

The Goa I live in is very different from the one experienced by ephemeral visitors. Within a few months of my arrival, I found a job as an editor of a monthly magazine, a position I held for eight years. I soon discovered that beneath the gloss there was much that was gross. Legal threats and abusive phone calls are stock-in-trade for any editor. But provincial meanness can take some absurd turns. In one instance, when I refused to publish a clearly defamatory letter by a young college lecturer, he sent me eight foolscap sheets of invective—in red ink, in stylish cursive and on both sides of the paper. I saw at close quarters the tussles of politicians with their daft dreams of transforming Goa into 'another Singapore', the struggle for Konkani to achieve official first language status in the state, the wanton environmental degradation by iron ore miners, the ruinous fallouts of unplanned tourism, the most repellent avarice in both the higher and lower ranks of government, and builders and property developers trampling over the fragile ecosystem with sickening boorishness. The colour of corruption and venality is the same everywhere. For some, Goa is paradise; for others, who have always lived here, it is indeed paradise lost.

Of great concern to the community are the wild distortions about Goa blazed abroad by the media and popular cinema and fanned by the demands of tourism. In my Introduction to *Ferry Crossing: Short Stories from Goa*, I wrote: 'Such has been the gilded smokescreen created by tourism and its avaricious auxiliary industries. It becomes necessary, therefore, to clear the air and place the facts as they are. Few in the rest of the country even realize that the Catholic community in Goa is very much a minority; that the most widely spoken language in Goa, Konkani, is an official language under the Eighth Schedule of the Constitution; that the caste system (the word is derived from the Portuguese 'casta') remains deeply rooted in the Catholic community too; or that the tiresome eulogising of vapid, risibly moralistic pop stars has been at the expense of some of the finest Goan exponents of Indian classical music.'

Another misconception is that inter-racial marriages were common and widespread in Goa. The truth is, except in the early years after the conquest of Goa in 1510, when Afonso de Albuquerque favoured such unions between the Portuguese and the native population, miscegenation was rare, and looked down upon by both sides. In the Introduction I also point out howlers on Goa in Anita Desai's *Baumgartner's Bombay* and in the otherwise admirable *A Son of the Circus* by John Irving. But so deeply ingrained is the brochured image of the place that even an astute observer like William Dalrymple, the award-winning and seasoned British travel writer, goes into starry-eyed overdrive. In his *At the Court of the Fish-eyed Goddess*, published in 1998, the same year as *Ferry Crossing*, here is his description of Fontainhas, the 'Latin Quarter' of Panjim, much touted as a tourist attraction in coffee-table books:

Wandering through the quarter in the evening you come across scenes impossible to imagine anywhere else in India: violinists practise Villa Lobos at open windows; caged birds sit chirping on ornate art nouveau balconies looking out over small red tiled piazzas. As you watch, old men in pressed linen trousers and Homburg hats spill out of the tavernas, walking sticks in hand, and make their way unsteadily over the cobbles, past the lines of battered 1950s Volkswagen Beetles slowly rusting into oblivion.

I spent well over three years in this same area, editing that magazine from a small, poky office from 1986 onwards. I've seen nothing resembling Dalrymple's rosy description. The residents of Fontainhas, in fact, routinely complain of the inadequate sanitation facilities, the poor ventilation in their houses and the constant flow of noisy traffic. And as for the famed 'cobbles', I discovered that nobody could recall seeing them since the beginning of the last century! All I saw were a few potholes.

More worryingly, Dalrymple shares the widely held Western fallacy that most Goans did not desire freedom from Portuguese rule. He derives this conviction after a few interviews and a conversation with a quaint, anachronistic old lady who dwells entirely and most blissfully in the Portuguese past. Such cockeyed perceptions are inadvertently disparaging of the Goan community at large, and more so to the spirit of the seventy-two martyrs and the thousands incarcerated and tortured by the Portuguese police in jails in Goa, Portugal, Angola and Cabo Verde during the state's long and arduous struggle for liberation.

Both the horizontal world of prose and the vertical one of poetry have been a part of me. I write poems because I need to. It is not an act of will, but must come, as Anne Stevenson says of love, as naturally 'as a Ferris Wheel to its fair'. Poetry is for me an internal stabiliser and that moment is unmatched when some ephemeral, drifting wisp of thought and image is snatched miraculously from midair and made palpable on paper. Goa has not gifted its poetry to me. I have written poems here, of course, but they have no 'setting' and could have been written anywhere. I cannot write obvious Socialist verse, of 'the blood in the street and blood in the bread you eat' kind. To me Paul Celan is an infinitely greater poet than Pablo Neruda. And though Ted Hughes' last book, *Birthday Letters*, was to me a huge disappointment, his birds and beasts speak to me as lucidly and disturbingly as they did those years ago. In Goa the sunsets are gold and saffron, the seas opalescent, the rivers sinuous and silvery and the greenery riotously green. But there is no intrinsic poetry in external beauty.

The provenance of poetry lies elsewhere. There's an avocado tree in our backyard. Planted by my neighbour, a Scotsman, several years ago, it is tall and spindly. Lovingly tended, it flowers every year but never bears fruit. I've been told that it's the female of the species, and for it too bear fruit it must cross-pollinate with its male counterpart. No amount of water and fertiliser will bring that tree to real fruition. Native chicku, cashew, bora, guava and mango trees flourish everywhere; wild, fecund as the mongrels in the neighbourhood. But not that solitary, spinsterish tree, alien to the rocky terrain of the place. There's the seed of a poem in this somewhere. But I can't get to the root of it. Poems are like that— elusive, sentient creatures. Teasing, disparate images floating about, very rarely dovetailing into place.

There are other pictures: a cauliflower vaguely brings to mind the human brain (vegetable?); a brinjal wears a Roman helmet; a panicky centipede on the widow grille is a rollercoaster or the wagons of a goods train; windscreen wipers swish to and fro and I'm reminded of an umpire signalling a boundary; my twelve-year-old daughter's asthmatic lungs are a guttural tremolo; her sore throat is emery paper. Singly, these are showy, empty pictures. But linked and anchored to a comprehensible reality, to a wider human canvas, and tautened by language and the tug of emotion, these images can grow to meaningful metaphor, claiming a living identity of their own. Poems are not merely ways of seeing but ways of feeling too. Those colourful shreds of cloth scattered on the floor of a tailor's shop can easily be stitched into a wall-hanging, but into a usable garment—free-size? That's a little more difficult.

The use of the ingenious hyperbolical simile has been raised to a delectable art by the English poets, Craig Raine and Christopher Reid. There's even a name for it: 'The Martian School of Poetry', after a poem by Raine called 'A Martian Sends a Postcard Home', in which an alien, in honest and child-like bewilderment, sends back his report on Earth. I've never written a full-fledged 'Martian' poem, but I find that kind of imagination at work profoundly attractive.

A reviewer once complained that I was retreating further and further into the self, into an eventual state of aphasia. But before I'm condemned as an escapist recording the sound of his own heartbeats for an audience of one, I would like to let on that even in my most absent moments, I look at my world quizzically. Last year a poem came to me, unannounced and almost fully-formed, after a nerve-wracking fallow spell, and goodness me, it was all about Goa:

Stills from Baga Beach

Vast freckled Englishwomen
Pylon-limbed
Thaw in the sun. Their breasts
Loll out like baby
Sealions.

Flabby leftovers of Valhalla
Diet on bread and bananas,
Their dozing blue eyes stroke
Small boys in torn
Pyjamas.

The German studies the Vedanta
In translation through chromax
Dark glasses, her oozing
Tattoo mobbed by
Bluebottles.

The temple elephant, vermilion
Swastika on its domed
Forehead, lumbers
Unblinking over the buff
Sands.

I don't visit Baga and the other beaches of Bardez too often. Tourism has disfigured the place into facelessness. The shady invasion of the beach umbrella seems unstoppable. Every few yards, there's a hotel, a boutique, a shopping centre and a beauty parlour—reminiscent of any city. My wife feels the degradation much more keenly—she has irretrievably lost the places of her childhood. At Anjuna, the flea market is a regular bazaar with stalls selling Rajasthani and Tibetan handicrafts. No one plays Bob Dylan here. But I don't mean to be a killjoy. The seas are still relatively clean and the air eminently breathable. And when the breeze blows the coconut palms do sway. The dress code is very informal, but it is not recommended that visitors roam the streets in their underpants like some of the lager louts from England. And if you are into Goa Trance and Techno, the state's latest large-scale export to the west, the place pulsates with it. 'Adrenalinn drum-Xperimental Goa from Unnatural Recordings'; 'Techossomy—Synthetic Flesh from Flying Rhino'; 'Holy Mushroom from the High Society label'; 'Trance Psyberdelic from Moonshine'; 'Deck Wizards Goa Gil-Kosmatrator from the Psychic deli label'—this is the new cosmic beat, born in Goa and exported to the UK, Sweden , France, Germany and Finland.

I've been to only one Rave party and consider myself fortunate to be living out of earshot, in Dona Paula, near Panjim, in an eyrie of a house overlooking the Arabian Sea. The monitor lizard population has dwindled sharply and in their place stand luxurious bungalows, row houses and hotels, rising pellmell from the crushed pre-Cambrian rock. I live in an older, more orderly area, one of the pioneering settlements in the place. Dona Paula is filled with myth and legend. They do not stir me. I know them for what they are: tall tales for the gullible tourist. I prefer to watch from my balcony, at night, the radiant clockhands of the Aguada lighthouse scything through the sky, marking time. With each passing year, I feel a greater reluctance to visit the big city.

The historic lighthouse has not imparted a poem. But lately, I found myself examining a bunch of keys. Old, rusted, I don't remember what doors and cupboards they once opened. But, unmistakably, I saw the stirring of a poem—a skeleton key that opened a doorway to the past and the present. A poem speaks for itself. Once written, it does not belong to its creator. Often, when I come across my old poems in anthologies and periodicals, I find myself wondering which person wrote them. This poem is too fresh in my mind for that otherworldly detachment. To me, it traverses both Bombay and Goa, and unlocks a part of my heart:

Anniversary Poem

A few click into place
From this ring of rusted keys
Like a child's stick-drawing
Of the human race.

This one, brittle as nicotine-scarred
Teeth, unlocked photographs
Silverfished, sepia with age—
A schoolboy's album of hills,

Lakes, embroidered gold
Colours on maroon blazers;
And that stray picture of a scrawny,
Long-haired creature

In a narcotic haze, dreaming
Of escape first into a neon
Forest, then into colliding
Waves, spindrift in the face.

But that flat iron key, its bit
A city skyline, opened doors
To a chain of empty rooms,
Cobwebbed calendars, uncleared bins,

Unread books, unwritten poems,
A young man's wavering silhouette
At a darkened window, toxic eyes
On a key lost in a gunmetal sea.

The master-key that came, warm steel,
Fully rounded, sprung ajar a grey
Shutter to sunlit waves, arms, hands,
Gentle as clouds, shutting down

Room after empty room.

Contributors

Alexander Hamilton, the Calvinist Scotsman, visited Goa in 1692 and in 1704.

Anthony Monserrate was part of the first Jesuit Mission to the court of Akbar in 1580.

Carre Barthelemy, a French priest, arrived in Goa in December 1672 to free a group of his countrymen held by the Portuguese viceroy.

The Scottish theologian **Claudius Buchanan** arrived in Goa in 1808.

David Tomory, born in London and brought up in New Zealand, visited Goa in 1976.

The French priest, **Denis L. Cottineau de Kloguen** was in Goa in 1827.

Duarte Barbosa, a Portuguese official and brother-in-law of Ferdinand Magellan, was stationed in India between 1500 to about 1517.

A soldier, missionary, and a friend of St. Francis Xavier, **Fernao Mendes Pinto** accompanied the body of St. Francis Xavier on its last journey to Goa in 1554.

The French navigator **Francois Pyrard de Laval** landed in chains in Goa in 1608.

The Florentine merchant and slave trader **Francesco Carletti** visited Goa in 1600-1601 when he was twenty-one years old.

The French physician **Gabriel Dellon** was tried and incarcerated by the office of the Holy Inquisition in Goa in 1675-1676.

The Italian Doctor at Law **Gamelli Careri** visited Goa in 1695 during his travels round the world.

The famous English author **Graham Greene** visited Goa in 1964.

Helene Derkin Menezes came as a tourist to Goa in 1994 and stayed on for good.

The American Unitarian Minister, pacifist, writer and social activist, **Homer A. Jack** covered the Satyagraha movement in Goa in August, 1995.

J. Albert de Mendelslo, an attaché with the German embassy, visited Goa in 1639.

The Dutch pastor **Jacobus Canter Visscher** visited Goa around 1717.

The French linguist and botanist **Jean de Thevenot** visited Goa in 1666.

The Frenchman **Jean-Baptiste Tavernier**, a famous jewel trader and intrepid traveller, spent seven days in Goa in 1641 and two months in 1648.

The Dutch traveller **John Huyghen Van Linschoten** arrived in Goa in September, 1583 and left five years later, in January, 1589.

Jose Nicolau da Fonseca, originally from Colvale, was a doctor in Bombay. His book remains one of the most popular tomes on the Portuguese in Goa.

Katharina Kakar runs the Goa-based NGO, Tara Trust, which is involved in the education of deprived children.

Lora Tomas is a Croatian writer, indologist and translator based in Zagreb and Bangalore.

The Croatian Jesuit priest **Nikola Ratkaj** (Nicolaus Georgii) was in Goa between 1623 and 1629.

The distinguished Portuguese historian and geographer **Orlando Ribeiro** visited Goa in 1956 and discovered a place at odds with the dictator Oliveira Salazar's rose-tinted view.

Pierre du Jarric, a French Jesuit, was a professor of philosophy and theology at Bordeaux and a chronicler of the Jesuit Missions that arrived at the Moghul Court in 1580, 1590 and 1594.

The Italian traveller **Pietro Della Valle** arrived in India in January, 1623 and left in November, 1624.

Ralph Fitch, England's pioneering traveller in India and Burma, arrived as a prisoner of the Portuguese in Goa in 1583.

Richard Burton, the English scholar and chronicler, travelled through Goa and the Nilgiris ('the Blue Mountains') in 1847 and in 1876.

Acknowledgements

The essays which comprise *Goa Travels* have been excerpted from books, or from periodicals in which they first appeared. Given below is a full list of the sources, and the editor, as well as the publisher, are grateful for permission to reprint copyrighted material. While every effort has been made to trace copyright holders, this has not been possible in all instances. We would be grateful for information on any omissions, and will ensure that it is updated in all future editions.

'When the King dies four or five hundred women burn themselves', from *The Book of Duarte Barbosa: An Account of the Countries Bordering on the Indian Ocean and Their Inhabitants*, Mansel Longworth Dames (trans. and ed.). New Delhi: Asian Educational Services, 1989.

'A magnificent Christian spectacle', from *Peregrinação*, Fernao Mendes Pinto.

'King Akbar most devoutly kissed the Bible', from *The Commentary of Father Monserrate, S.J., on his Journey to the Court of Akbar*, J. S. Hoyland (trans.), S. N. Banerjee (anno.). London: Oxford University Press, 1922.

'Worshipfull and bountifull houses', from *The Voyage of John Huyghen Van Linschoten to the East Indies*, volume 1, Arthur Coke Burnell (ed.). London: The Hakluyt Society, 1885.

'A great trade in spices, drugs, silk...', from *Ralph Fitch: England's Pioneer to India and Burma*, John Horton Ryley. London: T. Fisher Unwin, 1899.

'They eat from porcelain plates' from *My Voyage Around the World: The Chronicles of a 16th Century Florentine Merchant*, Francesco Carletti. Herbert Weinstock (trans.). New York: Pantheon Books, 1964.

'Lady Mary is worthy of great veneration', from *Akbar and the Jesuits: An Account of the Jesuit Missions*, Pierre du Jarric. C.H. Payne (trans.), F. Denison Ross and Eileen Power (eds.). Oxford: RoutledgeCurzon, 2005.

'Singing, laughing, and performing a thousand antics', from *The Land of the Great Image: Being Experiences of the Friar Manrique in the Arakan*, Angel Manrique. Maurice Collis (trans.). London: Penguin, 1945.

'A Kingdom lying in the midst of Barbarians', from *The Travels of Pietro Della Valle in India: From the Old English translation of 1664, by G. Havers*, Edward Grey (ed.). London: The Hakluyt Society.

'Remember me in your prayers', from an unpublished manuscript by Nikola Ratkaj. Lora Tomas (trans.). Original text translated from Latin and Italian into Croatian by Mate Krizman.

'Chastity is so strange a virtue in those parts', from *Mendelslo's Travels in Western India (1638-1639)*, M.S. Commissariat. New Delhi: Asian Educational Services, 1995.

'They all become Fidalgos or gentlemen ...', from *Travels in India*, Jean-Baptiste Tavernier. Valentine Ball (trans.), William Crooke (ed.). London: Oxford University Press, 1925.

'Some of them worship Apes', from *Indian Travels of Thevenot and Careri: Being the Third Part of the Travels of M. de Thevenot into the Levant and the Third Part of a Voyage Round the World by Dr. John Francis Gemelli Careri*, Surendranath Sen (ed.). New Delhi: National Archives of India, 1949.

'A thousand insults and indignities', from *The Travels of Abbe Carre in India and the Near East, 1672—1674*, volume 1, Charles Fawcett and Richard Burn (eds.). New Delhi: Asian Educational Services, 1992.

'The sharp dart of excommunication', from *A New Account of the East*

Indies: Being the Observation and Remarks of Capt. Alexander Hamilton from the year 1688-1723, volume 1. New Delhi: Asian Educational Services, 1995.

'Reduced to a miserable condition', from *The Globe Trotter in India Two Hundred Years Ago, and Other Indian Studies*, Michael Macmillan. London: Swan Sonnenschein & Co., 1895.

'Great lovers of fine titles', from *Letters from Malabar to Which is Added an Account of Travancore, and Fra Bartolomeo's Travels in That Country*, Jacobus Canter Visscher. Heber Drury (trans.). Madras: Printed by the Gantz Brothers at the Adelphi Press, 1862.

'My object all this time was the Inquisition', from *Memoirs of the Life and Writings of the Rev. Claudius Buchanan, D.D, Late Vice-provost of the College of Fort William in Bengal (1817)*, Hugh Pearson. London: Oxford University Press, 1817.

'Most regular and exemplary in their manners...', from *An Historical Sketch of Goa, the Metropolis of the Portuguese Settlements in India*, Denis L. Cottineau de Kloguen. Madras: Gazette Press, 1831.

'Intolerably dirty and disagreeable', from *Goa, and the Blue Mountains; or, Six Months of Sick Leave*, Richard Burton. London: Richard Bentley, New Burlington Street, 1851.

'A flourishing city...gradually swept away', from *An Historical and Archaeological Sketch of the City of Goa Preceded by a Short Statistical Account of the Territory of Goa*, José Nicolau da Fonseca. Bombay: Thacker & Co. Limited, 1878.

'I was seized with an universal and violent trembling', from *The Land of the Great Image: Being Experiences of the Friar Manrique in the Arakan*, Angel Manrique. Maurice Collis (trans.). London: Penguin, 1945.

'Hunting satyagrahis', appeared as 'Death of a Satyagrahi' in the *Hindustan Times*, New Delhi, August 19-20, 1955.

'Meagre presence of the Portuguese language' from *Goa em 1956: Relatorio ao Governo,* Lisboa, 2000, from the website: www.reocities.com.

'A certain bitterness remains after "liberation"', first appeared in *The Illustrated Weekly of India,* Bombay 1964.

'Psychedelic conquistados', from *Hello Goodnight: A Life of Goa,* David Tomory. Victoria: Lonely Planet Publications, 2000.

'Like no other place on earth', from *Inside/Out: New Writing from Goa.* Saligao: Goa, 1556 & Goa Writers, 2011.

'Sex on the beach', from *Moving to Goa,* Katharina Kakar. New Delhi: Penguin Books India, 2013.

'The shady invasion of the beach umbrella' appeared as 'Drifting on a High Tide' in *Tehelka,* New Delhi, June 2004.

Editor's Note

I extend my thanks and appreciation to the Sahitya Akademi, New Delhi, and the Directorate of Art and Culture, Goa, for grants given to me; to Lilia Maria de Souza for help in some areas of research; to Lora Tomas for the discovery of the Croatian traveller Nikola Ratkaj; and to Anurag Basnet of Rupa for his editorial patience and perseverance.